Studies in Teacher Appraisal

Glenn Turner and Philip Clift

School of Education
Open University
A project funded by the Leverhulme Trust

D1100885

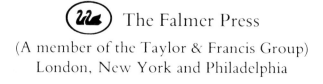 The Falmer Press
(A member of the Taylor & Francis Group)
London, New York and Philadelphia

UK   The Falmer Press, Falmer House, Barcombe, Lewes,
East Sussex, BN8 5DL

USA   The Falmer Press, Taylor & Francis Inc., 242 Cherry Street,
Philadelphia, PA 19106-1906

© G. Turner and P. Clift, 1988

First published 1988

British Library Cataloguing in Publication Data

Turner, Glenn
    Studies in teacher appraisal: a project funded by the Leverhulme Trust
[and carried out in the] School of Education, Open University.
    1. Great Britain. Teachers. Performance. Assessment
    I. Title   II. Philip Clift   III. Leverhulme Trust
    IV. Open University. *School of Education*
    371.1′44′0941

    ISBN 1-85000-267-3
    ISBN 1-85000-268-1 Pbk

Jacket design by Caroline Archer

Typeset by Chapterhouse, The Cloisters, Formby L37 3PX

Printed in Great Britain by
Redwood Burn Limited, Trowbridge, Wiltshire

Contents

Preface

This book is one of the outcomes of a two-year research project, funded by the Leverhulme Trust and carried out in the School of Education at the Open University. The other major outcome of the project was *A First Review and Register of School and College Based Teacher Appraisal Schemes* (Turner and Clift 1985), subsequently updated (Turner and Clift 1987).

The project was part of a programme of investigations into approaches to the improvement in the quality of education provided in schools and colleges. This programme resulted in a number of publications, including a book *Studies in School Self-Evaluation* (Clift *et al.* 1987) and two Open University courses (Curriculum Evaluation and Assessment in Educational Institutions, E364 and more recently Educational Evaluation, E811).

We hope that this book will be of value to practitioners, both the LEA officers and advisers who will have to set up schemes for the appraisal of their teachers and the heads and teachers who will be intimately involved in the process. We also hope that it will be of value to the academic community and particularly to teachers involved in advanced study as part of their professional development and in-service education.

We would like to express our gratitude to all those who helped in this research: the teachers in the schools and colleges who provided us with the information about their schemes and who generously allowed us to observe their appraisals; the Directors of the Leverhulme Trust for supporting the project financially; our colleagues in the School of Education, especially Desmond Nuttall, Chairman of the Educational Evaluation and Accountability Research Group; and Rita Bowden, who assiduously deciphered and transcribed our tape recordings.

Introduction

One of the most significant developments in the maintained sector of education in the 1980s is the decision to introduce the *systematic* appraisal of the professional competence and performance of teachers. There have been precedents, of course: developments in individual schools and colleges in the 1970s (see for instance Clift *et al*. 1987) which could be characterized as appraisal schemes, or which at any rate laid the foundations for such schemes, but it is only in this decade that systematic appraisal has entered the arena of *national* debate.

Pressure from central government for systematic teacher appraisal was first evident in DES policy statements such as 'Teaching Quality' (DES 1983) and 'Better Schools' (DES 1985a), and, as the decade progressed, became increasingly evident in the proceedings of certain major conferences (North of England in 1984, Education for Industrial Society in 1985, Better Schools in 1985, British Educational Research Association in 1986) and in the media generally. This has culminated in the proviso included in the teachers' recent pay settlement (DES, 1987), obliging them to take part in an agreed national scheme, once its form is decided upon. At the time of writing (1987), it is intended that such a scheme should be operational by the autumn of 1989.

This attention has had the effect of stimulating a major debate among professionals engaged in education at all levels, and an increasing number of practical initiatives are being reported in individual schools and colleges, for example Bunnell and Stephens (1984), Samuels (1984), Green (1984), Delaney (1986). These tend to be 'insider' accounts, mostly by Headteachers who have initiated schemes in their own schools. Other than these, the bulk of what has been published about appraisal to date is based upon opinions rather than direct experience.

More recently, however, there have been indications of a quickening of interest in research into the nature and effectiveness of appraisal schemes and with the advent of LEA teacher fellowships this increase seems likely to continue. At the time when we at the Open University, though, made a start on the work reported in this book (1984), very little British research had been undertaken. Indeed, since the phenomenon was so new in the UK, most of the material on which we were able to draw when preparing a commissioned chapter for the 1986 World Yearbook in Education (Turner *et al*. 1986) described American experience, which has developed mainly out of procedures for the initial certification of teachers. By contrast, in Britain schools seem to be culling most of their ideas from commercial or industrial practice, and the Industrial Society has been very influential in this.

Our interest in teacher appraisal was not prompted by the burgeoning national debate, although naturally we were very aware of it. It had arisen rather as a result of our earlier research into school self-evaluation (SSE, see Clift *et al*. 1987). The School Self-evaluation Movement was for the most part characterized by the denial of any association with the appraisal of individual teachers. The rhetoric had it that institutions not individuals were the legitimate objects of critical review. In reality this distinction was always difficult to sustain: how, for instance, is it possible to make judgments about the work of, say the Mathematics Department in a comprehensive school and not at the same time implicitly praise or blame the Head of that department and to a lesser extent also his or her colleagues? Thus towards the end of our programme of research into SSE, increasingly we came upon schools in which the appraisal of individual teachers was being explicitly included in the review process.

Although most LEAs are now developing policies with regard to the appraisal of their teachers, few have made much headway and many still have no explicit policy, in part because of the teachers' industrial action throughout 1985 and 1986. As a consequence, most of the practical activity to date consists of experimental schemes being developed and tried out in individual schools on their own initiative. This research therefore has concentrated solely on the schemes developed by individual schools or colleges and does not attempt to investigate LEA schemes and policies with regard to teacher appraisal.

The Leverhulme Research Project

In October 1984 the School of Education at the Open University set up a research project into 'the nature, impact and effectiveness of school or college based schemes for teacher appraisal'. The project was directed by Professor Desmond Nuttall and Philip Clift, and employed one full-time researcher, Glenn Turner. The Leverhulme Trust provided funding for the project for a two-year period, from October 1984 to September 1986.

The aims of the project were as follows:

1   to collect information about pioneer schemes for teacher appraisal and to classify them in terms of their salient characteristics;
2   to carry out case studies of schools whose schemes are representative of this classification;
3   to assess the impact of these schemes on the schools and their benefits in terms of school improvement;
4   to disseminate information about teacher appraisal as it develops.

To achieve these aims the work was done in two stages. The first stage was one of information gathering and classification. For the second stage, the impact of the schemes selected on the basis of this classification was investigated in a series of case studies.

Stage 1: The Review and Register

The first stage of the project resulted in the production of *A First Review and Register of School and College Based Teacher Appraisal Schemes* (Turner and Clift 1985: a second edition was subsequently produced, Turner and Clift 1987). This register contained skeletal information about fifty-six different appraisal schemes operated by a variety of different institutions, ranging from the primary through to the post-compulsory phase. In order to obtain the information for this register we placed a number of advertisements in the educational press in September 1984. The publications concerned were: *The Headteacher's Review, The Teacher* and the *Times Educational Supplement.* The advertisement requested schools and colleges which had set up a scheme to contact us and to send information for inclusion in this register. In addition to placing the advertisements, we also made direct contact with schools and colleges which we knew to be operating some kind of scheme and made use of existing publications and data-bases.

Of course, to draw statistically valid inferences about current trends in schools nationally it would have been necessary to undertake a national survey. We believed this to be inappropriate to our purposes, which were two-fold. Firstly, we wished to produce an initial classification of the *variety* of school- and college-based schemes. By publishing information about them in the form of a register, we hoped to aid in the creation of a network in which persons interested in setting up a scheme or investigating existing practices could do so by contacting the appropriate schools or colleges. Secondly, it was our intention to explore the main issues to do with teacher appraisal by conducting case studies in a 'theoretical sample' of schools and colleges, that is one selected in such a way as to encompass this variety. (There has in fact been a small-scale survey, of 233 schools in seven LEAs, conducted by Chris James and Joe Newman at the School of Education in the University of Bath, see James and Newman 1985).

We did not impose boundaries on the sorts of appraisal scheme in which we declared an interest, consequently a wide variety of different types of scheme have featured in our research. Clearly the nature of a scheme depends very much on the *purpose* for which it is intended. Some appraisal schemes have a definitely 'judgmental' quality; in others review is seen as linked solely to professional development. In any case terminology varies: quite often, innocuous terms such as 'staff development review' are used in schemes the nature of which is very similar to those which call themselves 'teacher appraisal'. Similarly, the terms 'dialogue' or 'discussion' are sometimes used in preference to 'appraisal interview', yet all of these may amount to something very similar in practice.

For our 'Review and Register' we developed a data-base of information about the fifty-six schemes. This was brief since our intention was to summarize the nature of each. Each entry contained information on the following:

name of school or college
address
Head or Principal
initiator(s) of schemes

person who made contact with the project
type of school
number of pupils on roll
age-range of pupils
date of introduction of scheme
the purpose(s) of the scheme
who is appraised
whether the scheme is voluntary or compulsory
the level of focus of the scheme
what appraisal methods are used
what other information is used
what forms and documents are used
what records/reports are kept
who has access to records/reports
the frequency of appraisal
what changes have been produced by the operation of the scheme
miscellaneous information
how (or if) the scheme has been altered since its inception
what publications about the scheme have been produced.

Stage 2: Case Studies

Undertaking case studies enabled us to elaborate on most of the basic issues included in this summary, making use of information from the observation of appraisal in practice and investigating the perceptions of teachers with experience of different approaches. In this our intention throughout was to explore and present the *variety* of approaches and reactions to appraisal, not to attempt to tease out its relationship to the idiosyncrasies of particular institutions. This approach to the reporting of cross-site case studies had the added advantage of enabling us to preserve the total anonymity of those involved, highly desirable by reason of the delicate nature of what we often observed or were told.

The way in which we present the results of this study is thus by issue not by institution. Information about the individual schools and colleges taking part is confined to the minimum considered sufficient in order to illustrate the variety from which data are drawn. A brief review of the structure of this report follows.

The first three chapters deal with the background to teacher appraisal, the sample from which the data is derived, and the methodology which we employed. The rest of the report deals with the major issues.

Background

The context in which this study of school- and college-based teacher appraisal took place is one of continuing public debate about standards in education, which had its origins in the mid-1970s. Following a brief review of the literature on teacher appraisal, this debate is discussed in the first chapter of this report. The School Self-Evaluation Movement is introduced and reasons considered for its apparent lack of success in bringing about school improvement. It is suggested that this failure led both to the political pressure for the introduction of regular and formal teacher appraisal and to the development of their own procedures by certain schools and colleges. The chapter ends with a discussion of the current position on formal teacher appraisal as a concomitant of teachers' pay and conditions of service.

The nature of school-based schemes

In the second chapter the rationale is presented for the choice of the eight case study institutions as a 'theoretical sample', based on information included in our 'First Register and Review of School and College Based Schemes for Teacher Appraisal'. Details of the nature and operation of the schemes are presented.

Methodology

The procedures by which we undertook case studies of school- and college-based schemes and the microcomputer procedures which we developed for analyzing the resulting qualitative data mainly derived from interviews are described in the third chapter.

The Issues

Following these introductory chapters, the rest of the report deals with what we have identified as the major issues of systematic school- and college-based teacher appraisal. We begin with a review of the strategies by which schemes have been introduced and developed, and go on to discuss the purposes of appraisal, as seen by the different participants. This is followed by a review of appraisal interviews, of the strategies adopted for gathering evidence about teachers' professional performance for use in the course of them and of the various ways in which teachers' involvement in schemes has been brought about. We then move on to the vexed issues of the appraisal of Headteachers and the corporate appraisal of school senior management teams. Finally, we review the range of teachers' perceptions of appraisal and their attitudes towards it, its impact on the life of the institutions in which it occurs, its costs in time and resources, and draw conclusions about its value as a means of bringing about improvements in educational provision.

The introduction and development of the schemes

The origins of the eight schemes, the nature and motivations of their initiators and the subsequent development of the schemes are presented in Chapter 4. The influence on each scheme of the institutional context — school size, prevailing ethos, characteristic modes of communication and decision-making processes, school organization and staff hierarchies — is discussed.

The purposes of appraisal

The purposes of teacher appraisal are considered in Chapter 5. The discussion includes the more extreme of the 'political' positions, specifically linking appraisal with contracts of service, promotion and possible dismissal as well as the more moderate 'professional' stance which associates it mainly with professional development and in-service training. This discussion is illustrated by reference to the schemes in the case study institutions and to the declared purposes of their initiators.

Appraisal interviews

Appraisal interviews are at the heart of all of the schemes included in this study. In Chapter 6 the issues of preparation for interviews, the setting of an agenda and who controls it, target setting and the vexed matters of the records kept and who has access to them are considered.

Strategies for collecting evidence

Appraisal interviews generally include the consideration of evidence concerning a teacher's professional performance. In Chapter 7 the range of evidence collected, whether deliberately or incidentally, is considered — consultation with others; the use of existing documents and information, including job descriptions; the observation of teachers as they go about their various duties in and out of the classroom.

Involvement in appraisal

The conducting of appraisal and being appraised, the skills and problems, the extent to which involvement in schemes is coerced (whether explicitly or implicitly), the time that systematic appraisal takes and the issues considered are discussed in Chapter 8.

The appraisal of Headteachers and college Principals

The appraisal of three Headteachers and the Principal of a college are compared and contrasted in Chapter 9 and the vitally important issue of who is the most appropriate appraiser of such people is considered.

The appraisal of a senior management team

The experimental appraisal of the senior management team in one of the case study schools, a large comprehensive, is described in Chapter 10. This provides an important organizational link between institutional self-evaluation and the appraisal of individuals: like most such teams, this senior management team functioned as a corporate entity. It is suggested that the most appropriate level of appraisal in such circumstances is at that corporate level, rather than as individuals, since individual actions were evidently closely circumscribed.

Teachers' perceptions of appraisal

The range of teachers' attitudes towards appraisal are discussed in Chapter 11. These include suspicions, feelings of professional threat, and positive views.

The impact of appraisal

The effects of appraisal on schools and individual teachers are discussed in Chapter 12: the targets set; INSET provided; positive and negative effects; career decisions made; dissatisfactions; changes in the school routines and structures; impact on teaching.

The costs of appraisal

Despite protestations to the contrary, all innovations have their costs. The costs of appraisal, in resources, time, what was 'pushed out' in the institutions studied are considered in Chapter 13 and an attempt is made to balance these costs against the benefits, claimed or substantiated.

Conclusions

In the last chapter we reflect on the lessons learned about teacher appraisal from the study; the benefits and the problems and the implications for the forthcoming LEA and 'national' schemes.

Chapter 1

The Background to the Project

Introduction

In this chapter we look at two aspects of teacher appraisal which together formed the background to the research reported in this book. Firstly, in order to place our work in its academic context, we present a brief review of the literature on the subject, mainly of American origin. We then go on to an interpretation of the motives behind the move towards the statutory introduction of the appraisal of teachers in this country, culminating in the recent (1987) setting up by the DES of pilot projects in six Local Education Authorities, intended to develop a national scheme acceptable to all parties.

The Literature

Although teacher appraisal has only recently become a significant educational issue in Britain, it is already well established in parts of the USA, Australia and South Africa. The influence on the development of appraisal practices in schools in Britain, however, does not seem to have been educational practice in other countries but rather local industrial practice. Nevertheless, there is quite an extensive literature stemming chiefly from the USA and many of the issues raised in this literature are pertinent to the issues discussed throughout this report.

The purposes of teacher appraisal

What tends to make the issue of teacher appraisal a complex and controversial one is that particular schemes are often intended to serve several purposes. In the USA a recent survey by the Educational Research Service revealed that the majority of school districts had four main purposes in mind when developing appraisal schemes (Wood and Pohland, 1983). These are: (1) to help teachers improve their teaching performance, (2) to decide on renewed appointment of probationary teachers, (3) to recommend probationary teachers for tenure or continuing contract status and (4) to recommend dismissal of unsatisfactory tenured or continuing contract teachers. Broadly these purposes fall into two categories: formative (1) and summative (2–4).

Formative appraisal serves the purpose of professional development — the improvement of practice — whilst summative appraisal is geared to career decision-making. In the United Kingdom, emerging schemes in schools seem to be almost exclusively geared to professional development (see Chapter 5). However, in the White Paper 'Teaching Quality' the government has stressed the importance of career decision-making and in particular the removal of incompetent teachers from the profession. The White Paper states that:

> Concern for quality demands that in the small minority of cases where, despite in-service training arrangements, teachers fail to maintain a satisfactory standard of performance, employers must, in the interests of pupils, be ready to use procedures for dismissal. (DES 1983, 25)

This particular issue has caused much controversy and arguably has slowed down developments in many LEAs by antagonizing teachers. It will be interesting to see how far schemes developed by LEAs in Britain will deal with this issue.

Contrasting trends

Staff appraisal seems to be taking a very different form in Britain from that in the United States for a number of historical reasons. In the USA staff appraisal has developed mainly along summative lines as a basis for initial certification of teachers and for the renewal of contracts. Concern over the competence of teachers to carry out their jobs successfully led some teacher training institutions to develop competency-based teacher training programmes. The notion of competency-based teaching has now spread throughout the USA, and beyond initial training to the appraisal of practising teachers. Many States have developed their own programmes of competency-based teaching, in many cases mandated either through legislation or through State Department of Education regulations. Assessment is carried out by a team of experts, usually experienced teachers, using agreed instruments of appraisal such as observation schedules and knowledge tests. On the basis of assessments made, contracts are renewed or terminated. In some cases tenured staff might even be dismissed on the basis of an adverse report. The desire to reward effective teaching has also led a few States to adopt systems for awarding 'merit pay' to those teachers considered to be achieving standards of excellence (see for example Burke 1982).

In Great Britain staff appraisal has traditionally been the responsibility of Local Education Authorities and is carried out by a team of local inspectors or advisers who usually have considerable experience in teaching. The purposes of such appraisal of individuals have tended to be to assess probationary teachers, to advise on appointments and promotions and to look into cases of poor performance. Periodical appraisal of non-probationary teachers does not normally take place, although many LEAs carry out inspections of schools. Staff appraisal is also undertaken in a sense by Her Majesty's Inspectorate as part of their own inspection procedures or in cases where they are invited into schools because of problems. However, individual teachers are not identified in reports of HMI or LEA inspections: concern is with the school as a whole rather than the performance of individual teachers.

Periodic appraisal of individual teachers by senior personnel within schools has been a recent development in some British schools. It seems to have emerged as a management tool designed, in many cases, to promote redeployment and boost morale at a time of falling rolls. To some extent staff appraisal has developed out of moves, mainly by LEAs, to promote curriculum review and institutional self-evaluation, and so far it seems to have had much more impact on secondary schools than on the other phases of education. The models of appraisal adopted owe more to schemes in use in industry and commerce and much less to initial training systems than those in the USA. Courses run by Education for Industrial Society have helped to promote management-oriented models, with an emphasis on staff development and training rather than hiring and firing. Those schools in Britain which are adopting schemes seem to have borrowed many ideas from industrial practice and there are striking similarities between the school schemes revealed by recent research (Turner and Clift 1985) and the industrial schemes revealed in company surveys such as that of Gill (1977). Common features are the use of appraisal interviews, 'target setting' and delegation of appraisal to 'middle managers'. Appraisal through observation of lessons is a feature of few British school schemes although the idea of mutual observation by teachers for the purpose of improvement of practice does seem to be developing and in a recent Schools Council publication (Schools Council 1984) a section is devoted to the techniques of mutual observation. However, the notion of competence-based teaching does not seem to have caught on in Britain at all despite promotion of the idea by the Further Education Unit (FEU 1982).

Research into teacher effectiveness

Staff appraisal in both the USA and Britain has to some extent been informed by research into what constitutes an 'effective teacher'. There has been a considerable amount of research into this in America; indeed it has reached such proportions that a recent annotated bibliography reports on no fewer than 3,041 studies of teacher effectiveness (Powell and Beard, 1984). According to Farrar *et al.* (1984), however, most American effective schools programmes are based on research into elementary urban schools serving low-income and minority groups. In the USA teacher effectiveness has been assessed partly through systems for rating teachers, however, these have been subjected to considerable criticism particularly on grounds of validity (Soar *et al.* 1983). Attempts to validate many ratings schemes in the past were not successful (Barr 1935; Medley and Mitzel 1959). Research on expert opinions of good teaching has also raised doubts about the validity of teachers' own notions of what constitutes effective teaching. Coker *et al.* (1980) found that expert opinions about good teaching correlated in many cases with decreased pupil achievement! Perhaps one of the least surprising findings is that of McDonald (1977) — that the most effective pattern of teaching differs according to the subject matter and grade level.

Flanders (1977) has shown that there are many logical and technical problems in research which has sought to establish the parameters of teacher effectiveness and Borich and Madden (1977) have identified several measurement problems in product-process research on teacher effectiveness. Borich (1977) argues that the evaluation of teacher effectiveness must be based on information gathered from multiple sources and should take into account four stages of the teaching process: (a) the pre-operational; (b) the immediate; (c) the intermediate; (d) the product. According to Borich, few schemes in the USA deal effectively with more than one of these stages.

In Britain the effectiveness of different teaching strategies was examined by the ORACLE project (Observational Research and Classroom Learning Evaluation). Initially concerned with the effectiveness of different styles of science teaching, the ORACLE project team devoted considerable attention to primary education (see Galton *et al.* 1980). It revealed that teaching which was geared to promoting individualized learning tended to be routine, managerial and didactic in its nature, and less educationally stimulating than whole-class teaching. This tends to be more true the larger the size of the class. In classes of over thirty, many pupils spend considerable periods of time working in isolation. The study emphasized the need for flexibility in teaching and for attention to be given to the quality as well as the quantity of pupil learning.

Research into competency-based teaching

Competency-based teaching in the USA has also been the subject of considerable research. Borich (1977) argues that the relationship between a competency and pupil change must be established by empirical data. Teacher appraisal must be based on validated proficiency levels. However, research so far has validated few of these. Rosenshine and Furst (1971) identified eleven teacher variables that showed some relationship to gain in cognitive achievement, the main five being clarity, variability, enthusiasm, task-oriented behaviour and opportunity for learning. However, these are all high-inference variables involving a very large element of subjectiveness in their assessment. In Britain the idea of competency-based teaching has been criticized as being based on a model of teaching which is extremely narrow in its conception. Elliott (1983) has argued that evaluating teaching in this way conceptualizes it as a simple technology which ignores the need for imaginative and reflexive skills on the part of the teacher. Similarly, Wragg (1984) argues that teaching is not just the transmission of knowledge but includes fostering interest in learning, the success of which can only be assessed in the long term. He objects to existing programmes of competency-based teaching on the grounds that they simply reduce teaching to a narrow set of skills.

Existing Methods of Teacher Appraisal

There have been several recent reviews of staff appraisal methods (Haefele 1980, Kyriacou and Newsom 1982; Soar *et al.* 1983; Darling-Hammond *et al.* 1983). The methods that have most often been used in teacher appraisal are: assessment of pupil performance, observation of teacher performance, assessing teacher knowledge and appraisal interview. Particular schemes, of course, might well employ more than one method.

Assessment of pupil performance

Perhaps the most common method of staff appraisal in the USA is to attempt to measure teacher effectiveness by some system of assessing pupil performance. The main problem in adopting such a method is to select out only those effects which can be attributed to the performance of a particular teacher. Many different systems for appraising teachers by examining pupil gains have been adopted in the USA, but most of these have met with objection. Haefele (1980), Kyriacou and Newsom (1982), Soar *et al.* (1983), and Darling-Hammond *et al.* (1983) have all criticized appraisal based on pupil performance and it seems that whatever form the assessment takes raises questions of reliability and validity. Furthermore, there is a tendency for pupils who have performed well at one particular time to perform less well on the next occasion and vice versa. Soar *et al.* (1983) argue that this regression effect makes assessment of pupil gains problematic if it is to be used for the appraisal of teachers. Brophy and Everston (1977) observed the behaviour patterns of teachers known to be effective in terms of pupil performance and found that there was a relationship between teacher behaviours and pupil outcomes in some schools but not in others. Klein and Alkin (1977) have approached the evaluation of teacher effecttiveness by comparing pupil gains produced by one particular teacher with the average gains produced by all the teachers being appraised but the problem here is being able to tell how good the average teacher in a school is. Good and Grouws (1977) divided teachers into two groups — more effective and less effective — using pupil gains in tests as the basis, but found that no single method was used by either group. They concluded that pupils did not seem to suffer from contact with the less effective teachers! In Britain the assessment of pupil performance has not been a formal part of teacher appraisal since the days of payment by results and, given the adverse effects of that system on teaching methods and the criticism it provoked, it seems unlikely to re-emerge as an appraisal method, except perhaps covertly in terms of appraisal of teachers according to the performance of their pupils in public examinations, although the possibility of making use of data from the 'bench-mark testing' provided for in the current Education Act certainly exists.

Observation of teachers

Appraisal systems which are based purely on performance testing can be criticized for taking a 'black box' view of teaching: they examine the product but ignore the process. Glass (1977) has argued that process rather than product measures are the most stable index of teacher effectiveness. Schemes which utilize lesson observation as a method of appraisal vary from those akin to interaction analysis, which list a set of attributes for the observer to look for, to those where the observer conducts the appraisal purely on an intuitive basis. Both systems have weaknesses as a basis for staff appraisal and research into different observation-based schemes has revealed that observers can be extremely unreliable and may be biased in how they interpret teacher actions (see Rosenshine 1970; Brophy and Everston 1974; Haefele 1980; Soar *et al.* 1983). If observation is conducted without a predetermined set of categories it is difficult to discover what criteria are being used. Much staff appraisal in Britain seems to operate in this way and its validity is assumed to lie in the fact that a Head or senior teacher or Adviser conducting the appraisal has sufficient experience to be able (intuitively?) to detect the characteristics of a good teacher. However, according to a study by Lloyd (1981) Headteachers have shown reluctance to observe their teachers for evaluative purposes. Observation of teachers by Her Majesty's Inspectors also seems to be of a high inference nature. Although the criteria used by HMI when observing teachers has recently been publicized (HMI 1982), what has not been made explicit is how judgments are arrived at. American competency-based schemes tend to be much more explicit in terms of the criteria selected and the basis upon which judgments are made. Many State programmes include detailed observation schedules which have been subjected to many years' trial and development — see for example that of Florida (1983) and Georgia (1984). Soar (1977), however, argues that we can only assess classroom processes if a relationship between product and process can be empirically confirmed and Scriven (1977) has criticized many existing American classroom observation techniques because they concentrate on procedures which have not yet been shown to produce growth in pupil attainment. Not all State programmes are validated or subjected to tests of reliability, although that of Georgia is an exception.

Assessing teacher knowledge

It follows logically that a teacher cannot possibly teach what he or she doesn't know. It also follows that a teacher needs to have sufficient knowledge of how to teach — what has sometimes been termed pedagogical knowledge. Some staff appraisal schemes base assessment on teacher knowledge, nearly always on subject knowledge. An obvious example is the National Teacher Examinations in the USA. In some States where such examinations form a part of competency-based teaching programmes, a score below a certain level is considered to be adequate grounds for dismissal. This has caused considerable controversy since many of the teachers who have failed to achieve desired scores have successfully completed teacher training and in many cases are considered to be very good teachers by their Principals (McDaniel 1977)! Kauchak (1984) has criticized these examinations on the grounds that they discriminate against black teachers. Many State programmes utilize paper and pencil tests designed to assess teachers' knowledge. Nevertheless, research which has tried to demonstrate the relationship between teacher knowledge and teacher effectiveness has produced inconclusive evidence (Byrne 1983).

Appraisal interviews

In the USA appraisal interviews sometimes form part of a programme for summative appraisal. One particular interview system which has been used in the USA is the Teacher Perceiver Interview (TPI). According to this method, interviewers apply certain techniques which are designed to tease out the extent to which a person is likely to be a good practitioner. Even though it could perhaps be used for routine evaluation of existing staff, the TPI was designed as a recruitment device. How far it is a valid system of assessing the qualities of a good teacher has, however, been questioned (Haefele 1978).

In Britain (Turner and Clift 1985) the appraisal interview tends to be used more for periodic evaluation as a basis for professional development rather than for summative appraisal. In some of the schemes developed by particular schools, it includes a large element of self-assessment by the teacher being interviewed. As well as classroom practices, other aspects of the teacher's job tend to be considered, such as planning, marking, curriculum development, management tasks and extra-curricular activities. The main emphasis of many interview-based appraisal schemes in Britain is to bring about improvements in practice and the responsibility for improvement is assumed to rest with both the appraiser and the person being appraised. In some cases both parties are expected to agree on targets for future action, the success of which can be evaluated at a subsequent appraisal interview.

Although such interviews can identify problems, priorities and training needs, much depends on the knowledge and skills of the interviewer and the ability and willingness of the teachers appraised to discuss and evaluate their own performance. The potential weakness of a system which relies exclusively on interviews is that it can become simply a formality and the interviewer may well have not direct evidence of the classroom performance of the person appraised.

In summary, what emerges from this very brief review of the literature on the appraisal of teachers is hardly reassuring. The use of direct evidence on teachers' performance in the process seems to be relatively rare. Where attempts are made to gather such direct evidence the problem arises of the lack of empirically established criteria on what constitutes good practice. This is compounded by the apparent falli-bility of expert opinion on the matter. Despite these manifest shortcomings, teacher appraisal is attracting a great deal of political and professional attention at the present time. In order to understand why, it is helpful to trace its origins in the way in which education has been viewed by politicians and the public over the past two decades.

The Political Background to Teacher Appraisal in Britain

Until the early 1970s little was heard of any anxiety about what schools were achieving. On the whole politicians appeared to be confident that the education service was providing what they and the public wanted. There seemd to be a comfort-able general assumption that a constantly expanding education system was serving the needs of the people of Great Britain well enough. Large numbers of teachers were in training and the once endemic 'teacher shortage' seemed likely soon to be a thing of the past. The school leaving age was raised to sixteen in 1968 and there was talk of raising it to 17 or possibly to 18 in the not-too-distant future. This general spirit of optimism and satisfaction culminated in the 1972 White Paper, 'A Framework for Expansion' (DES 1972), for which Margaret Thatcher had ministerial responsibility. Amongst other things this promised nursery education on demand and generally set the scene for an education service that was going to continue to expand, seemingly without limit.

In the early 1970s, however, there was a series of crises concerning oil supply and there was a huge increase in its price. The reaction of the industrialized countries was to inflate their economies, with the consequence of economic disruption, confounding public expectations of a constant improvement in standards of living. Reductions in public expenditure were sought and in Great Britain education was an obvious target. It was an obvious target because it was enormously expensive and because people were uncertain as to precisely what it meant to them and precisely what it did for them. Further, with the confounding of expectations of ever-increasing prosperity, a conviction grew that education was 'letting Great Britain Ltd down', that the needs of industry were not being met, that standards in schools were not as high as in earlier times or at any rate not high enough. This feeling led to the establishment, by the Department of Education amd Science (DES) in 1974, of the Assessment of Performance Unit (APU). The purpose of this Unit was to monitor standards in schools and to do so globally by a process of light sampling which would not identify individual children, teachers, schools or even Local Education Authorities, but be of such a nature as to give a picture of the general standards of education at the specific ages. The APU was given a task of answering two questions: Was education as good as it used to be, was it better, or was it not as good? and However good it was, was it good enough for present needs?

The first of these questions was in its nature impossible to answer. Data from yester-year, with which the APU's measured standards could be compared, simply did not exist. At a more subtle level, even if such data had existed, it would have been difficult to make sensible comparisons because of societal changes over the years. The second question could certainly be answered, and for some years now the APU has been providing precise information about what children generally currently know and are capable of doing at particular ages.

Moving on to 1976, we then had the James Callaghan Ruskin speech. This was the first speech by a major politician in recent times which referred to a direct link between education and the economic health of the nation. The wealth-creating function of education was stressed in this speech, and in 1977 there was a series of local 'Great Debates', later summarized in the Green Paper of 1977 (DES 1977a), in which a major topic was how education might better meet the needs of wealth creation. In 1977 also the Taylor Committee reported, stressing the accountability of schools to parents. In 1978 and 1979 national surveys of primary and secondary schools by Her Majesty's Inspectors of Schools (DES 1978, 1979) were published. These tended to go against the demands of those who wished the schools to 'go back to the basics', pointing out that the schools had never really departed from the basics and indeed there was an awful lot of boring and tedious work in the basics going on and it might be a good idea if some of this were set aside in favour of something more imaginative and more closely linked to the perceived present needs of children. In the General Election of 1979, however, attention was again turned to the way in which education was failing to meet the needs of the country. The rhetoric had it that progressive education (seen as synonymous with 'permissive') was the product of socialist thinking and was producing a sloppy-mindedness in children and in turn in the adults into which they grew, thus undermining the economic life of the country.

The new administration soon moved to increase accountability in the education service. In 1980 and 1981 two Education Acts were passed. The first required schools to provide more information about themselves to parents than had generally been the case, and the second required them to publish their results in public examinations. In 1981 Sir Keith Joseph, Secretary of State for Education, announced that from then onwards HMI reports would also be made public. These reports had always been restricted to the school in question, its LEA and to the Department of Education and Science.

Reviewing the ten years between 1970 and 1980, they could perhaps be summarized as follows. There had been a change in the popular mood over the decade, from one of a general lack of anxiety over the quality of education provided by the State, to a mood in which schools were suspected of being inefficient and ineffective institutions and teachers in general suspected of being lazy or incompetent, or both. There were demands for more inspection but inspection is a very costly activity and certainly in the detail and in the breadth that was being called for, probably impracticable. So in various DES policy documents around that time (see for instance DES 1977b) schools were exhorted to inspect themselves, that is to adopt some form of school-based review.

By 1982 two-thirds of all LEAs in England and Wales had been involved in the development of schemes for school-based review and about forty of these LEAs had already published them. What is very interesting and significant now is that none of these schemes made any provision for the appraisal of individual teachers. Indeed, far from the appraisal of teachers being included, the reverse was true: many of the schemes specifically denied that such a procedure was part of school review. School review, the schemes claimed, is institutionally focused for an institutional not an individual accountability. Research carried out at the Open University (Clift *et al.* 1987) suggests that these schemes have been relatively ineffective in their impact on the quality of education in schools. What the implementation of these schemes may have achieved, however, is to develop a climate of opinion within the education service in which the introduction of regular systematic appraisal of teachers was feasible. There is evidence for this in the correlation between the places where such schemes have been used and where teacher appraisal seems now spontaneously to be starting.

An appreciation of the impotence of school-based review without teacher appraisal and of this receptive attitude may have encouraged the DES to advance the idea of teacher appraisal. Thus in 1983, the White Paper, 'Teaching Quality' (DES 1983 para 90) talks about the 'relationship between the structure of the salary scales and policies for promoting commitment and high standards of professional performance, greater rewards for the best classroom teachers as well as for wider responsibilities'. It goes on (para 92) to welcome recent moves towards self-assessment by schools and by teachers but

> employers can manage their teacher force effectively only if they have accurate knowledge of teacher's performance. For this purpose formal assessment of teacher performance is necessary and it should be based on classroom visiting by the teacher's Head or Head of Department, pupils' work and the teacher's contribution to the life of the school.

The Secretary of State gave further emphasis to the importance of teacher appraisal in his speech to the North of England Conference in January 1984. He said:

> I attach particular importance to the interesting and innovative work that is going on in the area of teacher assessment, I believe that every LEA should have accurate information about each of its teachers, vital for career development and that information should involve an assessment of performance based on classroom visiting, and appraisal of pupils' work and the teachers' contribution to the life of the school. I welcome the willingness of LEAs and teachers to grapple seriously with these difficult problems.

On a more sombre note he said of teachers 'whose performance cannot be raised to an acceptable standard', 'This is a matter of importance and public concern because of the damage done to the education of some pupils. The aim should be to remove such teachers from a profession where they can do so much harm.'

In March 1985 the White Paper 'Better Schools' was published (DES 1985a). In talking about quality in teaching it says, (paragraph 158):

> the employment of sufficient teachers fosters but does not guarantee quality in teaching, there is much excellent teaching in maintained schools, nevertheless the Government's view reached in the light of reports by HMI is that a significant number of teachers are performing at a standard below that required to achieve the objectives now proposed for the schools.

In paragraph 181 it states:

> the government welcomes the sustained efforts made by many parties to negotiate a new salary structure for primary and secondary teachers embracing new pay scales, a new contractual definition of teachers' duties and responsibilities and the introduction of systematic performance appraisal designed to bring about a better relationship between pay, responsibilities and performance, especially teaching performance in the classroom.

'The appraisal of teacher performance has been widely seen', it says, 'as the key instrument for managing this relationship with teachers' professional career development and salary progression largely determined by reference to periodic assessment of performance'. In paragraph 183 'Better Schools' hints at coercion. It says 'the Government believes that consistent arrangements across all LEA areas within a single national framework are needed for a teaching force with a tradition of movement within and between LEA boundaries'. It says that:

> this could be achieved through an agreement between the Authorities and the Teachers Associations but that the Government believes that it may prove desirable or even necessary to provide that national framework in the form of statutory regulations as is already the case for the probation of new teachers. It is proposed therefore that the Secretary of State's existing powers should be extended to enable him in appropriate circumstances to require LEAs regularly to appraise performance of their teachers.

Appraisal thus became a key element in the Burnham negotiations for 1985. In principle the salary structure that was on offer to teachers would have transformed the profession into one in which status was personal rather than institutional, as was currently the case. After a three-year probationary period, a teacher's further professional progress and salary increments would have been subject to satisfactory review. Responsibility for carrying out the review would have fallen on Headteachers, assisted by local inspectors (or 'Advisers') as moderators. In the event, the transformation of the basis of teachers' remuneration did not occur in the way intended. Although the 1986 pay settlement obliges teachers to take part in a national scheme for appraisal, once such a scheme is agreed, appraisal is not directly linked to salary.

The Six Pilot Projects

In order to determine what should be the nature of a national scheme, the DES has adopted what is becoming the standard model for national educational innovation. Local Education Authorities were invited to apply for Education Support Grants in order to pilot different approaches. The applications of six, Croydon, Cumbria, Newcastle, Salford, Somerset and Suffolk, were accepted. At the same time, an academic institution, the National Development Centre for School Management Training at the University of Bristol, was asked by the DES to take on the coordination of the work of the projects by supporting the trials of a range of approaches to the planning, implementation and monitoring of appraisal in the six LEAs and their schools and trying to ensure that a coherent national scheme results. In response to another invitation from the DES, Cambridge Institute of Education has taken on the role of independent national evaluator of the work of the six. At the time of writing (autumn 1987) little is known in detail of the schemes being developed and it is rumoured that progress is being retarded by antagonism on the part of teachers' unions.

This then is the current situation concerning teacher appraisal. Firstly, it will very shortly become a statutory requirement. Secondly, the methods to be used are still unclear. Thirdly, the direct attachment of salary to appraisal is still unresolved. Merit pay as such seems only to be a minor element at any rate for the present. Of course, there always has been an implicit link between some kind of appraisal, generally of a covert kind, and promotion hence salary. It may be that what we are seeing is some kind of return in spirit to Robert Lowe and payment by results, the Revised Code of the last century. It is all too easy to see a link between the National Curriculum with the 'benchmark testing' provided for in the current Education Act and the appraisal of the performance of individual teachers.

Conclusion

Evans (1951) argues that the best way to evaluate teaching is by a composite of different methods. However, the important question is what purpose appraisal schemes are put to. In this review a distinction has been made between formative and summative evaluation. The former is concerned with professional development whilst the latter is concerned with career decision-making. However, the two are not easily divorced and it is likely that any scheme will be adopted to some extent for both purposes.

It has been noted that in the USA staff appraisal has developed out of approaches to evaluating beginning teachers by institutions charged with initial training. Competency-based teaching programmes are increasingly being adopted by States for the summative evaluation of all their teachers and are being mandated through regulations or State legislation. The methods adopted in such programmes are mainly observation of classroom practice by experts, using observation schedules of different types, and pencil and paper tests to assess teachers' knowledge. There has been a considerable amount of research in America to establish the relationship between teacher actions and pupil gains, and thus to validate competencies. However, much of the evidence from such research is inconclusive and many competency-based schemes have been criticized on grounds of validity.

In Great Britain to date staff appraisal seems to be emerging in a different way to the USA. In addition to traditional assessment by LEA inspectors or advisers, schools are increasingly developing their own internal schemes, many of which seem to have been influenced by industrial practice. The primary aim of such schemes seems to be formative; they are designed to promote job satisfaction, indicate training needs and guide future professional deployment. The method most commonly used is that of an appraisal interview by a senior member of staff. So far the idea of competency-based teaching has not met with approval in Britain. Nevertheless, central government seems to be attempting to introduce systematic staff appraisal by employers for summative purposes. Legislation has been introduced into parliament to give the Secretary of State for Education powers to mandate the appraisal of teachers in accordance with a national scheme, once the nature of such a scheme is decided. At the time of writing, little is known as to how such powers will be used and how far responsibility for appraisal will rest with central government, with Local Education Authorities and with schools themselves.

Whatever the purpose or origins, however, it seems clear from a review of the literature that the greatest problem associated with the appraisal of teachers is that there is virtually a total lack of validated criteria. The seriousness of this lack should not be underestimated.

This issue will be considered again in the concluding chapter.

Chapter 2

The Nature of the Schemes Studied

Introduction

Before describing how the case studies were carried out, we first need to explain the basis upon which the particular schemes were selected and give some information about them. Initially we estimated that we could manage to study eight schemes. This number was later increased to ten, but exigencies reduced the number finally studied to eight again. The reasons for these changes are set out below.

The Population from which the Sample was Drawn

Our Review and Register (Turner and Clift 1985) provided both a population of fifty-six institutions from which a sample could be drawn for case study and a classification for 'theoretical' sampling. By this we mean rather than choosing schemes which were representative or typical, schemes enabling us to test out certain emerging theoretical ideas would be selected for study. Thus, it might be useful from this point of view to select a scheme which is untypical or even unique on the grounds that the data produced could highlight particular theoretical issues. It should also be emphasized that the research was qualitative in nature with a consequent emphasis on processes and perspectives rather than seeking to demonstrate statistically significant trends or test generalizable hypotheses. This report thus deals with the range and variety of school- and college-based teacher appraisal and of the reactions to it, not with the prevalence of different arrangements and reactions to them.

Factors in the selection of case study schemes

In thus making our selection of institutions for case study, a number of factors were considered likely to be important in terms of influencing the nature and effectiveness of processes of appraisal. Each of these factors is considered below.

The first and perhaps most obvious one is size. It was anticipated that large institutions would have a very different management structure and ethos from smaller ones and that this would strongly influence appraisal processes. A further and related consideration was the phase of education. We had originally intended to split the number of case studies equally between the primary and secondary phases. However, there are very few primary school schemes in our register and as a consequence we decided to concentrate more on different types of secondary school schemes. Furthermore, we thought it would be valuable to consider post-compulsory education and consequently selected a College of Further Education. Thus the case studies draw upon all phases of education from primary through to post-compulsory, though they are not evenly represented.

How far the nature and impact of schemes depends on their location, from the point of view of geography and particular LEA, was something we also thought needed to be taken into account. Although we were restricted to a large extent to schools which were within daily travelling distance of the Open University, we tried to include schemes from different LEAs and from as wide a geographical area as possible. To achieve this we chose two schools at a considerable distance which necessitated overnight stay facilities. It should be noted that the majority of schools studied were in urban locations as are the majority of schools in the register.

Turning to the nature of the schemes themselves, for our *Register and Review* we had devised a broad categorization of schemes according to how they operated. Four basic types of scheme had been identified:

a) appraisal interview with senior management;
b) observation and interview by senior management;
c) departmental review;
d) appraisal devolved to middle management.

In selecting schools and colleges for case study, it was at first intended to include two of each of these types of scheme in order to make up the eight. However, there seemed to be a trend towards devolving appraisal to middle management and this was being approached in many different ways. We therefore added two more schemes of this devolved nature to the original sample, thus ending up with ten.

There were other aspects of schemes which were thought to be important as selection criteria. One was whether participation in appraisal was voluntary or compulsory and we included an equal number of each type. We also tried to embrace a range of different purposes of appraisal, contrasting schemes oriented towards staff development and self-appraisal with those geared more to superiors making professional judgments on teachers' professional performance.

In keeping with the spirit of 'theoretical sampling', we tried to include schemes having special features which made them unusual or unique, for example schemes which included peer appraisal and even subordinate appraisal, ones which included the appraisal of the Headteacher, ones in which the role of a staff tutor featured, and so on.

Finally, we sought to achieve a balance between schemes which were at differing stages in development. We chose some which were at a very early stage in their development as well as others which had been operating for several years. Unfortunately, owing to industrial action, it proved impossible to study the process of a new scheme actually being introduced.

Practical problems in Selecting Case Study Schools

Given all the above considerations, it would have been difficult to achieve a perfect balance of contrasts in a mere ten case studies, even if conditions had been entirely favourable. Since our research coincided with protracted and often bitter industrial action, this was hardly the case and a number of pragmatic decisions had to be made with regard to the final selection of schemes for study. It was clear at the time the case study programme began that some of the schools and colleges chosen were not going to proceed with appraisal because of the effects of the action. The problem was whether to wait in the hope that the industrial action would ease or to try to find alternatives. The latter strategy was problematic since all schools were affected by the action in one way or another. However, we did take on two more case study schools (which we 'discovered' after the register had been published) at the eleventh hour and this helped to compensate for those which ended up being omitted altogether.

The industrial action was not the only source of problems. One of the schemes featuring departmental reviews had to be dropped due to the Headteacher leaving part of the way through the study. (We had however carried out a case study of a very similar scheme as part of an earlier project, see Clift 1987.) As a consequence of the problems encountered, the balance of different types of scheme altered somewhat from our original intentions.

We thus began the case studies in two primary schools, seven secondary schools and a College of Further Education. Of these, four dropped out altogether: three secondary schools and one primary. We subsequently added an upper school and another primary as replacements. The case studies finally included the following:

1   A primary school with an appraisal interview-based scheme
2   A primary school with an observation and interview scheme
3   A secondary school with an appraisal interview by Senior Management Team
4   A secondary school with appraisal delegated to Heads of Faculties
5   A secondary school with a departmental review scheme
6   A secondary school with freedom of choice of appraisers(s)
7   An upper school with appraisal delegated to Heads of Faculties
8   A college with appraisal delegated to Heads of Faculties

A more detailed description of the nature of each of these schemes is provided below.

Due to the industrial action, not only did some case study schools have to be dropped entirely: activities were also limited in many of them. The intention was to observe appraisal interviews and to interview a range of staff about their perceptions of the schemes and of appraisal in general. This did in fact happen in schools 1, 3, 6 & 7. In the other institutions activities were more limited. The Head of school 2 left in the middle of the project and only two appraisal interviews were observed. In school 4 only one faculty continued appraisals during the industrial action. We interviewed members of the faculty but did not observe appraisal interviews. School 5 presented problems because it merged with another school and the scheme lapsed. As a consequence, activities were limited to retrospective interviews with staff about the scheme. In scheme 8, appraisal interviews were not observed although several interviews with a range of different staff were carried out. Despite this volatility we managed to conduct a total of sixty-three interviews with teachers and to observe thirty-eight appraisal interviews taking place.

The Case Study Schemes

There follows a brief description of the schemes operated by the case study schools and the college.

1. A primary school with an appraisal interview scheme

This is a large primary school with over 550 pupils and 20 staff. The Headteacher conducts all the appraisal interviews and himself was appraised by one of his deputies and by one of the LEA's Inspectors. The scheme was introduced into the school in 1985 and it has a number of purposes — no fewer than twelve are listed on a document which was circulated to staff. Thus, review of past work, planning ahead, staff development, improving performance and career decision-making all feature. It was the Headteacher who initiated the scheme. Having attended a management course he began to counsel staff about in-service training. Initially he announced that he was available to talk to staff on this basis and left it to them to come to see him if they though fit. There was no response from the staff, however, so he decided to institute a compulsory annual programme of appraisal interviews with all teaching staff.

Prior to appraisal interviews, the staff fill in a brief form containing several broad headings: Classroom Organization and Management, Curriculum Development, Professional Responsibilities, Career Development, INSET and Conclusions. The form allows staff scope to decide what specific points to make under these broad headings. The Head also fills in the form and notes down what he considers to be important. Therefore the appraisal interview begins with both parties having independently completed the form. In the interview the points listed are then discussed in detail. Interviews last for an average of about an hour. The outcome is that a third form is then completed, by the person appraised, which records what has been agreed in the interview. It is returned to the Head. Both parties then sign it and it is kept as a record. The other two forms are destroyed. The record is confidential to the Head and the person appraised.

The appraisals take place in the summer term, but at the time of writing this was being changed to the spring on the grounds that it would then be possible for certain changes, agreed in the interview to be necessary, to be made well within the school year. It was thought that by the summer term it was often too late to implement changes that could have been beneficial. At the time the case study was undertaken (summer term, 1986) the staff were into their second annual appraisal interview and slight modifications in the process had already been made. The main change was in the form itself. Initially it had only three sections — Current Year, Development and Future Career. This was modified to the format described above, the most noteworthy inclusion being 'Classroom Organization and Management'. However, inclusion of this category did not mean that formal observation of lessons by the Head were undertaken as a part of the scheme, nor were there plans to introduce it in the future. It was, however, the Head's normal practice to make routine visits to classrooms throughout the school year.

The scheme had the approval of the teacher unions representing the staff and consequently was able to continue despite the fact that there was industrial action taking place throughout the case study period. Owing to the inability to create free time during the normal working day — a problem inherent in primary school organization — the appraisal interviews took place either at lunchtime or after school.

2. A primary school with an observation and interview scheme

This is a primary school of about 300 pupils and, in contrast with the school above, participation in the appraisal scheme is voluntary. A further difference is that formal observation of lessons is undertaken by the Headteacher prior to appraisal interviews. Although the Headteacher conducts all the appraisal interviews he has also instituted peer appraisal as an additional process. This operates by a system of pairings of staff who observe each other in the classroom and conduct follow-up debriefings. However, the industrial action had brought this to a standstill at the time of the case study programme and so we were unable to study it in operation.

The scheme was set up in 1983 and has as its main purpose staff development. The intention is that performance should be reviewed on an annual basis, consideration being given to how improvements might be made, to what in-service training might be necessary and also to career ambitions.

Prior to the appraisal interview the Head observes lessons. Rather than setting the number of visits he undertakes simply to spend 'as much time as I can observing the teacher in the classroom'. No observation schedules are used but thought is given to the six questions in the Open University pack 'Curriculum in Action' (P533), which are:

1   What did the pupils actually do?
2   What were they learning?
3   How worthwhile was it?
4   What did I do?
5   What did I learn?
6   What do I intend to do now?

After the observation the Head then issues to teachers a list of ten questions which act as the agenda for the appraisal interview. As can be seen from the list below, these are fairly broad questions which allow the person appraised — as well as the Head — to set specific topics for discussion:

1   How have you performed as a classteacher/post holder?
2   What are the barriers to more effective performance?
3   What has gone particularly well?
4   What has gone rather less well?
5   How do you feel about your job?
6   What do you like particularly?
7   What do you dislike particularly?
8   Is there any uncertainty or ambivalence?
9   What help do you need from me on courses?
10 What are your career ambitions?

These questions are dealt with at great length and the interviews tend to last for about two hours, being conducted after school. During the interview the Head makes notes and afterwards he writes up a brief report which is agreed and signed by both parties. There is no set season for the appraisals, which occur throughout the school year.

Minor changes were being made to the scheme by the Head but during the middle of the case study programme he left. It was some months before a permanent replacement was appointed and the scheme lapsed. However, the new Head has decided to continue the scheme with some modifications.

3. A comprehensive school with an appraisal interview by SMT

This scheme features an annual appraisal interview conducted by either the Head or one of the deputies. Its purpose is professional development — the identification of problems and in-service training needs, and to improve communication and keep staff records up to date. The word 'appraisal' is not used, 'staff development review interviews' being the preferred terminology. These interviews are compulsory for all teaching staff. The scheme was introduced in 1984 and was partly motivated by the school's experience of a whole-school review which took place a few years earlier. As part of this review one of the deputies had completed individual interviews with staff and such was the success of this that many staff suggested that it would be valuable to have such interviews on a regular basis. Very soon after the review, however, the Head-teacher left, but his replacement responded to the suggestions made and set up a scheme. Progress has nevertheless been slowed down considerably by industrial action which began just as the scheme was getting started.

The scheme features a brief set of guidelines and an interview preparation sheet which is completed by the person appraised and handed to the appraiser one week in advance. This sheet seeks information on subjects taught, in-service training courses attended and brief details of in-service activities. After this, teachers are asked to list what they consider to be the main responsibilities in their work that year. Then there are five questions to be addressed:

1   In what areas of your work have you gained most success, enjoyment and a sense of achievement during the last twelve months?

2   What areas of your work have been least satisfying during the last twelve months?
3   Are you interested in being involved in any other area of the school?
4   How do you see your career developing next year and beyond?
5   What action is needed to make your work more enjoyable and successful?

The completed form sets the agenda for the interview, at the end of which a summary sheet is filled in by the appraiser. This states what follow-up action is proposed (if any), personal aims for the next year and any other comments arising from the review. Some of these interviews have been fitted into a forty minute lesson period, whilst others have needed a double period. At the time of the case study a second session was being instituted to discuss the follow-up, the targets and so on. This was considered to be a better alternative to giving staff the summary sheets 'cold', since they are given out a week after the interview. The second session allows the interviewer to ensure that the summary sheet represents what was agreed.

The school has a staff development committee which was consulted over the setting up of the scheme. In 1985 the committee decided that it was not satisfactory for the interviews to be conducted solely by the Head and deputy.

They proposed to include Heads of departments in this and only to have the follow-up with senior staff. Senior management perceived two problems in achieving this: firstly the need for training Heads of departments to conduct the interviews, and secondly the problem of identifying which department some members of staff belong to. The latter difficulty was compounded by the fact that some departments are very small (consisting in some cases of one person) and there is no faculty structure. Owing to the industrial action the training of Heads of departments could not take place and at the time of the case study visits the scheme was still based on an interview by senior management — although there were still plans to evolve a delegated system as soon as conditions permitted.

4. A comprehensive school with appraisal delegated to Heads of faculties

This comprehensive school has adopted a delegated scheme of appraisal. Because of its size (about 1,500 pupils) the scheme began in a delegated form and has been operating since 1980. It is a compulsory scheme and all staff are appraised, including non-teaching staff. Who conducts the appraisal depends on where the person being appraised fits into the school hierarchy. Whilst Heads of faculties conduct most of the interviews, other people may be brought in, such as Heads of departments. In addition, senior management conduct reviews of departments on a regular basis. Therefore there is a two-tier system of appraisal, one top down and the other operating on very much a line management basis. A further complexity has been introduced by an attempt to set up peer appraisal using pairings in a similar way to the primary school described above.

The purpose of the scheme is staff development. Appraisal is intended to be a 'positive process', designed to rectify problems and to lead to in-service training where appropriate. The scheme was initiated by the deputy Head responsible for staff development and he evaluated it in the 1984-5 school year. In order to help appraisers to conduct interviews a detailed set of guidelines has been produced. There is also an interview *pro forma* (see below) which lists eleven items for discussion. This is not to be filled in, but rather is to help staff to think about aspects of their work prior to the interview.

DISCUSSION PLAN

I would like to discuss with you your plans for the future. Listed below are some questions I would like you to consider in readiness for our discussion. If you would like other things to be discussed please let me know before our meeting.

1　What are the main tasks which you have been working on for the past year?
2　How well have you performed such tasks?
3　What difficulties have you encountered in performing your job?
4　In what areas of your work do you feel you need guidance, and if so, what type of guidance?
5　In what areas do you think INSET would be useful?
6　What parts of your work do you particularly enjoy?
7　What aspects satisfy you least?
8　What skills do you have that you are not able to put to good use at present?
9　What skills would you like to acquire?
10　Are there any general comments that you wish to make about your present position?
11　What are your future plans, either in this school or elsewhere:

(a) Short term;
(b) Long term?

It is intended that these interviews should take place at least annually and that there should be some kind of written record, either a fact sheet or a summary of the interview. This record is to be signed and agreed by both parties and is confidential to the appropriate Head of faculty, the deputy responsible for staff development and the individual concerned.

Following the evaluation of the scheme carried out in 1984-5 it was decided to continue with the scheme in its existing form. However, it was stressed that appraisal should be seen as part of a planned programme of staff development. Suggestions were also made as to how to improve the effectiveness of appraisals. At the time of the case study programme, however, industrial action led to a situation where most faculties ceased undertaking appraisals and senior management has abandoned its review system. One faculty which continued with appraisals did so in response to a demand from its members.

The senior management team at this school have devoted much thought to the issue of management team appraisal. The history of developments in this and an experimental approach to such appraisal are described in Chapter 10.

5. A comprehensive school with a departmental review scheme

This scheme began in 1979 with a voluntary individual appraisal interview system based upon self-appraisal facilitated by the Headteacher. This developed into a departmental appraisal system which included appraisal interviews, observation of lessons and an examination of pupils' work. Given the scale of such reviews the two deputies were brought in, thus making it appraisal by the senior management team rather than just the Head. Thus what began as facilitated self-evaulation seems to have evolved into something more akin to internal inspection.

The scheme had operated initially simply by those who wished to be appraised opting in. For the departmental reviews a department was selected and, at a department meeting, agreement was reached as to whether to have an appraisal. There followed a negotiated agenda for the review, which included a questionnaire, an examination of pupils' work, staff interviews and interviews with pupils about their perceptions. This review was undertaken in the autumn term of 1983 and a report on the whole department was produced. Records of individual appraisals were kept confidential. The intention had been to go on to other departments but the scheme was suspended owing to amalgamation with another school. Individual appraisal interviews were also suspended on the grounds that the process could become confused with appointments for posts in the combined school. Owing to all the amalgamation problems and industrial action there were no plans at the time of writing to resurrect the scheme. There was therefore no possibility of studying a departmental review in progress. The research activity was thus confined to retrospective interviews with teachers who had been involved in the departmental and individual appraisals.

6. A comprehensive school with freedom of choice of appraisers

This scheme is in many respects one of the most interesting and unusual. It is not based on a top-down or a line management model but rather an approach involving peers. Although the Headteacher was perhaps the main stimulus behind the scheme the actual mechanics of it were decided by a staff committee composed of volunteers. The outcome was an approach which might be considered the least threatening way that appraisal could possibly operate. It is non-threatening in three respects: firstly, it is voluntary; secondly, staff can choose their appraisers; and thirdly, they set their own agenda for the interview. No lesson observation is conducted and in terms of frequency there is no pattern — opting in on one occasion does not result in any obligation to opt in again. The only element which might be perceived as even remotely professionally threatening is that an agreed report is kept. This is confidential to the parties concerned, however, and access to it, beyond those present at the appraisal, is at the discretion of the person appraised.

The scheme began in 1983 with the main aim being staff development. The method of appraisal is an appraisal interview which is supposed to operate as a two-way process. Staff not only choose their appraiser but they can opt to have more than one appraiser. Moreover, they are encouraged to seek the views of members of staff below them in the hierarchy. This makes it the only scheme in the programme to venture as far as subordinate appraisal.

Although the scheme operates very flexibly, the staff committee produced a set of topic areas and questions to help guide appraisals. Staff were encouraged to select particular issues which they themselves wished to pursue. The scheme began with a series of trial appraisals and then was properly instituted by the appointment of a staff development tutor. The first people who opted in tended to ask for the Head as appraiser and one of the aims of having a staff development tutor was to encourage and facilitate appraisal at lower levels. To help inform staff a guide to the scheme has been produced. A handbook for appraisers has also been produced to help them to develop the necessary skills. The staff committee had to suspend meetings due to industrial action but appraisals nevertheless continued since the Head managed to build in some time for appraisal within the school day. What further developments might take place once the committee meets can only be speculated upon at this point.

The Headteacher has taken a considerable interest in the issue of Headteacher appraisal and has taken part in several trial exercises with different appraisers. In the spirit of the school scheme he set up a panel of subordinate staff to conduct one appraisal, whilst on another occasion he involved an LEA Adviser (see Chapter 9).

7. An upper school with appraisal delegated to Heads of faculties

Although this scheme now operates in a delegated form, originally all appraisals were conducted by the Headteacher. Since 1984 the Head has only appraised senior teachers (scale 4's and above) and the rest of the staff are appraised by their Head of faculty. The emphasis of the scheme is on review and target setting. It features an appraisal interview based on a very broad framework as set out below:

1   Review of last twelve months.
2   Evaluation of successes in achieving objectives.
3   Discussion of methods of assessment in 2.
4   Selection of short- and long-term objectives for next year (linked to job specification and school initiatives).
5   Discussion of methods of assessment of 4.
6   AOB — agreed between colleagues before interview.
7   Write up, preferably by interviewee, soon after interview (copy to Head of faculty and Head).

The interview agenda is split roughly half and half with review of past work and selection of long- and short-term future objectives. In some cases separate interviews are set up to deal with each part. The scheme is compulsory but the person appraised has considerable freedom to set their own specific agenda within the broad framework presented above. Furthermore the person appraised writes up the report, which is agreed with the appraisers and then remains confidential to themselves, the Head and the Head of faculty. Access to it beyond these is at the discretion of the person appraised.

In addition to interviews the Head has been trying to institute lesson observation as a formal part of the process. Observation would operate in two ways, hierarchically with Heads of faculty observing their staff, then with peers observing each other. This was being instituted in the 1985-6 period but much of the peer observation suffered because of industrial action. What is interesting is the way in which knowledge derived from observation of lessons by Heads of faculties is now being brought to bear in appraisal interviews.

8. A college with appraisal delegated to heads of faculties

This college scheme dates from 1981. Its aim is staff development and it is based on an interview between Heads of faculties and teaching staff in their department. The interviews are termed 'annual reviews' and the intention is that they take place annually — although participation is voluntary. The review is designed to operate as a two-way exchange of views, resulting in an agreed plan of action. Targets which have been agreed can then be reviewed at the next annual review.

Reviews take place in the summer term and Heads of faculties circulate a notice to all of their staff inviting them to take part in the review. Thus, staff in effect have to opt out if they are unwilling to take part in a review. In the first review a form is completed stating the qualifications, experience and aspirations of the person appraised. A second form is completed at the next review which gives details of the individual's professional advancement in the period since the last review. These forms are confidential to the Head of faculty, the person concerned and the professional tutor. The record of the interview is written up by the Head of faculty, but it has to be agreed and signed by the person concerned. If agreement cannot be reached, the record must state this. The professional tutor's role is to provide necessary support and guidance and on request he can be present at annual reviews to act as an independent third party. Thus a safeguard is built in to the scheme in the event of a Head of faculty and a member of staff being unable to see eye to eye. The scheme was reviewed in 1983 and as a result further training for Heads of faculties was arranged. Since its inception the scheme has been refined but is basically unchanged.

Conclusion

In this chapter the rationale for the selection of case study schools has been presented and we have briefly outlined the nature of the eight schemes finally included. Attention has been drawn to some of the changes and developments which have taken place within each of the schools or colleges. An examination of these schemes highlights two important points which must be borne in mind when reading later chapters of this report. Firstly, the form which schemes have taken seems to be determined to a great extent by the prevailing ethos and management structure of particular institutions, something we will discuss in detail in Chapter 4. Secondly, all the schemes are continuing to change and develop but in different ways. The case studies therefore must be seen as snapshots of particular schemes during particular stages in their development. The questions of how schemes are changing, and whether we can identify general trends, will be considered in Chapter 4.

Chapter 3

Project Methodology

Introduction

Having considered the nature of the appraisal schemes included in our programme of case studies, it is now appropriate to describe how we undertook the research in the schools and college and how the data collected were analyzed. Since the appraisal schemes differ in fundamental respects, the nature of the research in each institution followed a different pattern. In every case, however, a similar basic strategy was adopted. This consisted of an introductory stage, where the nature of our research was explained, the negotiations of the specific case study, a series of visits in order to observe processes and/or interview participants, and finally feedback to participants.

Setting up the Case Studies

Having selected the schools which we wanted to include in the case study programme, initially we approached the 'contact' person (see our *Review and Register* 1985) in each school by letter, stating briefly our wish to conduct a case study of the scheme and what this would probably entail. There followed a visit to discuss the matter in more detail. If the contact person was the Headteacher or a member of the senior management team, this discussion usually took place with him or her on their own. In a minority of cases the contact person was not in this echelon and either a prior meeting was arranged with the contact only and what was decided was subsequently put to the Head for approval, or the Head was brought into the discussions from the very beginning. Owing to industrial action it was not possible to explain the nature of the research at staff meetings in most of the schools. In one case we did address a meeting of senior staff but in most cases information had to be communicated in writing. Thus either the Headteacher circulated information about the research being undertaken or we were asked to produce a document to explain the research to participants. Guarantees of confidentiality were given.

If the institutions were willing to be included in the research, we then went on to obtain clearance from their LEA. Since the schemes were devised by schools themselves and were not overtly influenced by LEA policies, this was in most cases merely a formality, requiring little more than a brief explanation of our planned activities. All LEAs granted clearance, several saying that they were pleased that the research was to be undertaken.

With LEA clearance, the next step was to firm up arrangements with each school. This was done in different ways given the differences in the schemes and the schools themselves. The amount to which the contact — usually the Headteacher — sought to guide or manage the research differed. In schools which had adopted delegated schemes, the firming up of procedures took place between ourselves and individuals immediately concerned, the Head in most cases allowing this to take place without being involved. We offered each school an explicit written contract if this was desired, stating what the research entailed and outlining the procedures to ensure confidentiality. Briefly, this last stated that information from individual interviews was confidential to the parties concerned and that no information would be used in any report which named individuals or in such a way that individuals could be identified, nor would the name of the school be used without prior consent. We also offered to return transcripts of tape-recorded interviews to the individuals concerned if they so desired.

Visits to schools

Once agreement over procedures had been reached, it was necessary to try and fit in a series of visits to observe appraisals taking place and to interview participants about their perceptions. This was not easy to do in eight schemes all in different locations. Fortunately the timing of appraisals differed from institution to institution and it was possible to have brief periods of intensive involvement in one at a time. In the interests of continuity and to maintain confidence, we tried to keep involvement with each scheme to one researcher, but this was not always possible.

In Chapter 2 we noted that we were not able to observe appraisal interviews in all eight schools. In some schools we were only able to interview participants about their retrospective perceptions of appraisal, sometimes a considerable time after their particular appraisal had taken place. The weakness of such retrospective interviews is that individuals may well have forgotten some of the important elements of the appraisal and might also reinterpret past events. The accuracy of the information obtained was thus in doubt, but these interviews were of the greatest value as a means of investigating perceptions of the long-term outcomes of appraisal.

In the schools where we were able to observe appraisal interview taking place, we tried to arrange a follow-up interview with the person who had been appraised as soon as possible afterwards. This was in order to discuss perceptions whilst the appraisal was still fresh in their minds. We also arranged interviews with appraisers, usually after they had completed a whole batch of appraisals. It was not of course always possible to arrange interviews at ideal times and in a few cases we were unable to interview certain individuals within the appropriate school term. Given that all visits had to be completed by the end of the summer term 1986, some interviews had to be abandoned.

Data Collection

Our preferred method of collecting data from appraisals and interviews was to tape-record them, at the same time noting anything purely visual which seemed to be of importance. The tapes were later transcribed in full. For this purpose the project employed a part-time audio-typist. We were aware that appraisal interviews are for many participants a threatening experience which our presence might well exacerbate. For many people, being tape-recorded is also a threatening experience. Despite this most agreed to have their appraisal interviews recorded, although some later claimed that it had unsettled them, mainly by inhibiting them to some degree. If they said that they did not want their appraisal tape-recorded we resorted to note-taking, although this meant that we did not have a comprehensive record. We tried to make allowance for the effects of our presence in various ways, and this is discussed in more detail later. In our efforts to make the process as unobtrusive as possible, a few of our tape-recordings were of a very poor quality and difficult to transcribe, with the result that there are many gaps in them.

In the follow-up interviews we sought to identify salient issues in the appraisal and to ask teachers to give their views on these. We also followed up any unsolicited issues raised with us. The strategy was deliberately open-ended and inductive, that is we tried not to impose issues but to find out what teachers themselves considered to be important. To do this we tried not to be directive in our questioning and we asked very broad 'open' questions, such as 'What is your own view of the school's scheme?' and 'What did you personally get out of the appraisal?' Such questions allow for a wide range of response. We had to be very flexible in the interviews and approach each one in a different way. This is not to say that we did not have an agenda and basic questions to ask. What we did was to fit these in where appropriate or omit them if they turned out to be irrelevant in a given situation.

In the case of teachers whose appraisal had not been observed, interviews were conducted in a similar open-ended manner. However, much of the interview was then aimed at finding out about the appraisal itself: how it had been conducted, what had been discussed, what had come out of it and so on. This was to put us in the picture and enable us to decide what questions would be appropriate to follow on with.

In one school we adopted a different approach for the study of the corporate appraisal of the senior management team. Since there were no available 'off-the-shelf' models, the school asked us to become involved in the process itself. The result was the adoption of an experimental 'action research' approach. We went further than mere interviews and observation for the purpose of the research project and actually shadowed members of the team for a day at a time to provide data for their own appraisal. We then evaluated the effectiveness of the strategy. The methods adopted in this particular study will not be discussed further here since methodology is an essential aspect of the report on the study presented in Chapter 10.

Reliability and validity

Three questions need to be asked about the validity and reliability of the data thus collected. Firstly, were the methods of data collection appropriate to the purpose? Secondly to what extent did the teachers included display the full range of possible responses to appraisal as practised in the theoretical sample of schemes? And thirdly, what was the extent of reactivity, what bias or distortion of the data resulted from our presence and the use of the tape recorder?

Turning to the question of whether the methods adopted were appropriate to the purposes of the project, we need to consider this in light of the alternative strategies available to us. Our purpose was to undertake case studies which would highlight different processes of appraisal and the perspectives of a variety of participants who had experienced different types of scheme. We chose to conduct the case studies by making several brief visits to schools whilst appraisals were taking place, or when we could talk to participants — preferably as many as we could fit into each individual visit.

An alternative strategy might have been to conduct in-depth studies in the true ethnographic mode — that it, by becoming an everyday member of the school, just as the anthropologist studies a culture by living within it. This would have entailed spending a very considerable time in each school thus working in far fewer schools, thereby reducing the variety of appraisal practices and perspectives which could be explored. We decided that it would be better to sacrifice depth for breadth.

Let us now consider the question of how representative the teachers in the sample were. In the case of voluntary schemes, one would expect that those who were confident and perceived that they were performing well would opt in. However, this would not mean that our sample would be biased towards such people, but rather that such schemes would inevitably tend to include such teachers.

Another consideration is that those who had initiated schemes would be likely, consciously or unconsciously, to try to present their scheme in a favourable light. They would therefore be inclined to direct us towards appraisals which were positive and productive in nature and perhaps towards individuals who had positive views about appraisal. However, there would be limits to the extent that they could do this. We asked if we could interview sceptics and people who had opted out of schemes and many such people were only too willing to talk to us. We certainly did talk to many teachers who were opposed to appraisal in any form or who objected to the particular scheme operating in their own school, or at any rate had misgivings about it. By giving guarantees of confidentiality we in fact made it easy for teachers to present negative views without incurring adverse reactions from seniors. However, it is likely that we spoke to rather more teachers who had favourable views about appraisal and their own scheme. Nevertheless, as noted earlier, our purpose was not to investigate a typical or universally representative sample of teachers but to talk to as wide a variety as possible of those who had actually experienced appraisal in different forms and to find out what issues emerged from different approaches and situations.

A final consideration is whether there was bias or distortion in the actual process of data collection. Bias on the part of the researcher can indeed affect not only the interpretation of the findings but the very process of interviewing participants and observing events. Here the use of tape recorders helped considerably, by making explicit how teachers were interviewed — so that biased questions and comments could be spotted and the responses of teachers consequently viewed in the light of this. Secondly, a tape-recording of an appraisal interview, even if incomplete, does at least present an unbiased record. It is only where we had to resort to note-taking that it would be possible for bias to affect what was recorded. As there are few such cases we do not see this as posing a serious problem overall.

Another way in which interviewer bias can be reduced is by utilizing more than one person in the research. The fact that two of us conducted interviews and observed appraisals therefore helped to some degree in this respect, although it must be admitted that, having worked closely together for some years, we tended to share opinions about the subject in hand to a very considerable degree!

Finally, the research itself can distort the actual processes by inhibiting teachers or forcing them, consciously or unconsciously, to act in uncharacteristic ways. This is extremely difficult to make allowance for and, beyond speculation, there is often little one can do about it. It is only to be expected that individuals will tend to present themselves in a favourable light and thus would be inclined to 'rise to the occasion' to some extent. Although there is no way one could ever stop this from happening, what one can do is try to keep the tendency in mind. Similarly with those who feel inhibited or threatened by the presence of researchers, there are ways of monitoring the effects of the research, even if these are far from perfect. Sometimes it is possible to explore reactivity in interviews with participants. We did this in a number of cases where reactivity seemed evident and as a consequence we have some data on the matter which can be considered. There seemed to be two factors which produced reactivity in the appraisal interviews: firstly the presence of an observer, and secondly the tape recorder if it was used. These factors are now explored in more detail.

The effects of the observer and the tape recorder on appraisals

The extent to which the observation of appraisals would distort the process did not only become apparent as appraisals were taking place. In the early discussions about the nature of our research, many Headteachers and others responsible for under-taking appraisals were quick to point out what they considered to be the likely effects of an observer. Here is an extract taken from notes made during an early visit to one school:

> The Deputy Head was concerned that my presence would change the interview. He believed that it would in 90% of cases because of things people are already saying i.e. people tend to say 'don't make a note of this' before going into something. Already people tend to come back to him and say 'what I said about such and such wasn't really accurate'. With an observer present it might end up becoming a 'public interview' where it is less possible to bring up delicate matters. He said he wouldn't himself

object to me observing but wouldn't want his own appraisal observed. The Headteacher said he would be willing to have me observe but that it would probably affect his behaviour.

(Field notes, GT)

As we have pointed out already, most of the appraisal interviews were not only observed but were tape-recorded as well. In one school at least it seemed that the tape recorder was more obtrusive than our presence as researchers and that it was the tape recorder that individuals were mostly reacting to. Given that appraisal interviews often went on for an hour or more, cassettes would reach their end and the machine would automatically switch off. At these moments we paid particular attention to whether or not there seemed to be any change. In some cases there was no detectable difference, but in others quite a marked change in behaviour was evident. The most notable case was where there was a pronounced look of relief and relaxation of tension both on the part of the teacher being appraised and the Headteacher who was conducting the appraisal. Indeed, afterwards the Head remarked that it was not the observation of the appraisal which affected it but the tape recorder. In a follow-up interview with the teacher who had been appraised I took the opportunity to ask about how the interview had been affected:

> R ... how far was it [the appraisal observed] typical of the kind of interaction you would have had with the Head were it not being tape-recorded and I had not been there?
>
> T The whole session was typical. At first I was conscious of trying to control my vocabulary etc., and I think he was too but after a while I felt we got into the swing of things a little bit and it lost its importance quite quickly actually. But I did, before I came in, try and adopt a view that it wasn't going to be threatening and I seemed to have mastered that almost.
>
> R Are there any things that you might have brought up that you felt somehow unable to?
>
> T No, none at all.

Here some of the specific effects of the tape-recording of an appraisal are voiced by the person who was appraised and it is interesting to note what these were. It seems that the content and style of the appraisal were largely unaffected but that use of vocabulary became subject to distortion. It is noteworthy also that it was claimed that the effects of the tape recorder diminished as the appraisal proceeded.

This teacher in fact agreed to have the follow-up interview with the researcher tape-recorded, as did most teachers selected for interview. However, there were cases when teachers expressed concerns about the use of tape. Sometimes we resorted to note-taking, for example one teacher claimed that she would feel inhibited by the presence of a tape-recorder and this was considered by the researcher concerned to make taping counter-productive.

Of course, when tape-recording an appraisal interview it is probable that the effects will be greater with one person than with the other. It may in fact have more effect on the person conducting the appraisal than on the person appraised. This extract from a follow-up interview suggests this:

T . . . when he [the appraiser — a Head of Faculty] was talking he was more aware of that [pointing to the tape recorder] than I was. I mean, you might not have noticed this because you don't really know . . .

R Oh I looked at that.

T I think he was much more aware of it being taped than I was, I might be wrong there.

R I noticed that the atmosphere didn't seem to change when it switched off. I have noticed a change in the atmosphere of an appraisal, you know a sigh of relief and a different kind of way of interacting when the machine ran out of tape but that didn't seem to happen, but maybe it was because it was you who was talking at the time and you didn't alter.

T I didn't even really think about it switching off actually.

With some teachers we discussed the appraisal interview but did not observe it. Here it was also possible to gain some insight about reactivity to observation by a researcher. The example below, from a discussion about an appraisal interview, is interesting in this regard:

R Would you like it to be a more critical approach, you know, more like an initial interview say, where you're put on the spot a bit?

T You didn't hear mine, did you?

R I think I would have needed a big bag full of tapes. [Earlier T had said that the interview lasted for three hours.]

T You would! No, actually, if you'd been here, you see, he probably wouldn't have gone on so much. It wasn't me, there were very long silences, because I said my bit ...

A further possible method of obtaining feedback about the extent of reactivity to observation and tape-recording of appraisals is to ask the appraiser for their view. Having conducted a series of appraisals which were observed and tape-recorded, one Head claimed that the tape-recording of appraisals had in general made them more threatening and less helpful to teachers. It is unfortunate that in order to research appraisal it is easy to end up adding to its potential threat:

HT It's interesting that, for what reason it isn't quite clear, [the appraisals] this year, I think were perceived as more threatening and less helpful than last year's.

R Do you know why this is so?

HT Well the most frequent cause is the recording, this I think was perceived by colleagues as being the threat. Not I hasten to add your presence — the human presence I think was not perceived as a threat, the all-hearing tape recorder was seen as a threat. Now whether that is true I don't know, whether the impact of the tape recorder was upon the appraisee or upon me I don't know.

The limitations of a tape-recording are also worthy of comment. Restricting the data to what is audible inevitably misses certain important visual messages and in this regard the following extract from a transcript of an appraisal interview is illuminating: a Headteacher is discussing a curriculum initiative with the teacher being appraised. The discussion moves on to the financial implications of the initiative:

HT I shall find a means of getting that money somehow from somewhere.

T Does that tape recorder take on smiles?

General effects of the research

Not only does the observation and recording of individual appraisals produce reactivity on the part of the individuals concerned; there are more general effects of a school taking part in research of this nature. Returning to the point made about individuals wishing to present themselves in a favourable light, this manifested itself in ways other than what was said in actual appraisal interviews. One potential effect, for example, was to keep certain individuals on their toes — especially the appraisers — and this was noticed by some of the teachers we interviewed. Below is an example, a discussion over the difference between this year's appraisal and last year's with a teacher who had recently been appraised:

T ... on a lot of the things on last year's, nothing happened and then a week before my appraisal this time, everything was very quick. Now I think it's been good for [the Head] to have a researcher because he knows that he's got to do something and he admitted this to me. I said I was surprised a week before this time, by gum you've been going round like a scalded cat.

R So what changed in that week?

T He came to me about a child that I had asked him about right at the beginning of school year and when I sort of very nicely reminded him during the year nothing happened and then suddenly, as I say, everything happened.

Perhaps of more importance, however, was the extent to which the research itself raised consciousness and influenced the actual development of appraisal schemes. It is extremely difficult to assess what changes were influenced by the project and what changes were about to happen anyway. Since many of the teachers who were responsible for the setting up and development of schemes were keen to have information from the project, it is obvious that to provide such information could affect their thinking about the future development of the scheme. It would have been churlish to have declined to offer information simply to prevent this from happening, and in any case one of the project's aims was to disseminate information as appraisal developed. Therefore information was given if asked for and we have tried to evaluate the extent to which the research project has thus influenced development in schemes. Again there are data which illuminate this. A Headteacher discussing changes that have taken place in the schools's scheme:

> HT A further development was that when we came to look at this year's appraisal, partly as a result of your coming in but also because there was natural development from twelve months ago, it seemed illogical that last year's appraisal, that the one issue it did not address was classroom performance and yet here was the central issue as far as teachers were concerned and it didn't really appear.

This extract indicates that there is a 'grey area' between natural developments in a scheme and the influence of the project. Here it seems that the research lent emphasis to something which was 'on the cards' already. The extract below suggests that the research had a much greater effect and that the Headteacher felt some pressure to be appraised himself as a result of discussions with us. Furthermore, having undertaken one appraisal he felt that he now had to include Headteacher appraisal in the annual cycle. The Headteacher describing his perceptions of having been appraised:

> HT I had some feeling of trepidation about it, it was almost as though I was ... when the issue first arose that you were coming in and it was clear that a lot of the research actually was pointing to the importance of the Headteacher's appraisal as part of the credibility of the scheme, which I accept, when actually we embarked upon the exercise and it was going to include me, when I actually made that decision it was just a little bit that I held my nose and jumped . . . . Having done that now, I have no reason not to continue the same exercise next year.

Conclusions concerning the collection of data

The above considerations point to ways in which the research undertaken needs to be interpreted, bearing in mind that there could be bias in the data collection, there could be distortion in events caused by the presence of researchers and the appraisals observed and the teachers interviewed might be untypical as a concomitant of their involvement in a research project. In our view these considerations do not invalidate our findings. By considering possible ways in which such teachers might be untypical, and the data might be influenced by the research process, we are offering some speculations about ways in which this report can be meaningfully interpreted.

The Analysis of the Data

As described above, the main means of data collection was by tape-recording, both of our interviews with participants and of their actual appraisal interviews. This resulted in well over a hundred tapes, the playing time of which varied between about half an hour and an hour. These collected, we were faced with the task of making sense of what they contained. In this we had all along intended to make use of a computer. Those readily available to us were Acorn BBC Bs equipped with 6502 Second Processors. Although more sophisticated machines might have been requested, we decided to see what we could achieve with these relatively modest machines. We engaged an audio-typist and installed a complete system, consisting of computer with 6502 second processor, the VIEW wordprocessor, monitor, disc drives, printer and tape player in the spare bedroom of her home. We impressed upon her the confidential nature of the work which we were asking her to do (though none of the teachers or schools were known to her) and as fast as we were able to gather taped material, sent it to her for transcription on to computer disc.

Transcription is only the first step in the analysis of data of this kind. The print-out of each transcript has to be read and its contents comprehended in the context of the research. To facilitate this, the transcription format we adopted was one in which the text appeared as a narrow column occupying only the left hand half of the screen (and the paper, when printed), leaving empty the right-hand half. As we read through the transcripts (on screen) we classified what was being said, vis-à-vis appraisal, at each stage. For instance, where teachers were describing to us their perceptions of how the particular scheme in their school had been negotiated, we noted 'introduction of scheme' opposite the beginning of the particular unit of dialogue. For our own convenience we termed such units of dialogue 'utterances'. This classification was 'typed into' the empty space to the right of the screen. In principle the amount of space available for this process was sufficient for about fifteen words of average length. Later, when this process of classification was automated (see below) the 'space' available was reduced to about sixty characters, perhaps ten words at most. In practice, to make use of as many as ten words to classify passages of dialogue would have been excessive and counter-productive to our later purposes.

As we read through each transcript, we thus gradually built up a 'thesaurus' of classifications to apply to later ones. This thesaurus grew rapidly at first as each new transcript introduced new concepts, but the growth slowed and came virtually to an end after about twenty had been dealt with.

The problem of access to the data was only half solved by this simple strategy. Some means had to be found to index these classified utterances so that we could quickly go to examples of each when the time came to conceptualize teacher appraisal and to write up the project. To do this we had all along intended to make use of Acorn's VIEWINDEX, which as its name implies, produced indexes from VIEW text files. This particular piece of computer software requires that each word or phrase to be included in such index first be marked in a special way. This 'marking' proved to be a slow and tedious process, much prone to operator error. Accordingly, a program in BASIC was written to automate it. This program proved to be very successful when applied to the marking of the classifications. The final index ran to almost eighty pages of A4 and gave us just what we wanted: immediate reference to any classified utterance in any of the transcripts.

The next stage in the process of data analysis and reduction was to group the various classifications hierarchically under a series of issues. This conceptual task took a very considerable time and when we were satisfied that we had a valid conceptualization we realized that the index, useful as it was, was only able to show us where illustrative dialogue could be found. Any further use of such 'snippets' to illuminate the issues would then either involve retyping them en masse or making use of scissors and glue on printouts. Encouraged by our success in developing a program for automating the marking of the original transcripts, we set to and wrote a simple program which automated the assembly of the categorized passages of dialogue as a series of 'compilation files' on computer disc, immediately accessible either for printing-out in toto or for sampling. It was these compilation files which then formed the raw material for the writing of this report.

Reliability and validity

As with the collection of the data, the issue of the validity and reliability of this approach to its analysis has to be addressed.

The purely mechanical, programmed processes of marking passages, producing an index and assembling compilation files are almost certainly entirely reliable. The Acorn BBC 'B' microcomputers all behaved impeccably and none of our discs became corrupted. It is the human classification of utterances (units of dialogue) and the subsequent conceptualization of issues based on this classification of utterances that has to be justified. We will deal with each in turn.

The classification of utterances   We worked closely together on the process of classification and quite quickly reached the stage where agreement was almost total. The process was thus reliable. This in itself was not sufficient to show that our classification was valid, however. We had become accustomed to one another's ways of viewing things, having worked closely together for some years. We therefore needed an outsider to validate our conceptualizations. In this we were fortunate to have a part-time Higher Degree student attached to us, whose doctoral study also involved research into aspects of teacher appraisal. We asked him to review our conceptualization at both levels and were gratified to find that he was in broad agreement with us. To an extent, however, he too was an 'insider', having shared ideas on appraisal with us for a year or more by that time. We therefore sent a number of the marked transcripts back to the participants with the request that they consider our classification of what they had said. Again, we were gratified to find that they were mostly in agreement with us, though some objected in principle to the process of 'intellectualization' of what they had viewed as 'conversation'.

The development of issues   As noted in the introduction to this report, we had developed an agenda of issues in relation to teacher appraisal for the *Review and Register* which had constituted the first stage of the project and from which the sample of schools had been drawn. One purpose of the case studies was to refine that agenda and 'colour it in' with illustrative material. We thus already had a conceptual framework into which classification of utterances could be fitted. What we needed to establish was firstly whether we could unequivocally assign classified utterances to these issues and secondly how far the case study material necessitated an expansion of that framework.

As to the first of these matters, as before we quickly came to an agreement about the allocation of utterances and issues and our Higher Degree student again concurred. Because of the relative openness to logical scrutiny of this aspect of the conceptualization of the data, we considered that this was an adequate test of the validity of the process. With regard to the second matter, the adequacy of the framework of issues, data analysis processes almost invariably involve data reduction. That is, material is invariably set aside in the cause of clarification and simplification. As will be seen from the chapters which follow, we did not feel the need to expand significantly on the original framework in order to present teacher appraisal as experienced in our theoretical sample of schools.

Conclusion

By the means described, we are satisfied that we had arrived at a sample of schemes which, within the limitations imposed by the scale of the project, allowed us to collect reliable and valid data about a very wide variety of schemes for teacher appraisal, operating in widely different kinds of settings. We are satisfied also that the processes we adopted or developed (whether human or mechanical) for the analysis of these data were valid and reliable. The rest of this report consists of the insights into aspects of school- and college-based teacher appraisal derived from these data.

Chapter 4

The Introduction and Development of Schemes

Introduction

As well as differing in their nature and the purposes which they are intended to serve, the appraisal schemes developed by the institutions studied differed considerably in the ways in which they were introduced and subsequently developed. There do seem to have been general patterns of development, however, and these were outlined in the *Review and Register* (Turner and Clift, 1985). In this chapter we look at the introduction and development of schemes, drawing on detailed information from the eight case study institutions.

As noted earlier, we had hoped to make an on-going study of the process of introduction of a scheme. Chiefly because of teachers' industrial action, this did not prove to be possible. As a consequence, the data on this topic which we present are retrospective in nature, that is, derived from interviews with teachers some time after the event. We accept that, because of fallible memories and the inevitable tendency to reconstrue past events in the light of their perceived consequences, this may yield an incomplete and possibly distorted picture.

With regard to the development of schemes, whilst this also was hampered by industrial action there were certainly developments taking place and we have been able to illustrate these.

The Introduction of Appraisal Schemes

That schemes for teacher appraisal require careful introduction has been stressed by the Suffolk research team (Suffolk Education Department, 1985), yet there is little in the literature to show what lessons can be applied. Most of what does exist consists of brief accounts by Headteachers (for example Samuels, 1984; Bunnell and Stephens, 1984). The issue of participation in deciding the nature of a scheme has also been commented on. For example, the Suffolk team assert that schemes should be introduced with the full cooperation of staff. The extent to which all staff were involved in the process in the eight case study institutions, however, varied considerably.

In order to provide a framework for considering how schemes have been introduced, we have produced a tentative typology indicating the potential range of staff involvement in setting up schemes:

1   Decision by Headteacher
2   Decision by senior management team
3   Decision by senior staff
4   Decision by Headteacher in consultation with SMT
5   Decision by Headteacher in consultation with senior staff
6   Decision by Headteacher in consultation with all staff
7   Decision by SMT in consultation with senior staff
8   Decision by SMT in consultation with all staff
9   Decision by senior staff in consultation with all staff
10   Decision by a staff committee representing all staff
11   Decision by all staff

Thus at one extreme a scheme may be introduced by the Headteacher without any kind of consultation: at the other there would be total staff participation in the whole process of decision-making. Even where appraisal schemes have arisen as a result of a democratic process such as GRIDS (McMahon 1982), however, the decision was not usually unanimous and one would therefore expect some dissent. Samuels (1984) for example notes that at Heathland school the decision to introduce a scheme for all staff was passed by the school policy committee by a majority of only one vote. Furthermore, even if the decision is made by all staff the initial idea or impetus is likely to have come from one person, although this might not always have been the Head (see Turner and Clift 1985). Thus, in most schools a situation exists where an initiator seeks to 'manage' the introduction of the scheme into the school, clinging to their original vision. This is something we shall consider later in the chapter.

In some of the case study schools the decision to adopt a scheme was made almost solely by the Headteacher. To varying degrees, these Headteachers also decided the nature of the schemes adopted. The amount of consultation prior to setting up such schemes in some cases appears to have been very slight. In one school, for example, the teachers were consulted only in the sense that a form for appraisal interviews was produced and they were asked to comment on it. There were no comments, thus teachers played no part in deciding the nature of the scheme.

How far staff were consulted in the eight case study institutions is evident from some of our interviews with teachers. The extent to which teachers were aware of their scheme and its nature seemed to reflect the degree to which they had participated in its setting up. Some teachers were not even aware that a scheme existed until they were actually appraised:

> T   I suppose I was first aware of that (the appraisal scheme) when I was invited for appraisal interview.

Other staff were simply informed about the existence of a scheme at a meeting or through a circulated document, for example:

R How was the scheme introduced to you personally?

T I think it perhaps was just mentioned, mentioned perhaps in a staff meeting or something.

and:

R Was there a general meeting of all the staff to discuss the scheme, or was it simply announced in the form of a letter from the Head?

T As I recall it, just a letter from the Head.

and:

R Was there any public discussion on the scheme in any formal sense?

T It's difficult for me to remember, we're talking about two years ago now. It was mentioned in a staff meeting. Whether it was open to discussion I can't remember — whether we were just told we were going to have it, or not, I really can't remember.

and:

T I can vaguely remember the subject coming up in a staff meeting and there may well have been a small amount of discussion on it but there wasn't anything like an open debate or anything like that and I don't think we were given the choice really.

and:

T The actual machinery of the thing being introduced, that is a hard one to think back to. I seem to remember that there was some kind of discussion and perhaps some guidelines, some discussion as to what staff felt ought to go on and what they thought might be advisable in terms of who was present and so on before they ever actually started. I really can't be too sure.

In all of these examples teachers seem to be unsure as to the extent and nature of any consultation, or whether they had had any real choice. In schools where there was a much greater degree of staff participation, however, there appeared to be much greater awareness about how the scheme was introduced. The greatest level of awareness seemed to be where introduction of the scheme had been placed in the hands of a staff committee. Even those members of staff who were not on the committee knew quite a lot about the nature of the scheme being developed:

T There's been quite a lot of discussion in the staffroom, apart from anything else. I'm not too familiar with, you know the actual workings of their team [the team responsible for the scheme] because obviously that's been reasonably confidential and it's been set up as a sub-committee and people who wanted to opted on to the committee . . . . So I mean it hasn't been a public thing except probably in the fact of the staffroom sort of thing, and you get some quite interesting, serious debate and conversation about it afterwards. We also had an open meeting chaired by the Head about the system.

R What followed on from the committee . . . ?

T There was an open meeting as to what people thought . . . as a staff feedback for the Chair of the Committee and I went to that.

R How many were there?

T About thirty people, I suppose.

Those teachers who opted on to the Committee had the opportunity to shape the scheme in the way they themselves wished to see it develop:

T I had made suggestions from the beginning and they'd been taken up or maybe thrown out but most of my suggestions were taken up actually.

This was true even of teachers who were in principle opposed to the idea of an appraisal scheme:

T Some people had come on to the committee because they didn't like the idea of appraisal at all and thought that they should be involved, either to express this fact, or to become convinced that it was a worthwhile sort of procedure.

R So it didn't just contain people who were keen on appraisal?

T Definitely not.

However, those members of staff who did not choose to be on the staff committee lost the opportunity to shape the scheme:

T I didn't feel I'd got the time to devote to the committee so I didn't put my name forward because I have a lot of other activities going on. It might well have been a sensible thing to have put my name forward so that I could have made it work the way I wanted it to. I didn't feel that I'd got the commitment to do it but when I heard it was getting going I was very concerned that it was going to go too much towards judgment and I felt reassured when I spoke to one or two of the people who had been involved in the earliest [appraisal] interviews where it seemed that it was going fairly sensibly, not always amicably but there was a fair balance of judgment, criticism, help and advice, which seemed to me fair enough. So then I became more interested in it.

Managing the introduction of a scheme

It is the process of managing the introduction of the scheme which seems to be crucial for its later success. We were aware (through our earlier work preparing the *Review and Register*) of schools where an attempt to introduce a scheme had failed. In one school (obviously not in the case study programme) the Headteacher tried several times to introduce a scheme without success. Firstly he introduced the idea to his senior management team, who raised various objections. He then introduced it to Heads of departments with a similar response. Finally he persuaded a member of staff to give a talk on the subject at a whole staff meeting, but the idea was rejected by the staff. Having failed to carry the senior staff with him, it proved impossible for the Head to gain support for the idea from the whole staff. In other schools, however, the 'climate' seemed to be right for the introduction of an appraisal scheme, as Samuels (1984) notes in the case of Heathland school. Despite this, he accepted that the scheme still had to be 'sold' to the staff and that this needed careful handling.

It seems that four main strategies had been adopted for the introduction of schemes in the case study schools:

1   Set up a pilot scheme, evaluate it then extend it to include all staff;

2   start up the scheme on a voluntary basis and later make it compulsory;

3   introduce the scheme in stages, adding further components as confidence grows;

4   start as you mean to go on!

It seemed that the introduction of schemes had tended to follow the usual patterns of management and communication in each institution and it may be that attempts to operate in untypical ways in order to set up a scheme are more likely to fail:

> T   When the appraisal business was set up in this school the Committee was formed. We're totally Committee, you know, Committee this, Committee that . . . !

The setting up of appraisal schemes in some schools seems to have arisen from other developments. There had not been a conscious intention to set up a scheme but other developments brought the issue to a head. Below are accounts by two Headteachers about how their schemes originated:

> HT1   The intention was not I think to institute a system of appraisal. I think it arose because I had over a number of years said to staff, 'If you wish to discuss any matter don't hesitate to come and see me', and for a whole

variety of reasons I suspect that people did not respond to that request. I became aware that there were years going by where colleagues who were long established in the school never got any opportunity to be able actually to sit down specially and talk about their careers, their place in the organization and expectations for the future. So really it started from that . . . but I had already been thinking about, separate from the school, the concept of appraisal and the two then came together, so that there was a logical association, but the initial impetus was that of my failure to actually sit down and talk to colleagues seriously about their careers.

HT2 The scheme here came out of a sort of academic stocktaking exercise which developed from two in-service training days at the end of my first year here. The Authority gave us two half days for in-service training, because I was relatively new and because we were making certain changes. We were doing something which in general terms we called a whole school review . . . One of the things that came up that the staff wanted to consider was what they called 'the teaching environment'. They felt that was something that everybody could discuss, could contribute to a debate and could improve. I think in the very earliest stages they were talking about the physical environment but they soon realized that the most important factor was the teacher.

[. . .]

After I'd been given the excuse by the staff talking about the teaching environment being the most important thing to be improved, we talked about self-appraisal and we decided at that stage that if we were going to evolve any scheme then the senior staff should show themselves to be interested enough to be the guinea pigs. So this is the third full cycle now completed but the year before that was the senior staff, scale 4s and above and me. So that we went through one year before everybody got involved but certainly everybody who was in the school this time last year has been through the whole thing once.

The first Headteacher describes how he eventually got round to setting up formal appraisal as a consequence of his own concerns about staff development, whilst the second explains how the setting up of the scheme was rooted in staff demands for some kind of review. Here the scheme was piloted with the senior staff before being introduced to all teachers: a particular example of strategy 1 (above).

In attempting to gain teachers' acceptance, various arguments were used by the initiators of schemes. Typical was the argument that appraisal would be mandated eventually by central government and that therefore the sooner the school adopted its own approach the better. This raises the question of the extent to which teachers really chose to accept a scheme of their own free will. There seemed to be a fear among many teachers that appraisal of a kind to which they were opposed would eventually be imposed upon them. The response was to try to evolve their own approach and present it as a counter to any national scheme. Thus many of the schemes adopted represent a professional response to pressure to adopt appraisal:

R Can I ask about how the scheme was introduced and how you came to hear of it?

T Yes, well now it must have been early in '83 that the proposal was raised among the staff, that we formed a committee to look into the whole question of appraisal and what could be done within this school. The thinking was that appraisal was something that was likely to materialize in all schools over the next few years. It was going to be unavoidable and it would be helpful to us if: a) we got to know a bit more about it well in advance, so that we knew what the possibilties were, and b) that in the event of things developing in an official, anything remotely resembling compulsory sort of way, that we should be in a position to perhaps have some sort of offering or scheme that was viable and that was going to be defensible and workable, which we could submit or whatever, or have in operation.

In some schools Headteachers introduced appraisal schemes 'through the back door' as it were. For example, one Head introduced a voluntary scheme and approached members of staff individually. The teacher in the extract below was one of those approached with the proposition that appraisal was to be mandated eventually so why not opt in now:

T Well, the Head explained to me that appraisals were coming, this was the thing and that ideally he would like to go through an appraisal with every member of staff . . . He did say to me that he was hoping to do all pastoral members of staff in time, on a voluntary basis. I thought, 'Well if the pastoral staff were going to take part, why duck out now?' Firstly it might cause animosity, if I think, 'Well I'm not going to do it so there.' Secondly if it's going to come anyway, why not get some advance experience!

Here, as in the case of the teacher below, once asked personally and directly to take part in appraisal it was difficult to refuse. The *personalized* approach avoids the danger of the general objections which might well be raised in a staff meeting.

T I could have ignored the invitation, but since the Head was the prime mover behind the scheme it does have a weight of authority behind it.

In different schools, different ways of setting up the scheme were adopted. Beginning on a voluntary and fairly non-directive basis is one way of attempting to introduce a scheme and gain the acceptance of the whole staff:

T1 I think we're taking a very soft approach here deliberately to try and get confidence built up. But I think there would be a move towards probably tightening things up. I would hate it to be a compulsory, strictly laid down system because I think there would be more resentment than ever.

T2 I think it's also the fact that a large proportion of the staff are extremely hostile to the whole concept of staff appraisal and therefore we were very careful not to frighten those members of staff who have a great deal of hostility built in. I think some staff feel that they are threatened by it and we didn't want to allow any sort of excuse for the feeling of threat and I think that in itself tended to prevent us from being completely open and frank.

T3 One Head of faculty felt that the Head had clear ideas and introduced it in a very low key manner. He said he asked us to think about it and come up with ideas etc. It is going the right sort of way and it is based on self-appraisal and people are talking to each other in a professional way about what they are doing and being able to give and take criticism. They are still in the process of evolving.

The example below suggests that for some staff it is not how the scheme is introduced which is the most important factor in its general acceptance, but whether the person who is to appraise them has suitable credibility:

DH When it was introduced by the Head, whatever it was, two, three years ago when he started the thing off, obviously lots of people had lots of doubts, worries, concerns about it. I don't think I ever had any really but then again I trusted the Head's way you see. I think he's got integrity, therefore what he said would actually happen. If he said it wasn't going to go any further, it wouldn't go any further. So I'm quite prepared to bare my soul, as it were.

Changes and Developments in Schemes

Having considered some of the ways in which schemes were first introduced, we will now turn to some of the ways in which they then developed. As we have indicated, some schemes were set up initially to include only those aspects considered likely to make them readily acceptable to teachers, with the idea that other, possibly less acceptable aspects could be brought in later. Schemes have also changed in the manner in which appraisals are conducted. One general tendency appears to be the move, after the first year or so, towards a more formalized or systematic approach. This was noted by many teachers we interviewed:

T1 Well I was apprehensive about the appraisal last year because this was the first time it had been done. I think a lot of us were, but I came away feeling that it was a cosy little chat, in a way, and he put us at our ease and he did that deliberately because he knew how we felt about it.

T2 This year's was more . . . professional, if I might put it like that . . . This time, obviously he'd thought about it and developed it. It was more serious, I suppose. It wasn't quite the cosy little chat . . . !

R Was it very different last year?

T2 I don't know really. I think possibly a little bit, I think it's a little bit more formal this year. Last year it was perhaps a little bit more like a general chat, whereas this year there's been a lot more questions asked.

T3 This year there's been a tightening up, making sure that people didn't just specify one area. You know if someone just said, 'I want to only talk about this' it would be suggested that was not particularly useful.

HT [Appraiser speaking about the teachers] They may get defensive, I don't know, we'll have to wait and see but as I say last year I think I was too gentle. This year I'm going to be more honest. I don't know, I'll try to anyway. I don't know whether it will succeed.

The rationale behind making a change towards a more formal or systematic approach appears to be that once teachers get used to the idea of appraisal they will feel more confident. Given greater confidence, the climate would then be right to go on a little further. That such a strategy is effective certainly seems to be borne out by staff comments. Many teachers claimed that they felt more confident after their initial appraisal and some actually wanted their appraisals to go further than the 'cosy chat' experienced initially:

T1 Having been through it once, I feel far more confident in dealing with it.

T2 I would also like to be told more about strengths and weaknesses.

R Would you want more criticism?

T2 Yes, because it's a help.

The aspect of appraisal which many teachers wished to see adopted was some form of observation of their work. Although many claimed that observation of lessons would be a very threatening prospect, it seems that after undergoing appraisal which did not include some element of deliberate observation, there was some concern that teaching activities needed to be seen by the appraiser. One reason for this was that the appraiser would then have direct evidence. It was also thought by many teachers that observation would make the appraisal interviews more profitable:

T1 Next year I would like to have another opportunity for the formal discussion with the Head but preceeding that I would like the Head to have been part of the teaching activities, to be involved in the teaching activities on at least four different occasions, four different sets of children, as fore-runners to the actual formal meeting. I think that would be far more meaningful from my point of view.

T2 If he could actually get out and see the classroom management and see how you are working . . . it would be nice to have an independant evaluation, for somebody to say, 'Well you say you're doing this wrong but I watched you and I don't think you are, I think you're on the right lines and you could improve it this or that way . . . ' At the moment you have only yourself as a point of reference, you haven't got anybody else because he doesn't come to see you at work.

There was a desire by some teachers to have a two-way system of observation with the purpose of enabling them to share ideas:

> T I think that as a start it's been quite good but there are a lot of developments that need to take place in the process. I think that there needs to be classroom observation, I mean the only person who's ever been in to see me teach was the Maths Adviser . . . I think there should be a two-way process in observation, I don't think it should be just a question of somebody senior observing the teacher teaching and then making comments on it. I think there ought to be the opportunity for the teacher himself to observe those senior to him teaching. I would like the opportunity to be able to observe my Head of Department teaching, for instance. Not that we can directly copy another teacher's techniques but you can still learn from them.

One appraiser did an appraisal of himself through a departmental questionnaire. It emerged that staff thought that he didn't get into lessons enough. The inclusion of observation is therefore a response to his own appraisal. Another Head introduced observation by delegating the decision as to how it should be carried out:

> HoD Now the idea is that at the end of this term we come up with some sort of composite policy on observation, which will not only have the agreement of the senior staff but, because of the way it's been done, at grass roots level, it will have the troops feeling that, quite rightly, they'd had an input into what's coming out.

Another notable change in appraisal schemes is in their agendas. Issues which were perhaps considered too delicate or threatening in the early days of schemes thus came to be discussed in later appraisals. Some of the forms used as checklists or aide-mémoires have also been altered. The incorporation of a new aspect on forms can also raise suspicions, however:

> T This classroom organization and management bit, you see, is new. We didn't have this last year. So because it's new, we wonder quite what he wants and what kind of things he's looking at.
>
> R Has the approach this year differed significantly from last year's appraisal?
>
> T Not really, only I noticed more emphasis on strategies and classroom management. He didn't seem to emphasize that last year at all.
>
> HT [Appraiser] It seemed illogical in last year's appraisals that the one issue not addressed was classroom performance. It's the central issue as far as teachers were concerned and it didn't really appear. So this was added to the form.

There have also been changes in procedure in some of the schemes to improve the nature of appraisals and to improve communication about the scheme:

HT There has been a response to improve the system to give guidelines on what staff should expect.

Another change noticed is that writing up the report of the appraisal has become the responsibility of the appraisees. There have also been changes in who takes the main responsibilty for setting the agenda. In fact appraisal in some schools operates as an organic process and is never the same two years running. Such schemes might be deliberately flexible in order to be able to deal with changing needs:

T1 It certainly isn't settled pattern, it's very fluid, it's changing all the time, demands and needs are changing and fluctuating all the time. We're feeling our way, well of course I feel I'm feeling my way as we go along and one hopes that we're learning and as you talk to colleagues you'll get reflections of that I'm sure.

T2 The appraisal scheme varies year to year mainly because the needs of the individuals being reviewed and the needs of the institution are continually changing, so from one year to another there is a slight sort of shift, so although you might have some criteria which broadly you can say you will apply to the whole review process, given fluctuating circumstances, within that criteria the aims change on a year-by-year basis and what I've just done is a sort of up-date for myself of where we stand in this faculty.

HT1 What I've got in mind is to evolve a scheme in the next three or four years which has many facets to it and the negotiation part at the beginning of the year, say September time, or even at the end of this term, will be to emphasize which aspects, which facets of the scheme are appropriate to the particular teacher, in the particular twelve months that's coming up.

HT2 I think we've got it on record somewhere certainly that in future, if this model were to be offered to people, we would suggest the questionnaire as a means of highlighting areas which could then be selected to be talked about in more detail. Because that's in fact the way our discussions did go. We didn't talk about the questionnaire as a whole: we tended to pick on one or two issues.

HT3 I think if I were doing another one, if I were asked to do another one without any preconceptions as to the pattern it would take, I would certainly offer the schedule of questions as a basis for negotiation without intending to go through all of them one by one as we have done.

Delegation

Perhaps the most common development in schemes in large institutions has been the delegation of appraisal from the Headteacher or senior management team to middle management:

HT1 Ideally I think there's no doubt it should be annually. But I think it would have to be very much more on a departmental basis for that to happen.

HT2 The staff development committee two weeks ago decided that it wasn't satisfactory just to have the Head and Deputy Head doing interviews and wanted to include Heads of Departments and have just follow-up with senior staff.

HT3 A long-term aim is that there will be a senior and middle management section of the school responsible for the work of a number of colleagues and responsible for interviewing, motivating, guiding, helping, supporting, monitoring those colleagues.

R So you're thinking of a line management approach . . .

HT3 That's right.

T Last year we didn't do it with Heads of Faculty.

R Oh I see.

T This was with the Head last year.

Appraisal seems to have been delegated in larger institutions mainly for the practical reason that it is impossible for the Headteacher, even assisted by deputies, to undertake all the appraisals:

HT It's got to be followed up and I think if it is developed — I'm talking about one person interviewing perhaps eight or ten rather than forty — then perhaps I think it's got far more chance of success, far more chance of being followed through properly.

In some cases an attempt has been made to try to find a more appropriate appraiser, given difficulties arising:

HT I should say that given the way the deputies work with me these interviews are the most difficult and —— [one of the deputies] said it was the most artificial. I gave the deputies an opportunity for an outsider appraisal and two of them found it more useful for the job applications side.

Conclusions

In this chapter we have considered, on the basis of retrospective perceptions, how the schemes in the case study schools were introduced to staff and we have gone on to examine the way that schemes typically have developed. It is evident that many were introduced without a great deal of consultation and this is reflected in the inability of many teachers to recall precisely how their scheme was introduced. This vagueness did not seem to occur where the introduction of the scheme was placed in the hands of a staff committee. Whether a great deal of staff consultation facilitates the setting up of a scheme, however, it is difficult to say. Acceptance by staff might have more to do with the nature of the scheme and the credibility of appraisers than the mechanics of its initiation. Moreover, schemes tend to be introduced in ways which reflect existing systems of management and consultation in particular institutions.

Whatever the extent of consultation, it is apparent that there are common strategies to the setting up of schemes. All of them seem to have begun in a deliberately non-threatening way, some being presented as 'pilot' schemes, others as 'voluntary'. Furthermore, the manner in which appraisals were undertaken seems to have been deliberately non-threatening in the first instance, beginning as a 'cosy chat' but later becoming more formal.

The developments in schemes also seem to follow a pattern with the gradual inclusion of aspects which would probably have been unacceptable at the outset. Most notably, the formal observation of teachers at work has tended to be added to the procedures and in schools where this had not happened there is evidence to suggest that many staff actually wanted it, seeing it to be a necessary component of appraisal. A very significant trend seems to be towards the delegation of appraisal. Most of the larger schools had evolved delegated schemes and others had plans to do so. There also seems to have been developments in the 'appraisal agenda' in many cases. New topics have been added which would have been considered to be controversial if they had been included in the first instance. This is reflected in the forms used which have been changed with new items being added. Alongside such changes have been many developments in procedures for appraisal.

Such developments suggest that no scheme will ever be in its 'final' form and that there are perhaps patterns of evolution through which it is necessary for every school or college to go. Appraisal schemes, then, are perhaps best seen as organic in the sense that they constantly adjust to the needs of individuals and institutions.

Chapter 5

The Purposes of Appraisal

Introduction

Inevitably the nature of any appraisal scheme is closely linked to its purpose. As we noted in Chapter 1, disagreements over the purposes of appraisal add considerably to its controversy. From our review of existing teacher appraisal schemes (Turner and Clift 1985) we noted that two basic purposes of teacher appraisal schemes can be identified. These are:

a) *Formative* appraisal concerned with professional development, the improvement of practice by identifying strengths, weaknesses, needs and interests.

b) *Summative* appraisal concerned with the selection, promotion, redeployment and dismissal of teachers.

This is a conceptual distinction, however, and in practice most schemes tend to serve both purposes to varying degrees. Furthermore, in addition to these broad overall purposes, schemes are perceived by participants also to have purposes of a more specific nature.

The success of an appraisal scheme has to be judged in terms of how far it achieves the purpose or purposes for which it was established. Those involved, however, may perceive the purposes of appraisal differently. Senior management may see it in terms of their need to manage staff whilst teachers at junior levels in the hierarchy might see appraisal more in terms of their own professional development. It is thus possible for there to be confusion as to what purposes an appraisal scheme is meant to serve, and teachers may well be appraised without fully understanding the rationale for the scheme in use. Clearly, how teachers perceive the purposes of appraisal will affect considerably how they respond to it and for this reason the purposes need to be fully understood and agreed by all involved. In the words of one teacher:

> I think it has to be clear in everybody's minds as to why we're doing it and what happens to the information afterwards.

Accountability

There seemed to be a fair measure of agreement among the teachers we interviewed about what the purposes of appraisal should not be. At the time of the study, in the context of the media debate provoked by the pronouncements of the then Secretary of State for Education, Sir Keith Joseph, most teachers in the school studied, including senior management, had come to reject the idea that the purpose of appraisal should be contractual accountability, involving any kind of sanction. Sir Keith Joseph had stressed in his speech to the North of England Conference in 1984, in relation to 'those teachers whose performance cannot be raised to an acceptable standard', that one purpose of appraisal should be 'to remove such teachers from a profession where they can do so much harm.' The reaction of many of the teachers in our study to this statement was to set their faces against co-operating with the implementation of any national scheme for appraising teachers. In all of the eight case study schools the issue of the role of appraisal in identifying incompetent teachers thus became impossible to ignore.

In response to teachers' concerns, Headteachers or senior staff in most of the eight case study schools had made it clear that appraisal was not in any way linked to disciplinary measures. Steps were also taken in some of the schools to ensure as far as possible that appraisal was seen as non-threatening and in no way imposed from outside the school. The positive aspects of appraisal were stressed and the accountability dimension rejected. Here is a comment from one teacher who played an active part in creating a school's appraisal scheme:

> We saw it very much in terms of something that was going to be positive to help us develop to the best of our individual capacities rather than seeing it as something that was to be imposed on us from outside as a measure to see that we were keeping up to scratch, as it were. It was going to be something that should push us forward rather than something from outside trying to pull us up.

He went on to say: 'As the scheme stands I don't think it has much of a significance in the area of accountability.'

The denial that appraisal was in a way connected with the dismissal of weak teachers served to put most people's minds at ease in the case study schools. However, a minority of teachers believed that removing such teachers was a necessary purpose for appraisal. Here are comments from two teachers:

> T1 Some [teachers] have got things that they want to hide, perhaps they're not doing their job properly and then I think appraisal is going to be a good idea. There are some weak teachers about and they are the ones that should be appraised and either their teaching improved or they should be pushed out somehow.

> T2 I don't think it's [the school's scheme] adequate. How are they going to sift out weak teachers?

R But is it about incompetence or professional development?

T2 Both.

Such views were not held by the majority of the teachers we interviewed. Indeed there was much concern that appraisal and any reports produced from appraisal be kept within the school and not passed on to the LEA. However, it could be argued that there was a substantial element of internal accountability involved in any scheme in the sense that they create a system whereby teachers are formally accountable to their seniors. In a large school scale 1 and scale 2 teachers would thus be accountable to their Head of department or faculty, who in turn would be accountable to senior management. This element of internal accountability was not always made explicit, but it was noteworthy that in the case of a Head of department who was perceived by the Headteacher to be weak, the role of the appraisal in forcing that Head of department to account for deficiencies was mentioned explicitly by the Headteacher in an interview with us:

HT I looked at how far the Head of Department could account for deficiencies. I wanted to produce evidence and then look at it. The object was to get the department to improve.

Staff Development

Turning to the 'formative' side of appraisal, most teachers saw the main purpose of appraisal to be professional development. Indeed, controversy about the summative potential of appraisal schemes led two of the case study schools to abandon the notion of 'appraisal' as the official term for the scheme and to substitute 'staff development' in its place. After having been appraised themselves, some teachers rejected the notion of appraisal:

T I suppose in many ways it didn't really cross my mind that it was an appraisal, I didn't see it in that light. I saw it much more as a discussion about my hopes and fears about my career and about the work of the faculty.

Professional or staff development, however, tend to be catch-all terms for a variety of activities and from our interviews it soon became apparent that teachers were using them in different ways. Some teachers considered staff development to be virtually synonymous with career development and thus saw it in summative terms — even if unconnected with disciplinary measures and dismissal. Other teachers considered staff development to relate to improving performance and to be quite separate from career advancement. Here are comments from three such teachers:

T1 I'm not looking at staff development in terms of career development. I tend to look at staff development in terms of people doing their job of teaching better.

T2 Staff development I would put in a slightly different way and say that I see that being maybe something where you actually get on and do the job of teaching, or you move to work in a different aspect of teaching.

T3 There's no doubt at all that the scheme as it stands is primarily directed at professional development and only secondarily towards thinking about career prospects. It has things to offer regarding that [i.e. career prospects] but much less easily definable than the area of professional development.

Yet it was obvious to most teachers that improving one's performance is bound to have implications for career development and that to try to separate the two, and to argue that appraisal was not about career development, is impossible. One teacher argued:

T I was trying to work out whether there was anything about career development in the scheme as opposed to just self-appraisal and so on, and I'd say
that's where it's weakest, because last year, I read through — —'s [a col-
league] stuff and he was criticized for over-emphasizing promotion! Now, I
find that a little bit hard to take from a man who was a Head by the time he
was 33, you know, and everybody who is ambitious obviously puts their
emphasis on being promoted, don't they? And obviously you are promoted
because you develop professionally and you have clear-sighted aims and so
on.

The divergence of opinion here is between those teachers who saw the purpose of appraisal to be improving performance as an end in its own right, and those who believed that appraisal should be linked explicitly in some way to a system of rewards. Teachers who wanted appraisal to be linked in this way argued that those who came out of an appraisal in a favourable light should gain in career terms as a result:

T You see one of the things which I'm not too sure about is that if you do have
an appraisal scheme and it's a successful one, then those people who are
showing talent and enthusiasm and all the rest of it should in some way feel
rewarded by the system of appraisal. Now, I don't think that is going to
happen here. Now, what's going to happen is we're obviously going to set
ourselves goals, review our progress and so on, but we are not in fact setting
up a situation where somebody who is appraised to be exceptionally gifted
then advances careerwise more than somebody that isn't.

This view can be contrasted with those of teachers who believed that an explicit link between appraisal and rewards would create problems. These teachers believed that such appraisal could be divisive and raised questions, such as what of those staff who are not rewarded? Will some staff be told to 'pull up their socks'? A reward system ultimately implies a system of merit pay, which most teachers in our study seemed not to favour. Here is one such view:

T Appraisal is good as long as it is done in a positive kind of way. I think a lot of us fear that we are going to be criticized for our performance. I think people fear it is going to be used for the way we are probably going to be paid later on.

Institutional Developlment

Appraisal schemes in most cases were set up by senior management and thus tend inevitably to have a managerial function. That appraisal has a vital purpose for the regular review and management of individual teachers is something of which many Headteachers and senior staff are increasingly becoming aware. Thus a school's appraisal scheme can be seen as an integral part of a system of management. The view of the Headteacher below is that appraisal is part of a strategy for managing change and is linked with other aspects of institutional development:

HT I see appraisal in a context, only as a strand in staff development. It is part of the control loop, part of managing change. It is false to pull it out as a separate issue. It would not be possible were not other strands in place.

Appraisal can be viewed as 'personnel management':

T Essentially in the current ethos of the school, personnel management is seen as an important function of a Head of faculty, therefore the appraisal is his task.

On the other hand, some teachers were suspicious of the managerial purposes of appraisal. Senior management might have the best interests of the school at heart but what of the interests of the individual? The view of such teachers was that appraisal would be used primarily for the benefit of the school rather than the individual:

T I really don't know whether he's [the Head] going to use it for the teachers' good or whether he's going to use it for the good of the school. I suspect for the good of the school.

Thus staff development might be a means whereby senior management can get staff to adjust to structural changes without actually involving them in the political decisions surrounding such changes. This was the view of one teacher:

T We're very much in favour of staff development, we've pushed and pushed for staff development, but it's not got to be done to accommodate structural changes, either in the school or in the courses, which all of a sudden are being . . . you know, happen to change tack every ten minutes, because of political decisions out of our control, but to actually aid people to find confidence to develop new skills in their teaching.

From this point of view staff development can be seen as a manipulative exercise, one of 'people processing' and changing attitudes to facilitate changes desired by senior staff. This seems to be an extremely suspicious view of the purposes of appraisal, but there were teachers who took this line, as illustrated by the comment from the teacher below:

> Some people feel quite strongly that the whole staff development process that has grown up is primarily intended to change attitudes and change attitudes in directions that aren't always made explicit and change attitudes in the direction which would facilitate changes which senior management have defined as being important or appropriate or the direction we're going to take. I don't want to use words like propaganda or anything like that, but some people have felt that staff development is a subtle way of processing them as people to serve the needs of the institution in a way that hasn't been made fully explicit and has not been fully analysed and evaluated.

Whether claims of such sinister motives are valid is difficult to assess. The notion of the senior management team as a sophisticated, conspiratorial group with dictatorial aims and Machiavellian means is one that some teachers in junior or middle management positions quite readily espouse, but one wonders whether in many schools senior management is able to adopt so pro-active a stance. The view from Headteachers and deputies is somewhat different. It is more likely, it seems, for the full implications of their appraisal scheme not to be fully understood at the time of planning. Moreover, many schemes change in response to needs and developments as we saw in Chapter 2. The purposes of appraisal, therefore, might be transformed over time and senior management may have to review its intentions in undertaking appraisal. Furthermore, the purposes which appraisers have in mind when approaching different teachers in different situations varies considerably. This was pointed out by a Head of faculty:

> I see it as several things. It's trying to set some aims and things for improvement all the time. I think if we're not trying to improve things, at least maintain a reasonable professional standard. I mean, if somebody is running a department really well then I wouldn't think it necessary to push them, when I think it's well worth their while having a pat on the back or I'd say to them, you know, 'You are doing a good job but how do you think you're doing and are there any things that you want us to help you with because you're working so hard' or whatever. For others it might be, 'Look I don't really think you are doing such a good job', so maybe it is trying to set standards because we're all trying to enforce some sort of expectations of high standards but it's also a two-way feedback on an information channel for us. In a faculty like this where I've got probably twenty teaching staff, you can't really know what they're doing all the time.

The notion of appraisal as a two-way process relates also to purposes. In appraisal the parties can try to resolve what they see the main purposes to be. The purposes therefore can be seen not as manipulative but rather the subject of negotiation. Here is the view of one Headteacher on the aim of the scheme in his school:

> The aim is to evolve a system of staff development, appraisal, work review, call it what you like, which will have a lot of facets and the negotiated part at the beginning will be between the junior and senior partner as it were, to negotiate which of the facets are appropriate to them.

If a scheme is flexible and multi-faceted there is scope for the specific purpose of individual appraisals to reflect the stage of development a particular teacher has reached. Therefore the emphasis might be career development, or improving teaching, or further training and so on, depending on the needs of the individual. Here is a comment from a Head of faculty who is involved in conducting appraisals:

> It's a review of one's own work with regard to perhaps pinpointing any strengths or weaknesses with a view to consolidating those strengths and suggesting ways of improving where there's a lack of experience or gaps or a need for extra training, or so on and it's also a staff development thing in that people are encouraged to look to the future. They know that this is part of the review process so it's not as if it's just without any warning, so that career development can be discussed and noted and Heads of faculty can then suggest ways of reaching identified objectives. This may be to do with career paths, it may be to do with courses or conferences or other forms of staff development which would be conducive to achieving those identified objectives but those objectives could be anything really. They could be to do with expertise in teaching a particular subject or it could be on the admin. or management side. Of course that would reflect the grade of the member of staff who's having the review.

Career Development

Of course in the case of voluntary schemes in particular, teachers come to appraisals with purposes of their own in mind and these may well be at variance with those of the appraiser. Whilst senior staff tend to view staff development as improving the performance of teachers in the context of their existing jobs, many teachers see it from the point of view of career development involving a move towards a different job and may well come to their appraisal interviews with particular career objectives in mind. One teacher, for example, opted for an appraisal purely in order to find out why she had been passed over for promotion and to find out how she could improve her future chances in this regard:

> T Myself, I had asked for promotion. Initially, I was told I was going to get it and then it was not given to me and I wanted to find out why and felt an appraisal system would allow me to find this out.

The scope which a Headteacher has to promote eligible teachers is of course limited. For this reason alone some Headteachers tried to get staff to see appraisal in a wider sense and not just in terms of seeking promotion. One Headteacher put it thus:

> The school has no points left and we are trying to get them to look at the scheme in a wider sense — personal development and not just promotion.

Another Head argued that promotions are granted whether or not there is an appraisal scheme:

> I've emphasized in many things I've said and written that promotion is the sort of thing that people will get whether we have an appraisal system or not and all it might do is give me better reasons or better arguments for it but I hope that staff generally don't view appraisal as just a way to get promotion.

If teachers perceive a scheme solely in terms of a vehicle for promotion there will be a tendency for those who are not actively seeking promotion to opt out of schemes if they can. Thus, the Head may have to persuade staff that they should opt in for other reasons:

> HT One of the people in the very first year didn't volunteer and I had a chat with him about why. He said that he didn't volunteer because he was turned 50 and he was going for early retirement when he was 55 and he couldn't see much point because he didn't want promotion and I said, 'Well hang on this isn't what it is about and I didn't know you wanted early retirement and it's about that as well' and he opted in on the basis that if I could get him early retirement he wanted to be in.

Job Satisfaction

Similar concerns were expressed by a Head of faculty in another school who had the role of appraiser. Here the importance of job satisfaction was stressed:

> I think we're looking, aren't we, at job satisfaction and changing if that person's been stuck in the same work and they don't feel that they can go on. It's not just promotion, you're looking at how far you can change course or be involved in something which is going on or new and getting something for that. So we're looking at much more than promotion. But that worries me, that: the perception of staff looking for promotion and that's up to me to try and change it.

It was not only appraisers and senior management who wanted to avoid the sole purpose of appraisal being perceived as promotion. Many class teachers wanted to see an emphasis on performance in the job rather than career development. Here is the view of one such teacher:

I have reservations now about how the system works in the school because to some extent it might seem that what we've actually got is what happens in terms of career development rather than perhaps how you're doing your teaching job.

Criticism and Judgment

Whether the prime purpose of appraisal be career development or improving one's performance in the job, there is disagreement among teachers about what might be considered to be a subsidiary purpose; criticism and the passing of judgments.

Whilst appraisers tended to see a role for criticism in appraisal, many were anxious to stress the positive side of such criticism and the fact that it had no link with disciplinary measures. As one Headteacher put it:

> It depends what you mean by criticism. If by criticism you mean a disciplinary issue then I would exclude it from any appraisal session. I do not think it has any part in an appraisal system. If by criticism you mean a comment as to ways in which person X might be able to improve his or her performance then I do see that as appropriate.

Similarly with the issue of passing judgments. Another Headteacher argued that judgment was necessary in appraisal but only as a basis for making constructive suggestions for improvement:

> There's a judgmental issue I suppose which is involved in appraisal but I think even with that, coming out of that must be the developmental side where you are making constructive and definitive suggestions for improvements in matters that have not been right.

From the point of view of those being appraised, criticism was in many cases seen to be not only necessary but desirable. In opting to have an appraisal many teachers wished to have a frank opinion from a member of staff. One teacher, addressing the appraiser, made this explicit at the beginning of his interview:

> I always encourage frankness in others because I like to be frank myself and this is an opportunity, perhaps, for you to point out areas where you feel that I might be letting myself down or I might not be contributing all that I might do.

In the view of many teachers appraisal has to include a judgmental element:

> R Do you think there is a judgmental side to it as well? How far is it a judgmental appraisal?

> T I think to a certain extent it is a judgmental appraisal scheme. It has to be because your Head has obviously got certain ideas about how you should

approach your work: you are going to be judged upon that. Although I don't think it would be judgmental in a negative way, I'd like to emphasize that, I still think it is to a certain extent, it has to be judgmental.

If the purpose is to improve performance then, in the view of some teachers, as well as highlighting strengths, the identification of weaknesses and the discussion of remedies has to be a major part of the appraisal:

> T I think the report is necessary so that the parties can mull over it and say well that's a strength, that's a weakness. Staff development, then this is how you improve strength, this is how you overcome the weakness.

Some teachers went so far as to argue that the appraiser should highlight weaknesses that appraisees were not aware of:

> T I think the appraiser should have some rights too. If they feel that the person being appraised has left out very vital areas [i.e. in their preliminary self-appraisal] where there are weaknesses, he or she should be able to say, 'Well I think it would be worth us discussing those as well, how do you feel about it?' because otherwise it could very much end up being a patting-on-the-back session for everybody, with nothing being achieved.

Feedback and Communication

Many teachers spoke of opting into an appraisal scheme in order to have some 'feedback about how they were doing', which also implies criticism and judgment, as well as acknowledgement of what they have done successfully and encouragement to keep up the good work:

> T1 The purpose of it was to find out how I'm doing: a bit of feedback. It's nice if you can have a formal opportunity to get some feedback.

> T2 I think we all of us like to feel, has he noticed things, have things gone as well as we thought they'd gone, or has he noticed when things have not gone so well. I think that gives us encouragement and I feel that's important to us as well. I think we like to know whether we're on the right lines or whether there's anything we can improve.

Linked with the notion of feedback is two-way communication between junior and senior staff. An important purpose of appraisal for many teachers was to improve staff communication or to set up a channel for communication:

> T1 I see it as making each one of us more aware of each other, communicating with each other and being able to further ourselves.

> HT The scheme was originally seen mainly as an opportunity to talk to senior staff.

An appraisal with a senior member of staff might be perceived as ultimately enabling teachers to evaluate themselves more effectively:

> T To a considerable extent it has got to be self-evaluation, I think. You're encouraged to pay far more attention and analyse far more how you approach your work, how you prepare it and evaluate it and examine what was good and what was bad and to me anyway that's tremendously important.

The purpose for which a teacher decides to opt into a voluntary appraisal scheme also has implications for who might be the best person to carry out that appraisal. In the school where teachers were able to choose their own appraisers, the choice could be made in relation to a specific purpose. The teacher below, for example, pointed out why it was not appropriate to go to the Headteacher for a particular appraisal:

> T Well my aim for the appraisal was to find out about my role as deputy Head of House, find out how I was performing and it wasn't for internal promotion. If it had been internal promotion I'd have wanted to use the appraisal interview to say this is how good I am at being deputy Head of House, how about giving me another job, then I might have had the Head in there as well, but his knowledge of my performance as deputy Head of House would be reasonably small.

If the emphasis is solely on how to bring about improvements and not career development, there is scope for a non-hierarchical approach to appraisal. It was in the context of trying to improve teaching by developing skills that one school set up a system of peer appraisal in addition to the hierarchical system. A senior member of staff described it as follows:

> The emphasis is on the need for training — it has to be skills-based and non-threatening. The emphasis is on methods to improve performance, put in a non-hierarchical context — pairings of staff at the same level in hierarchy.

Outcomes from appraisal

Whilst appraisal might be viewed as a valuable thing in its own right from the point of view of communication and feedback, some teachers viewed its purposes more in terms of producing specific and tangible outcomes. The extent to which appraisal is able to produce any concrete change is something we shall look into in Chapter 12. For the present it is important simply to note that there were teachers for whom the most important purpose of appraisal lay in the developments which follow and that unless such developments do follow then involvement had no point. This was clearly the view of this teacher:

> Appraisal is part of a pattern which includes development. There is no future at all in having appraisal for appraisal's sake if you're not going to do anything with it.

Development can also be seen in terms of learning from mistakes or identifying weaknesses in one's practice which can then be improved upon. In the words of a scale 2 teacher:

> I see evaluation as leading to something you put right — something done that was not happening before.

In this sense development is linked to job satisfaction. Some teachers see appraisal in terms of constantly updating their practice and avoiding falling into routines:

> One of the reasons I wanted to do it was that I don't want to get stale. I have been teaching three years now.

Long-term and short-term purposes

In some cases teachers were able to identify both long-term and short-term purposes for appraisal. Whilst there are improvements which it might be possible to make almost immediately after an appraisal, others are only attainable in the long-term. It is also possible to speak of medium-term aims, these being developments, say, within the next year or so. Long-term aims may not always be realizable, but certain shorter-term measures can be adopted which can help teachers achieve long-term goals. In this sense it is possible to view career development as perhaps one of the long-term aspects of appraisal:

> R Do you orientate it [appraisal] mainly to career, career development or to how to improve practice?
>
> T I think both things must be dealt with. You look at what's going to be best for the department and colleagues' survival in teaching, if you like, within what they are doing at present and then you look at the long term . . . it's worth while splitting it into long-term and short-term aims. Your long-term aims are probably more career based but your short-term aims are what's going to happen within the next year or in the next term or so. When I did mine I divided it into three: short, medium and very long-term aims but the long-term aim is the career one.

The limitations of appraisal

Having looked into the variety of purposes which appraisal may or may not serve, we have considered different perspectives from teachers across the whole range of different positions within the school hierarchies. The purposes may also be the outcome of negotiation whereby it is agreed that, for example, appraisal is not to serve the purpose of accountability. However, what is beyond the scope of appraisal from a practical point of view? Certainly teachers saw some things to be beyond the bounds of an appraisal. One, for example, did not think that the skills of teaching were something that could be passed on from one person to another and therefore appraisal could not be effective in that sense:

> I don't think basically you can teach people how to teach, I think it comes from within. There's just that ability there and you use it to a greater or lesser extent according to how involved you are. I don't think you can actually teach people to be better teachers, to be quite honest. I mean you can give them more information, you can give them better equipment, you can give them new schemes to work with but basically when it comes down to it, the individual teacher, it's all on them whether they can get it over. I mean because that's it in the end, it's whether you can get the children to understand what you want them to understand and if you haven't got the ability to impart the knowledge then you're on a loser right from the beginning aren't you? — and I don't think you can teach anybody that, I think it's a skill you just have.

Conclusion

In this chapter we have examined the purposes for which the appraisal schemes studied were set up, as perceived by those involved. Initially we conceptualized two overall purposes, formative and summative. It was noted, however, that in practice these purposes tend to merge and that appraisal designed for improving the immediate professional performance of teachers can have implications for their careers in the longer term.

Few teachers saw appraisal as having an accountability or a disciplinary purpose, although there is an extent to which appraisal is seen as a means of enforcing internal accountability within schools, making individual teachers more accountable to their superiors through a system of regular reviews of performance.

It was noted that teachers have different views as to the proper purposes of appraisal and that teachers at different levels in the school hierarchy are likely to see appraisal in different ways. Whilst individual teachers might want to be appraised as a basis for career development, those conducting appraisals might want to use appraisal in order to facilitate change or bring about improvements in the status quo.

The purposes of appraisal might also be negotiated between appraiser and appraisee. In addition to overall aims of improving performance and career development, teachers may come to appraisals with more specific purposes in mind which are likely to depend on the context in which they work and the stage in career development they have reached. Teachers will have specific needs at particular points in their careers and the purpose of appraisal can be flexible so that these needs can be addressed.

Whatever the specific purposes, however, most teachers accepted that there was a need for judgment and criticism to play a part in appraisal, but in a positive sense as a means of bringing about improvements. From this point of view appraisal can be seen as a system of professional support and feedback, enabling teachers to make the kinds of changes which can both improve their immediate performance and benefit their career in the longer term.

Chapter 6

Appraisal Interviews

Introduction

Having looked into the introduction and development of appraisal schemes in the case study institutions, we shall now turn to the actual processes by which the teachers were appraised. Central to these and all pervasive was the appraisal interview and this is therefore dealt with first. The evidence considered in these interviews will be discussed here only incidentally. In later chapters this evidence ar ' ie strategies by which it was collected will be dealt with in greater detail.

There were differences amongst the schemes as to which me   rs of staff were appraised and who carried out the appraisals. This is something \   will consider in some depth in Chapter 8. As we shall demonstrate, the status of both the appraiser and the appraisee has a considerable influence on the nature of the appraisal interview. The majority of the appraisal interviews which we observed were conducted by Headteachers, however. Of the remainder, most were conducted by Heads of faculties and a few by Heads of years or houses. As for those appraised, we were able to observe a broad range of teaching staff, from (the erstwhile) scale one teachers up to deputy Heads. Headteacher appraisal is considered separately in Chapter 9. We did not observe any appraisals of non-teaching staff.

Terminology

Appraisal interviews are common to virtually every scheme we have so far identified, even if their nature differs considerably. Not all schemes had adopted that terminology, however. Some had preferred to avoid the term 'appraisal' deeming it to be controversial, even provocative at a time of industrial action and suspicion among teachers about the intentions of central government. Alternatives in use included 'annual review' and 'staff development review interviews'. One scheme had even avoided giving the interviews a title at all! It is interesting to note that, despite this delicacy, in their written follow-up to interviews, most of the teachers in this last school actually *did* use the term 'appraisal'. Terminology, however, gives little indication of the nature of the process and schemes adopting quite markedly contrasting terminology followed practices of an essentially similar nature.

The Physical Context

The physical setting in which it takes place has implications for appraisal interviews. An interview held in the Headteacher's office will be different from one held elsewhere, perhaps even in makeshift accommodation. Furthermore, the way in which a room is set out physically can be important in shaping the type of interaction which occurs. If the appraiser sits behind a desk this may make the interview more formal than if easy chairs are used. It was noticeable that none of the Headteachers observed did use their desk and many took pains to ensure that the appraisee was comfortable and relaxed. Below are some notes made by one of us (researchers) during a typical appraisal interview:

> Relaxed environment — 2 easy chairs, both smoking cigarettes, sitting casually and at the same level. They are close together and there is lots of eye contact. Very good rapport — no occasion where disagreement emerged.

Attempts to ensure a relaxed and informal interview were certainly noticed by those being appraised:

> T Well, it was an informal interview, the Head adopted standard tactics, refusal to use the desk to be on an informal level. I had my ashtray because I smoke and we sat and it was very informal, very pleasant, there was no unpleasantness.

Headteachers could readily create a pleasant atmosphere by having their own room, by being able to make use of easy chairs, and so on. Moreover, Headteachers were better able than their subordinates to ensure that there were no interruptions during the interview. In schools where appraisals were delegated to middle management, however, appraisers sometimes had to fall back on less congenial and suitable consitions. Metcalfe (1985) reported that sometimes even corners of staffrooms became the venue of an appraisal. We did not come across anything this extreme, but clearly in many cases those conducting appraisals had to make do with far from ideal settings. For example, one Head of faculty included in our study, who was responsible for carrying out appraisal interviews, had a tiny cramped office with just a glass partition separating it from a busy corridor:

> R Do you do the interviews in here?

> T Yes.

> R Don't you find it's a bit restrictive?

> T Well I've got that big 'do not disturb' notice up. Yes it's something I've often said to the Head. Actually I pull the curtains across a bit sometimes.

In some cases there were many telephone interruptions. The following comment was made by an appraiser after two telephone interruptions:

There's nothing I can do to stop phone calls coming through, external ones I can but internal I can't.

Despite such problems, many appraisers in middle management positions preferred not to use the Headteacher's office for appraisal interviews — even if encouraged to do so by the Head. The reason for this, again, was to create a relaxed informal atmosphere:

R I suppose if you were to do it in the Head's room it would be like . . .

A We were going to today in actual fact but . . .

R Do you think that takes it a bit out of context and makes it something a bit different, a bit too formal?

A I think there would probably be less honesty. It's difficult: it's a question of pitching it just at the right level, isn't it?

Preparing for the Interview

Before examining appraisal interviews in process it is necessary to consider what preparation might take place beforehand. Just as with teaching itself, appraisals can be well prepared or badly prepared and the amount of time taken in preparing for interviews in our case study institutions varied considerably. Moreover, the appraiser might devote more time to preparing for the interview than the appraisee, or the opposite might be the case.

The schemes certainly differed in the extent to which they included explicit *guidelines* to facilitate appraisal interviews. In the case of delegated schemes, clear guidelines are essential if appraisals are to follow a common pattern. Such guidelines may prescribe how both interviewer and interviewee are expected to prepare for the appraisal. Such preparation might include the observation of lessons, consultation with other professionals, collection and examination of documentary evidence and a written up self-appraisal.

However, the data collected from interviews with teachers in our case studies indicated that in practice many appraisal interviews began with little preparation. The teacher in the extract below pointed out that both he and his appraiser had been inadequately prepared for the interview:

T It was all very informal really and it was ill-prepared. It was ill-prepared on my part and on his part and there has been no follow-up since.

In the case of delegated systems there were cases where appraisers were unsure at first as to what was expected of them:

R Was that the first time you'd been asked to take part in an appraisal?

A1 Yes and I felt very ill-prepared in a way because I was asked towards the end of the week before half-term. I spoke with — — who does the co-ordination etc., to find out what it was about. The only connection I had with that sort of thing before was when we had a meeting with the Headmaster and he produced these documents, which we had to look at, with a questionnaire. I would have liked to have seen that but it wasn't available, so I must admit I felt a bit in the dark and a little apprehensive about whether I was perhaps, well, sufficiently qualified to do it.

A2 Well I had a brief interview with the member of staff responsible for staff development the day before half-term and said can you tell me a little of what this entails. I was at the meeting, which must have been all of eighteen months ago, about what this questionnaire was and I'm not even sure whether I did have a copy but if I did it's now stuck under a ton of paper.

One of the main reasons appraisers gave for the lack of preparation was insufficient time:

A1 I hadn't thought about this very much until yesterday, purely and simply because I just did not have the time to do it and I spent probably about an hour and a half last night just jotting down things that I knew had to be done.

A2 Now we had rather more time to try and organize the previous one, of which that's the report and we attempted to follow a fairly elaborate scheme of consultation, which almost worked. This time round we don't have quite that sort of opportunity, and so that degree of consultation and pre-planning has not been able to take place.

One aspect of preparation, therefore, is consultation between the parties prior to the interview to ensure that both are aware of what is to be discussed in the interview. Some teachers argued that it was important that the agenda was known in advance and that neither party be in the situation where something could come up unexpectedly in the interview:

R So you wrote down the specifics of what you wanted to bring up and then you gave it to him first. How long before?

A1 The beginning of the day before.

R He had time to see it first, it didn't surprise him or anything?

A1 Oh no, that's why I gave it to him early because I know that forewarned is forearmed. But, fair enough, he's had the chance to look at it as far as I'm concerned.

A2 I don't think you should get something sprung on you in an interview, that wouldn't be fair. I mean both parties should state what they wished to discuss or the appraisee should say what they wished to have discussed and the appraiser then has time to come back prior to the interview and just say you know would it be helpful to do this or that. It shouldn't be done actually in the interview because that's not fair, I mean the whole point of this is that it's planned, thought out, logical and not just an incoherent ramble.

A3 I'm a great believer in not getting any surprises in interviews like that because I think there's enough potential tension anyway and I've encouraged people to get together before an interview, if they want to do. (Headteacher)

On the other hand there were some teachers who were of the opinion that a great deal of planning prior to the interview was unnecessary:

T1 I don't really think there's an awful lot you can prepare for, I think it's just a case of going in and discussing the points.

R Having taken part in one on a trial and error basis, are there any ways you would do it differently if doing another or, if taking part yourself, would you like to see it done in a different way?

T2 I think I would feel better about it generally by being better prepared and having a few more guidelines and not literally having to sit there and think up my own guidelines but then again I don't know. Having said that, perhaps it did me good because I had to sit there and think, well what areas do I know about, what can I comment on? Whereas if I'd had certain headings in front of me I'd have been more or less filling up boxes with ideas.

To avoid the problem of prescribing too closely what takes place in an interview, some schemes included guidelines which were merely suggestive. They were meant to give some ideas as to the areas which might be covered in an interview but did not have to be followed slavishly:

T The professional tutor has put together a kind of checklist which people might want to run through a couple of days before they had their annual review in order to clarify things that they might want to ask and things that they might want to say.

R A sort of interview agenda?

T Yes, that's right. You could ignore it if you wanted to it might just stimulate you to talk about some things that you might not have thought of.

On the other hand there are some teachers who found their scheme to be too broad and would have wanted more structure to it:

T The Handbook for Appraisers has only surfaced this morning and so there was very little preparation. I mean — — [the appraiser] said what am I going to do and I said well just pick up on the conversation because it will be quite straightforward because my starting point was how am I doing and then it would have taken it on from there.

R You'd not filled in any forms or anything prior to it?

T No, nor at the end.

R Do you think it would have been better to have done so or do you think it was just okay on a 'try it and see it basis'?

T I got something out of it, I got quite a bit out of it but the structure of it was very loose. In fact sometimes . . . I mean, looking through the system sometimes I think that in places it is a little bit too loose, it allows teachers just a bit too much leeway.

An important element in preparation is deciding the agenda for the interview. The question of what the agenda of an appraisal interview should include is something which needs to be considered in its own right.

The Agenda for the Appraisal Interview

The dilemma confronting any creator of an appraisal scheme is whether to impose an agenda for appraisal interviews or whether to allow participants to come with their own. To some extent this relates to the question of whether the appraisal scheme is a mandatory one, in that allowing individuals autonomy over deciding an agenda does seem to go hand in hand with voluntariness. However, there is a further dilemma here, that of flexibility versus consistency. If an appraisal scheme is to encompass individuals of varying status and responsibilities, and to cope with a range of circumstances, then it needs to be flexible. On the other hand there is a danger that an appraisal interview could amount to almost anything if there is no attempt at standardization.

Below is an extract from an interview with a teacher in a school with a very flexible scheme. The rationale behind the approach is to ensure that the scheme is able to respond to the needs and concerns of teachers themselves:

Throughout the development of our scheme we've been concerned that it be a teacher-motivated and not a scheme-motivated approach. We wanted the concerns to emerge from the staff so that they should come to the scheme and say look I want to look at these aspects with regard to me, this is where I feel my need is, my concern is . . . and asking respectfully enough for the appraiser to be able to say, 'Yes, right, we'll do that, although I think you ought to consider this too.'

On the other hand such flexibility can result in the scheme becoming distorted out of all recognition. In the following extract a Headteacher explains why he is concerned not to devolve the scheme too far in the interests of standardization:

> H I haven't moved away from the Head of faculty [i.e. conducting appraisals] because I fear devolving it to too many people will dilute, alter, change, make moderation more difficult, make comparison more difficult and I've engaged myself in some training of those four people, not because I think I know how to do it but because I want them all to do it in the same sort of way. Now the minute you give people freedom of choice of course, or a wider choice, then you increase problems. I feel that once you start spreading it to too many people you've got different sorts of interpretation creeping in.

From our observations and interviews it is clear that the agenda of appraisal interviews does differ widely from person to person. This is only to be expected in the sense that teachers with different responsibilities are bound to be appraised in terms of such responsibilities. The emphasis of an appraisal interview, therefore, may vary:

> T . . . [appraisal interviews] could be to do with expertise in teaching a particular subject or it could be on the admin. or management side. Of course that would reflect the grade of the member of staff who's having the review.

One consequence of selecting the main aspects of a person's role in the school might be that for a senior member of staff there would be little or no attention paid to his or her actual teaching:

> A The negotiation part at the beginning of the year, say September time, or even at the end of this term, will be to emphasize which aspects, which facets of the scheme are appropriate to the particular teacher, in the particular twelve months that's coming up. For instance it's pointless me spending hours watching —— [one of the deputy Heads] teach, because that's a very minor part of his overall role in this school and I know he's a pretty good teacher anyway.
>
> R To what extent did performance in the classroom feature in your appraisal?
>
> T It didn't because I'm a reasonable teacher and nobody wanted to talk about that because there was no necessity to.

Thus in some cases competence in the classroom might be taken as read and therefore omitted from the agenda altogether:

> R Was it an appraisal of you as a class teacher or more an appraisal of general matters like your contribution to extra-curricula activities, organization, preparation and so on?

T1 It was largely the latter. I suppose it depends on the individual concerned but I don't have an awful lot of problems in my classroom teaching.

T2 I don't think think that came up an awful lot in my appraisal, you know if you are good at teaching or what you do is the right thing . . . No, I wouldn't say we actually talked about the teaching.

Of course, virtually all teachers do more than just class teaching, and most of the schemes were geared to a wider emphasis than merely concentrating on the teacher in the classroom:

T1 A teacher is more than just an operative in the classroom, much more than that, and so we didn't give it undue weight in our scheme.

T2 If one has an overall type of assessment — it's teaching, it's relationships with staff, with pupils, with one's commitment, perhaps including what one does in one's own time. I think that's a much broader and more rounded picture of the teacher being appraised.

On the other hand some teachers criticized their schemes for failing to grapple with the issue of class teaching. One Headteacher in fact introduced 'classroom organization and management' as an item on the agenda for appraisals in response to such criticism:

HT It seemed illogical, in last year's appraisal, that the one issue we did not address was classroom performance and yet here was the central issue as far as teachers were concerned . . . so this was added to the form.

This change was certainly noticed by the teachers:

T I noticed the emphasis on strategies and classroom management. He didn't seem to emphasize that last year at all.

In some cases appraisal interviews concentrated on such matters in considerable depth:

T He asked the strategy you used . . . your aim for each lesson, for your teaching. He went into quite a lot of detail about that. When I decided to teach as groups, why did I decide on that strategy rather than on a formal class lesson, how did I decide, he asked, which I found quite difficult to think of there and then, after school yesterday. It does make you evaluate, it did make me think.

Consideration of teaching in the abstract is something many teachers claimed to find difficult. In schemes (the majority witnessed) where no direct observation of teaching took place, many teachers found discussion of classroom teaching to be vague:

T I wasn't sure what he [the Head] really wanted there, so I had worked out my ideas of what I wanted in the classroom. But it's more 'theory' than practical, concrete ideas. I found that all a bit 'airy fairy'.

It may be that the intended emphasis of a scheme is on matters of curriculum in which case much depends on the breadth of the appraiser's knowledge. In a secondary school, it is almost inevitable that the appraiser will be a non-expert in the subject discipline of many of the appraisees. Given such a lack of knowledge, the strategy of the appraiser was sometimes to narrow the agenda to the *techniques* of teaching rather than subject matter. Below is a comment from a Head of a Craft Design and Technology faculty, in connection with the appraisal of an Art teacher:

A I'm not appraising the subject as such, I'm appraising their methods; I'm appraising their approach to the teaching situation. Whether they were teaching History, Geography or whatever, there would be certain things that I would want to look at — were the organizational structures, the ad-ministrative structures that they put together to enable the thing to work: were they sound; were they the right approaches; etc. Obviously there's an expertise with people, like —— —. I wouldn't say that I knew more about Art or GCSE in Art than him, I would rely on his expertise and his advice on that.

Whoever conducts appraisal is bound to have some gaps in their expertise. It could be argued, for example, that delegating appraisal interviews to Heads of faculties or departments is bound to lead to more of an emphasis on a curricular rather than a pastoral agenda. Some schemes have built up a parallel structure so that a pastoral ap-praisal takes place in addition to the academic one. If a scheme is fairly flexible a teacher may be able to select pastoral matters for attention at a particular time. In the extract below, taken from an appraisal interview, a teacher is asked why he wishes to concentrate on an agenda consisting solely of pastoral reponsibilities:

T I'd like the appraisal to be on my role as Deputy Head of House. I would like to be told how I am doing.

A I'm surprised you are only picking the Deputy Head of House role and not other aspects, why is that?

T It is an area of my role I am not good at assessing myself in, I can generally assess the success of a lesson but not in this area.

That an appraisal interview might have a specific focus at a particular time has much to do with changes and developments in a teacher's work. A teacher who has recently taken on new responsibilities may want those particular responsibilities emphasized in the appraisal agenda:

T Well my particular interest in an interview at this stage was after one year as Head of department and so my interest was very much in the work in the department and my position as a new Head of department. My previous interview was concerned with broader issues. I think possibly this time we've got something a little more definitive to focus on although there are broader things that come in.

In some schools the agenda for the interview consists of the appraisee's job description. In such cases the agenda for each person will differ, but it will be based on what have been agreed are essential aspects of the job rather than random elements chosen at whim. However, the level of detail in any job description tends to vary. Some teachers have a list of specific responsibilities whilst others have a rather vague paragraph. Concerns were expressed by some teachers as to whether job descriptions were flexible enough and others were not of the view that having a job description was a good idea. Nevertheless, one could argue that for an appraisal interview the responsibilities of the person appraised need to be clearly understood and that the main elements of the job need to be clear even if some aspects of it are subject to negotiation and change over time.

Of course there is always the possibility that important things might be omitted from the agenda which one party wanted to discuss. In addition, if the emphasis is on specific things there may be little opportunity to examine teachers' general contribution to the school:

R Do you think you had the opportunity to say the things you wanted to say?

T1 Yes, but at one point I was worried that my contribution to the school as a whole was going to be missed out. We went from my responsibility area to my classroom management and I wanted to squeeze it in.

T2 Not entirely. I like to divide it up into how things have gone outside the school in the County system and then how things have gone for us within the school and then within the Faculty and then within the Department and then my own personal appraisal. I like to look at it from that point of view because all those things are very important and you can see it as a whole then, how you fit into the whole scheme, but that didn't happen.

School policies and the appraisal agenda

The second extract above raises the question of how far appraisal interviews should focus on the individual as opposed to the wider context in which the individual has to work. Appraisal interviews provide an opportunity to address the extent to which individual teachers feel that they are being supported or frustrated in their work by school policies. It is fascinating how quickly roles can become reversed in appraisals so that the person being appraised seizes the chance to air grievances about school policies:

T I talked about sanctions, for a short time, detentions, this type of thing, the school detentions which have been abandoned, I mentioned that, small points about my own personal timetable. I was concerned about the fact that I had too heavy a timetable this year and I would hope that I would get a less heavy timetable next year.

It is difficult to see how one can divorce the evaluation of the work of a teacher from the general policies of the school. Certainly the teachers we interviewed saw school policies to be appropriate matters for the agenda of an appraisal interview:

R The appraisal interview got on to school policies as well, didn't it?

T Yes.

R Do you see that as appropriate in an appraisal interview?

T I think so, really, because it brings out your personal feelings, doesn't it and surely isn't that what an appraisal is supposed to be?

What should not be on the agenda

So far we have looked into what appraisers and appraisees choose to discuss in an appraisal interview. However, the reverse side of the coin is what should *not* be discussed. Deciding a specific agenda is a highly effective way of excluding matters from discussion. It is apparent from our interviews and observations that many teachers believed that there were matters which should not be dealt with in appraisal interviews. In some cases both appraiser and appraisee had agreed (whether tacitly or otherwise) to exclude a delicate matter from the appraisal. Sometimes problems or weaknesses were passed over in the appraisal, to be dealt with separately:

T I've had a fairly difficult time emotionally and financially etc. and I'd left quite a few exercise books unmarked. I just hadn't had the time to do them. Now the Head saw me about that point separately to the appraisal. Now I think this is good because I was being appraised as a Head of Year, not as a Geography teacher. So my appraisal was focused on my role as Head of Year.

There were also cases where the person appraised was of the opinion that the appraiser had brought up a matter which should not have been raised in an appraisal interview. The following extract is taken from an appraisal interview between a Headteacher and a member of middle management. The interview had been amicable and was about to end when the Headteacher suddenly brought up a such a matter under 'any other business':

A Can I then mention just one more thing, ask you to reflect on your relationship with pupils. Do you feel that there are times when you've flown off the handle?

T Yes.

A Too easily?

T It has happened, not so much recently but certainly the Fifth Year have been a trial, some of them are very difficult to handle.

A I'm thinking about that lady [a pupil] who came in to see me on Monday . . . she said she was upset because of the way that you'd reacted.

T No, I hadn't flown off the handle at her. No, all I said to her, and she's a sensitive young lady, I accepted her wish to change subject options because what I'd given her was her third choice, Dance and Drama, and I said to her that I'd given her that and I understood therefore the reasons for wanting to change and I simply explained to her that I'm sorry but she'd come to me too late. I mean it was last thing Friday afternoon and it had been a hectic week and I didn't fly off the handle too, I just said that it involves quite a lot of work to effect the change but I would look into it. Now where I had less time was for the other young lady, who'd been given exactly what she'd wanted and where she'd asked for it and then came to say that she couldn't cope with it . . . I'm sorry, it's a pity that her mum hadn't spoken to me about it and I could have explained it.

A Well, that's how parents often work though, because they don't feel they're going to go into a confrontation and say things that they don't really mean.

T I mean I've always been someone who speaks my mind and . . .

A Well it's just something that I felt I ought to bring up.

Whether or not appraisal interviews are an appropriate occasion for bringing up matters such as that in the above extract is clearly debatable. The fact remains that the teacher claimed afterwards that he felt it was inappropriate with the consequent effects it might have on relationships and of course willingness to go into another appraisal interview in a positive frame of mind. One argument against the inclusion of such matters is that, at least in the above school, an appraisal interview is an annual event and therefore not the time to bring up transient incidents irrespective of their recency — even though they are bound to be at the back of participants' minds. In some schemes it was a matter of policy not to do this in appraisal interviews. The view was taken that the interview is an opportunity to view the whole year in perspective and that transient incidents should be dealt with on an ad hoc basis. The very fact that an appraisal interview is an annual event shapes the agenda:

T My annual review takes a certain form and I think the form is influenced by the fact that it's annual. In other words very large-scale, slow-moving things get discussed rather than minute-by-minute, week-by-week things. If I had a termly review then I might very well start talking about projects which only lasted a few weeks or things which are happening now or might be different next term.

Another potentially taboo topic for appraisal interviews is teachers' lives outside school. The following extract is taken from a discussion between one of the researchers and a teacher who had been appraised:

> R To what extent then do you believe that an appraisal system like this should raise issues concerning your non-school work in that it represents a burden on your energies?

> T I don't think it's possible to avoid this, quite honestly . . .

> R Yes, but let me give you a parallel. In a school I was visiting recently, with regard to appraisal again, the appraisee was a keen member of the Labour Party, a local councillor and a football referee and this kept being raised in the appraisal interview in terms of how much commitment, energy he had got to devote to the school. Now do you consider that's a proper part of the appraisal?

> T If it's to be thorough then I don't see that that can be avoided and in saying that I think that both sides have got to recognize that that is bound to be raised. The danger as I see it is that a teacher put in that position will feel himself being compromised, will feel a threat of judgment is being made in that sort of way. I think it's important that both sides recognize the area and the legitimacy of pursuing those areas but what slightly concerns me is any tendency towards the approach that is to be found in the business world of the man who is prepared to put in seven days a week, sixteen hours a day, the sort of pressure that can be seen in the American business world where the man who is prepared to work himself to a state of almost getting a coronary is going to get the promotion or whatever because he is prepared to give himself so much.

The issue of personality

Perhaps just as contentious is the issue of whether teachers' personalities should be included in the appraisal agenda.

> T When I was thinking about it I tried to keep personalities out of it — I didn't really feel appraisal was the time to bring up personalities and this sort of thing.

> HT I am loath to put in personality issues into appraisal. I think it is fraught with difficulties to attempt to try appraise somebody and to bring in issues of personality.

Other teachers were of the view that, even if the issue of personalities were best avoided, it may be inescapable if it has a bearing on work. This is especially true of teachers working as part of a team:

R Would you just prefer to keep personalities out of it altogether?

A As much as possible but if they're affecting the way I'm working and they're affecting the way the nursery is working I think it's inescapable that they come in, but I think perhaps it's best to keep names out . . . . I think it depends on the level of it, how much it's had an effect, really. I would rather not bring personalities in but sometimes I think it's inescapable when you're working as a team.

In appraisal interviews teachers would sometimes raise matters of personality themselves, especially when discussing frustrations. Matters of personality are what some teachers consider to be essential elements of a good practitioner. Patience, for example, might be seen as a virtue, but there are limits to everyone's patience:

T I find I'm not as patient as I feel I ought to be at times, that's one thing where I feel there is a bit of a problem. I have to bite my tongue at times on Friday afternoon and not to tell them to go away and leave me alone but I find them very, very demanding, which you don't get with the older children and in such a way that I find it very irritating.

Yet teachers would accept that such qualities were such that one could do little about their lack:

R I wondered whether when the issue of say patience came up, whether these are things you can actually change?

T1 I don't think so, I think it's in our basic nature, isn't it?

T2 I can't really see where one can go any further, taking personalities into account because you're not talking about inanimate objects, you're talking about personalities and certain personalities won't respond and you can be sure they won't respond to certain ways of treating — it will only exacerbate the situation.

The view of some appraisers was that such matters should only be raised if there are strong reasons for doing so and that ideally it ought to be the appraisee's decision:

HT I think that it is only an issue if the appraisee sees it as an issue. I mean there are plenty of people who would say either it's none of your business, which is in fact legitimate, or say but it isn't a problem and I mean unless the appraiser has got some very strong reason for raising it . . . I wouldn't raise it unless the appraisee had already said it or expressed some concern about it.

The issue of relationships

A similarly fraught issue is that of relationships among teachers. Although some teachers were of the view that one should not discuss relationhips in appraisal interviews, sometimes they were deemed to be the main reason for a particular difficulty. The following point was made by a teacher who had been appraised by a panel of staff:

> T I had an idea that people would talk about what they felt was important, which I think happened. They felt that the most important thing was that my relationships with the staff had not been as friendly as might have been, which was unfortunate. That was what would stop my promotion.

Relationships are perhaps a more productive topic for appraisal interviews than personality, even if controversial, in that one can at least change one's orientation to another person. The following extract is taken from an appraisal interview:

> A How about [relations] with X?
>
> T If I re-lived it I would have done it differently. Obviously she did feel steam-rollered. I would want to try different methods, I felt there was a danger of her feeling she wasn't contributing. I have tried to talk through things more with her.
>
> A How did you try to talk about ideas?
>
> T I tried to talk it through with her rather than introduce my own ideas.

Let sleeping dogs . . .

Finally on the issue of the agenda for appraisal interviews, is the point that to consider some issues might have *negative* outcomes and might therefore best be left alone!

> T Obviously there are things that one doesn't say in a review simply because you know that despite the fact that it's supposed to be confidential that it might be going to worry the Head of faculty unnecessarily, that he might do something as a kind of panic measure which would be inappropriate.

Thus far in our consideration of appraisal interviews we have concentrated on issues to do with the reviewing of the past and present state of affairs. Unless the main purpose of a scheme is mainly summative (see Chapter 5), there is little point in this unless it leads to proposals for the future, even when such proposals are in effect to maintain the status quo. This brings us to the considerations of target setting.

Target Setting

One result of the spread of industrial ideas and practice to schools has been the adoption of 'target setting' as a component of appraisal. The Industrial Society has been very influential in this respect with two booklets published in 1983, one of them devoted entirely to the question of setting targets (see Trethowan 1983). The purpose of a target setting exercise is, having reviewed past performance, to set specific tangible goals which can be tackled over a defined period of time. This ensures that there is some *outcome* from appraisal interviews and that they do not become oriented solely to review.

Although targets tend to be set for fairly short periods of time — usually the next academic year — in some cases longer-term targets are discussed, especially if career issues form part of the agenda. One of the case study schools has a scheme which is explicitly divided into review and forward planning, and for some teachers each forms the basis of a separate interview. However, in many cases setting targets is given far less attention than the review of past performance. Indeed, in some appraisals the setting of targets did not take place at all.

Perhaps the key point about appraisal targets is that they should be agreed between both parties, since it is considered that teachers would have little commitment to ones which were imposed. Once agreed it is necessary that the agreement is recorded. This brings us to the subject of record keeping generally in which regard agreement between parties is also important.

Records Kept

The subject of recording appraisal interviews is one which, certainly in the early days of a scheme, seems to generate concern among teachers. Whilst many were of the view that there was little point in having an appraisal interview if no record was produced, the nature of the record, who has access to it and where it goes, are all matters over which teachers tended to agonize. In some schools, teachers were initially given the option as to whether a record was kept or not. This was one way of trying to entice them to volunteer to take part in the scheme. The view of some teachers was that it might be best not to have any written record if staff could thereby be persuaded to have an appraisal:

> T   It would be nice if we could persuade more people to risk it [an appraisal] even if they insist that there's not going to be any written record in the end, which is perfectly admissable.

However, even if no formal record is made, some way of noting the conclusions of the interview was found to be necessary, if only to act as a reminder of things which needed to be done by way of follow up:

> A   I don't make a report but what I do is to make a few notes to say, must see so and so, such and such a time in the year.

The agreement of targets might require a further interview. This of course increases the amount of time to be spent on appraisals. In one case study school a notable change in their appraisal scheme was the setting up of a follow-up session to agree targets. However, finding time for these sessions turned out to be a problem, as the Headteacher pointed out in the extract below:

> The people whom I saw in the summer term — I did not organize my time, I suppose, right — I did not give myself the time to follow it up with them, to produce the summary documents and to go over it with them. Now I can blame all sorts of pressures that one is under during that summer term, but basically I suppose it comes down to me organizing my time.

In some cases the explicit recording of targets was thought to be problematic. Even though the Industrial Society booklet suggests that targets sheets should be kept, and an example of one is provided (see Trethowan 1983), in the case study schools this practice was not always adopted. The following extracts point to some of the arguments against the practice:

> A1 I could keep a copy of their aims but if I did so maybe people would look on it as their, sort of, spy in the sky, sort of thing. I don't know, I think there might not be so much honesty about it if I was actually keeping a copy and referring to it.

> A2 We aren't sure whether it is a good idea to keep targets on record. We don't do it normally, except areas on the pro-forma [document used in conjunction with the appraisal interview]. There is also the problem of someone failing to achieve a target. Also people will tend to compare targets and this can lead to all sorts of problems, for instance, why one teacher at scale 1 seems to have targets leading up to their becoming a Head of department whilst another has targets set to deal with mastering the basics in the classroom.

But if the appraiser does not keep any record of the targets agreed there is no way he or she is able to ensure that there is any tangible outcome to the appraisal. It is of course possible for the writing of a record to become an end in itself. Many teachers stressed the need for the interview to lead to actions:

> T If this is just going to be a record that's made and then that's it, it is clearly a waste of time, apart from what he knows now about the situation and what he might do informally. I would hope that we both would look at what we've said . . . that we can at least come to some agreement about what things need following up.

If targets are not recorded they cannot easily be reviewed in a subsequent appraisal interview. Unless the same appraiser is present, the appraisee may choose to ignore progress with past targets. Thus one advantage of keeping a record of the appraisal is to enable the appraiser — even if it is a different person — to place the appraisal in context with what has preceded it. Thus last year's record may form the basis of this year's agenda:

A1 [At the start of an appraisal interview] I wonder whether it would be an idea to take the conclusions and recommendations of the previous report and to give this something of a context within which to work.

A2 Starting from scratch it will be useful for me to see their background because although I have access to their personal files, some of them are very scanty.

Keeping records also enables both appraiser and appraisee to make comparisons with several previous years and to note trends over time:

A I was struck by the differences between what you've said this year and what you said last year.

T Do they always put last year's in?

A Yes, they do so that you can see . . . Yes, I assume they do. Probably after a while they start to throw it away but I know — [another teacher]: he had three or four years of records and we could say, 'Look I've been saying that for years.'

The above extract raises question of whether after a period of time records should be destroyed. Pointing to developments over time might be valuable in one sense, but it might also be the case that old criticisms are hard to counter. Despite making changes the appraisees might find that mud sticks:

A Did you while considering these questions also consider your own classroom control, discipline, whatever? I mean this was an area that we talked about in the previous appraisal and — did refer to problems of classroom control and relationships and the question of personality, or 'eccentricity' . . . . Have you as a result of that made any conscious modification of your approach to classroom teaching?

T Those references go back several years and really described initial difficulties when first I came to the job. Finding a style, finding something that could represent me as an individual and teaching within that style so that there was something in front of which the pupils could clearly identify, then organizing reasonably effective teaching. I don't think that has been a problem really now for a few years. I think I have solved most problems and I feel quite happy that I have classes well enough under control to at times to be able to do quite absurd things . . .

Thus, a record can become an albatross of sorts round a teacher's neck. In some schools, however, much of the threat of having a record made was avoided by giving the task of writing the record to the appraisee. It also has the advantage of reducing the work load of the appraiser:

A I think there are lots of strengths in allowing them to write their own, certainly I think it's removed a lot of the threat in the school to let them write their own. It's certainly reduced the job of the people who are doing the interviewing because they don't have to write fifteen or sixteen of these. (Headteacher)

In other schools the system was changed from one of appraiser recording to appraisee recording, perhaps mainly to reduce the amount of time spent by appraisers, but also on the grounds that since the record had to be agreed by both parties the question of who writes it is less significant. Either party could ask for changes to be made:

R You produce a record of this do you?

T Yes.

R Which is agreed by both parties?

T That's right, yes.

R Does that mean you get together again to decide what you're going to put down on paper, or is it a matter of him writing the report and you saying fine or change this sentence or whatever?

T1 The first time he wrote it and I thought it was perfectly okay and that was the agreed report. Subsequently he's asked me to write it and he's made minor modifications and that's what's been agreed.

T2 The Head made notes during the interview and he asked me first of all did I mind him making notes, or whether he should try to take it all in and write it up afterwards. Now looking back I don't think he did make notes. I think the offer was there and I said I didn't mind either way but after the interview he did prepare an account of the appraisal and he gave a copy to me to read and either agree or disagree with. Now looking back again there were about two or three lines which I did disagree with and I took it back to him and said well I don't agree with this for these reasons and he had it changed. So the actual final copy was an agreed copy between myself and himself.

T3 We had the full appraisal interview itself from which a report was written, which in fact I wrote and submitted to the other three for their comments, which were then agreed.

Where agreements cannot be reached over the record the solution often adopted was simply to record the fact of the disagreement:

A After the interview I write it up as soon as it is finished, get it typed and a week later we both look at it. If we agree we both sign it and both have a copy of it. There are only two copies. The reason for the one week between writing and signing it is to have a period of reflection.

R If there is any disagreement do you try to resolve it?

A Any disagreement in the interview is noted in the record and the record is then agreed. It might be noted in the record that we disagreed on some issue.

What should be included in the record

There are variations between schemes as to what was included in records and the amount of detail. In some cases only basic conclusions were recorded, whilst in others a precis of the actual discussion was attempted. There were divergent opinions as to how detailed a record should be, and of course one result of allowing the appraisee to write it is records of very varied length and quality:

A They vary from half a side of A4, which simply says short and long term a, b, c, d, e and a, b, c, d, e last year was alright, although there aren't many like that. But I can certainly think of a couple which are eight to ten sides that take me about an hour and a half to read. The system might be one of the problems, after all if somebody wants to write eight or ten sides then I suppose they should be allowed to. Equally if somebody wants to hide whatever they hide by only writing half a side I suppose somebody should know what they're hiding and that should be accepted. It's one of the weaknesses of allowing individuals to write their own . . . . Report writing generally, I think, could be much more structured. It might well be simply a case of reminding them what's on the framework sheet and then at least they'd have half a dozen headings under which to make comments, but writing of reports I think is something that we could certainly discuss. (Headteacher)

The purposes of records

The question of how detailed a record should be and what should and should not be in it depends on the purpose of keeping it. Is it simply a summary of what was said in the appraisal interview or does it have some specific purpose? Can it for example become a form of window dressing?

A Some of the reports, I'm thinking of one report that I've seen that went from the member of staff who was interviewed by me, went through. It didn't really reflect what we'd talked about, which was at a sort of honest level, but was done obviously to impress. It didn't say anything wonderful; it fully admitted there were lapses and so on, but it was obviously written in a way to impress.

Just as we saw with the agenda of an interview, the report made can become the basis of airing grievances or for making demands. In the extract below a Head of faculty and a scale 1 teacher end up using the record of the appraisal interview as another opportunity to note that the teacher appraised deserves an additional scale point for his or her responsibilities:

A   All the more reason for giving you a point for doing all the hard work.

T   Exactly my own argument.

A   You will note all this down on your report?

T   Yes I will

Access to records

Clearly the issue of who has access to the record of an appraisal has implications for what is put into it. In most cases those who have access are the appraiser and the appraisee and the Headteacher as well if he/she is not the appraiser. Such records will then be confidential to these parties. However, the issue of confidentiality can be more complex than at first meets the eye. What, for example, if the appraiser is a Head of faculty and a new Head of faculty takes over? Are the records of departmental appraisals automatically passed on to the new Head of faculty? What if the new Head of faculty is an internal candidate who now has access to the records of appraisals of former colleagues and friends? It may even be the case that the new incumbent was criticized in these appraisals. The main issue here is the ownership of records. If the person appraised owns the record then they can ensure that it is not passed on to anyone without their permission. From our observations the issue of ownership was not always clear to those involved in conducting appraisals. In the following extract a Headteacher had to remind a new Head of faculty that he did not have automatic access to records of past appraisals of departmental staff:

HT   [In our scheme] the information belongs to the person who writes it. Now if X wants you to have it, that's his decision. If he wants to start afresh, so be it. Now we made this point particularly when you were taking over as Head of faculty because Y [the former Head of faculty] came to see me one day and quite innocently said, 'Oh I'll be able to get rid of all this job', you know, give it to you and I'm sure it was without thinking, said, 'I'll give him the write-ups.' So I said, 'Well hang on, that's not for you to decide,' and as soon as I said that he realized that he'd committed a slight faux pas and I simply said, 'You go back to each one in turn,' and he did, I know he went back to each individual, and said did they mind if you have this copy and whatever they said then abided by that. So we've got to stick to this feeling that whatever is written is the property of the person who wrote it, even though there is a copy in that file and a copy in the Head of faculty's file presumably. Now it might well be that because of the relationships people don't want past records to be used and so they've the right to destroy them and start afresh. I simply want to underline all the way through this that it is the individual's property, if they decide you can use it, fine.

As for those being appraised, there were cases where we interviewed teachers who had no idea as to how confidential the record of their appraisal interview would be:

> R What about this agreed statement, the summary, what's its status, is it going to be confidential or is it open?

> T I've no idea. You tell me, I don't know.

Confidentiality might be essential to ensuring a frank exchange of views during an interview, but it can also act as a barrier to setting targets in cases where other teachers need to be involved. Achieving targets might mean 'spilling the beans' with another party. There is also the problem of how far it is possible to have corporate planning on the basis of individual and confidential targets. Some schools have attempted to produce a general report reflecting for example all the appraisals of persons within a particular department. However, even veiled and vague general criticisms can easily be deciphered by members of departments and be seen as a singling out of particular individuals. In the extract quoted below a teacher explains what happened when the senior management team produced a general report from appraisal interviews held with staff in the department:

> T We did have meetings as a group after everything had been written down, typed out. We were all given an appraisal document which recorded exactly what had been said about each member of the Department and then we went into this meeting and had a fight, you know, and it was the case of the Head of department trying to defend himself and his department against individuals and there were quite a few people who were quite hostile towards him because he had dropped people in it here and there.

The production of this report for all staff obviously breached the confidentiality of the individual appraisal interviews. This pinpoints the dilemma in attempting to produce targets for the department based on individual appraisal interviews. Another teacher in the same department claimed:

> T Obviously they are not really confidential because if there's anything to come out it must be talked about later on.

Such problems might have been avoided if the teachers involved had been consulted and given control over what information was to be released from their appraisal interviews. If individuals wish to keep their interviews completely confidential it may be that corporate review and planning has to be informed in other ways.

Conclusions

In this chapter we have focused on the main strategy by which appraisal takes place in the case study schools, the appraisal interview. What emerges strongly from this data is the enormous variety of practice, not only from school to school but from individual to individual. We looked at the physical context of the interview, what preparation takes place beforehand, what is discussed during the interview, and we ended by looking at records kept and target setting and their implications for individual and corporate planning. All of these elements gave rise to wide variations in practice and relate to policy decisions. The basic questions are: where will appraisal interviews take place? what will the agenda be? who decides the agenda? how flexible is it? what should *not* be discussed? are targets to be set? what if there is disagreement? will a record be kept? if so, what kind of record? how detailed should it be? who writes it? how confidential is it? who has access to it? how do individual appraisals relate to whole school policy decisions? These are some of the issues to do with the appraisal interview which have to be faced by anyone intending to set up a scheme.

It is clear that no single prescription can be given here to ensure that appraisal interviews are successful. In any case a lot will depend on the skills of the interviewer and the interviewee — something we will discuss later. However, what this chapter has done is to highlight the issues which need to be carefully thought through when deciding the details of an appraisal scheme. Not only does the basic framework for appraisals have to be clear, but all elements of the *process* need to be fully thought out and guidelines provided for appraisers and appraisees. The comment was made by several teachers earlier in this chapter that appraisal interviews should contain no surprises for either party.

Chapter 7

Strategies for Collecting Evidence

Introduction

In the discussion of appraisal interviews in the last chapter, incidental reference only was made to evidence about teachers' competencies and about how well they had carried out their professional duties during the review period. We now turn to this issue and how it was dealt with in the case study institutions.

It is arguable that the main weaknesses of most of the schemes for appraisal which we studied is that they provided little structure or guidelines for the systematic collection of evidence for use in appraisal interviews. In some cases we observed appraisal interviews taking place where there was little or no mention of evidence and much depended on the opinions of the persons concerned. The processes by which such opinions are formed in schools and colleges are intuitive, nebulous, circumstantial and anecdotal. Above all, they are highly subjective.

Few publications to date have said much about a need for valid and reliable evidence in teacher appraisal, let alone how one might go about collecting it. The Suffolk report for example largely ignores the issue in a general sense (Suffolk Education Department, 1985), although much is said in it about the need for *observation* of teachers as they go about their duties to be a part of appraisal procedures. Yet observation is only one source of systematic evidence about teachers for use at the appraisal interview. Other sources which were seen to be in use in our sample were student or pupil outcomes, teacher 'inputs', curriculum option choices, consultations with third parties and the use of existing information, including school documents. These are now discussed in turn.

Indicators of Outcome and Input Quality

A number of teachers included in our studies pointed to particular outcomes which they believed reflected their 'input'. One teacher in the College of Further Education claimed:

> As far as an assessment of my work is concerned that could happen in a very brutal kind of way: if none of the students that I am teaching on their second year manage to get into higher level courses then I shall know I've gone wrong.

However, not every aspect of a teacher's work culminates in a clearly definable end product. The teacher quoted above went on to say:

> There are people in the college teaching on courses, maybe in a 'servicing' faculty, where they don't have any direct connection with the end product of what they are doing, so they haven't got that kind of yardstick against which to measure their work.

Some teachers interviewed, in fact, were not of the view that appraisal should be based on pupil outcomes:

> I think appraising teaching generally is very difficult because teaching is a very flexible thing. I think one of the comments that —— [his appraiser] made right at the beginning was very interesting, saying 'Oh we can appraise by results in the classroom — if the pupils have done well, you know we have succeeded . . .' I don't think I necessarily agree with that.

Examination results

In secondary schools one of the most obvious outcomes by which one might measure the success of a teacher's performance is examination results. If the results are good the implication is that the teacher's performance was too. If they are not, then the appraiser might be able to point to an aspect of performance which requires improvement:

> A I'm in the process at the moment of doing some analysis of the examination results of the different groups within the department and then going into some statistical breakdowns of the various marks that the groups have got. Mine aren't looking very good at the moment. I haven't finished the figures yet by any means but I'm not convinced that the actual class teaching has been as precise as I would like it to be.

Examination results present evidence of a very general nature, however. The appraisers in the extract above conclude that the teaching might not be as 'precise' as it could be. This might not be obvious from the results but rather very much a speculation. The problem here is how one interprets examination results and to what extent they directly reflect a teacher's performance. Consider the following extract:

> A I'm looking forward to the next twelve months, I think the faculty is on the verge of developing very successfully.
>
> T Can I just say that I think this year's exam. results are going to be pretty disastrous.
>
> A Yes but in a sense exam. results reflect what went on some time ago rather than what is going on now.

The concluding comment acknowledges that examination results are a measure of a long-term process and therefore should be viewed with caution in the appraisal of an individual teacher. An alternative strategy might be to assess more specific aspects of learning in the short term. The teacher below outlined one such strategy:

> T It's no good having your short-term goals unless you can assess whether those short-term goals have been achieved and that's really the thing we have sought . . . Obviously every teacher wants to do things in a different way but we wanted to identify certain key elements that we can test as we go along. For instance we've started certain key exercises in the half term's work, so you could have something to compare over, say, the whole third year.

A major objection to the use of pupil outcomes as a basis for appraising the work of teachers is that it is always difficult to say whether particular pupils could have done better with a different teacher. There might be cases when despite poor results the teaching has been good or where a good result might be achieved by pupils despite the teacher concerned. Some teachers certainly believed this to be so:

> T If you have a good teacher and they give him a CSE bottom group, grade 4 is a fantastic achievement for those children. If you are a bad teacher but you have an O-Level group, some of the children go on and get A's what-ever, so it's no assessment of the teacher to look at the grades of pupils in external examinations.

There is also the problem of singling out the effect of a particular teacher on the performance of pupils. This was noted in the literature review (see Chapter 1). The difficulty is that teachers operate as a team and in secondary schools pupils are taught concurrently by a number of teachers. This raises the issue of the context in which teachers operate. As one teacher pointed out, performance can vary considerably in different contexts:

> T There's a question of end product and a question of efficiency. You can be very efficient in one school and very inefficient in another, yet you're the same person, it's a harder school.

Nor should we assume that all examinations necessarily represent objective evidence of performance. Internal examinations in particular might be marked to different standards. This might present the appearance that one teacher is more successful than another, especially in subjects where it is easier to be imprecise, for example music:

> T I think there could be a number of reasons why there are differences in marks. In the marking of the practical part of the music examinations it's quite clear that one member of the department was marking higher the whole way through, with a higher average. It's obviously statistically sig-

nificant. Now we've got to ask whether it was a really good music group or whether the teaching for that group was much better or whether — — [the teacher] was simply adopting a different standard of marking.

Measures of input

So although examination results seem to offer an objective measure of a kind they have to be interpreted with care (see for instance Gray 1982). They are a very crude reflection of an individual teacher's input. A direct measure of input which we came upon was the extent to which a teacher had managed to cover the syllabus. Consider the following comment from a Head of faculty:

A There's a big difference in the way people try to assess. — — was dreadfully worried that he hadn't covered everything and being that sort of person, he wants to cover all the syllabus. Other people aren't so worried about that.

Thus, one could point to having completed the syllabus with a group of students or pupils as evidence of efficiency. But it could be argued that in itself this indicates very little and that it is the *quality* of learning that is important rather than the *quantity* of material covered. Since quality is a very difficult thing to identify, however, one can understand the desire to find evidence in ways which though crude are at least tangible.

Low ability pupils

One of the most difficult things to provide evidence for is how successful a teacher has been with low ability pupils, underachieving pupils and pupils with 'behaviour problems'. Since one would expect such pupils to perform badly in examinations what outcomes might suggest that a teacher has had some measure of success? Perhaps one could point to aspects of progress other than in academic terms. Here are two examples:

T1 I think they have actually benefited from the course. They're much more relaxed with equipment and quite competent with equipment, even if they can't comprehend what scientific principle should leap out at them. Their practical skills have certainly improved and socially they've got on, I mean immeasurably. — — in particular is much more fitted to go out into the real world now than he was a year ago, and — — too, but in terms of what physics either of them have learned, that's negligible I think.

T2 When I first came here I had a poor group and I just slogged them through these Social Studies and out of seventeen we got seven or eight who got Grade One. Now that might be counted as success, but I wouldn't have said that because they got those results I was successful. I don't feel particularly proud of that success: it was just a case that they were a group that needed controlling rather than teaching.

Pupil Option Choices

In comprehensive schools pupils usually have to choose between different curricular options in their later years of schooling. The number of pupils opting for particular courses was taken as providing some evidence of teacher performance in some of the schemes on the ground that pupils often choose a course for the teacher rather than the subject (see Woods 1979). Travers (1981) highlights the fact that in the earliest recorded days of formalized teaching, the ability to attract students was considered to be the true indicator of a good teacher. In the following extract the evidence for the success of a General Science course is taken to be the fact that pupils have opted for it — or at least have not opted out!

> A Yes there hasn't been hundreds of kids clammering to get out of General Science, they've been clammering to get in, so obviously it's quite successful.

But such evidence could equally point to the fact that General Science just happened to be a popular choice that year and that many pupils chose it because their friends did (another tendency noted by Woods 1979). One could even imagine a situation where the success of a traditionally unpopular subject was the fact that pupils chose it at all! The difficult question to answer is how far it is the quality of the teacher that is influencing particular option choices. We will look into the issue of pupils' views of teachers later in this chapter. Suffice it to say here that the number of pupils opting for a course constitutes dubious evidence of a teacher's effectiveness.

In many of the appraisal interviews we have observed, input evidence was presented in much vaguer terms than so far discussed. This was particularly the case when evidence for the success of particular lessons was provided. Much seemed to be made of 'how well the lesson went' from an intuitive point of view. It was sometimes difficult to comprehend exactly what teachers meant by this. When asked to provide more detailed evidence, teachers usually alluded to the fact that the pupils seemed to enjoy the lesson. Here are three examples taken from appraisal interviews:

> T1 It was successful on the level of all the kids enjoying it. They liked it: I got a lot of work out of them.

> T2 Well I suppose you always evaluate lessons in an intuitive way. If you feel you're getting some positive feedback, with children saying they enjoyed something . . . or if we've all enjoyed it . . . I do feel I've had some successes in the sense that I know we've done something worthwhile and they've said they'd enjoyed it.

T3 I think if you feel that it's been an enjoyable relationship with the kids and they seem to respond in a favourable way then I think you can say it has been a reasonably successful lesson.

And the following comments made by appraisers:

A1 It has been very evident that the bubbling enthusiasm of the children for what they've been doing, which obviously has spilled over in the quality of what they've been doing as well, their general attitude, which I think has been excellent, certainly I detect a lovely working atmosphere around the group.

A2 [Addressing an appraisee] I think one of the obvious ways of evaluating your success is the response of the pupils in the classroom. I think where youre successful, and I'm particularly impressed, is that you do create lots of learning situations which the kids respond to because of the high level of imagination you put into it.

Such evidence of teacher input and pupil outcomes would probably be seen as far too vague and subjective to satisfy 'hard-nosed' appraisers. But if evidence of a more concrete kind is problematic what is the alternative? Some teachers were left with the view that one should fall back on one's 'gut reaction':

R This is a thorny issue, how do you recognize a good teacher?

A Oh well, yes. You certainly can't do it just on examination results and you can't do it on discipline alone either: you get a school in Central London that's going to be quite different from, say, a Grammar School in the West Country . . . it's a sort of basic gut feeling.

Consulting Third Parties

Another strategy for obtaining evidence for use in appraisal interviews is for the appraiser to consult third parties about a particular teacher's performance. The advantage of this strategy is that it provides a view additional to that of the appraiser and appraisee. The person consulted ought obviously to be someone who has considerable knowledge of the appraisee. Evidence from such a source is highly relevant where the appraiser does not work closely with the appraisee and does not routinely see them at work. Thus a Headteacher in a large comprehensive school might do well to draw on the knowledge of Heads of departments when appraising junior staff. This strategy of consulting a third party is an explicit procedure in some schools' appraisal schemes.

One of the problems with such a strategy is that it is open to bias. The individuals consulted may or may not be favourably disposed towards the person being appraised. The appraiser may or may not be aware of the state of the relationships that exist which are likely to colour the views of persons consulted. Even if there is no formal procedure for consulting other members of staff such practices tend to occur informally. It is possible for third parties to deliberately try to influence an appraiser in a particular direction. One teacher interviewed was aware of this process operating in his own institution:

> T Senior staff or team leaders or anyone who could provide more detailed evidence or information, they're not actually built into the [appraisal] system. So some senior staff I think abuse the system in that they will go out of their way to feed certain information to the Head of faculty if it happens to be one of their favourites. It's quite a damning thing to say but I'm forced to say it because I think it's true. The Head of faculty will get lots of plus signs and lots of plus sounds about a particular person from a particular senior member of staff. That's okay if it's quite certain that the appraiser has the professional maturity to take an objective view of what's said.

The concern here is whether the appraiser, who has little knowledge of the person appraised, has access to reliable and objective opinions about the appraisee. Another concern expressed by teachers was whether appraisers in this position did seek information from staff who work more closely with the appraisee. If a judgment on performance is being made how is that judgment arrived at? Unless the appraiser hears something significant about the person he or she is appraising the assumption might be simply that the person concerned is an average performer:

> T I actually said to him, 'How do you know whether I'm doing a good job or not?' because I had the feeling that he wasn't always aware of how individual members of staff were getting on. His answer to that was, 'Oh well, don't worry if you were either doing brilliantly or doing terribly I'd have heard about it!' which wasn't really terribly encouraging. It meant that I hadn't caused any awful disasters but hadn't done very well either.

This last quotation is interesting when considered alongside some of the rhetoric about appraisal having as one of its main functions the motivation of 'average' teachers: those who fall between being excellent performers and those whose performance leaves something to be desired. If the aim is to give more attention and time to such persons, then leaving it to information passed on informally is unlikely to do more than endorse existing perceptions.

In some appraisals the appraiser cited what was in some cases little more than 'gossip' picked up from a variety of sources, for instance the school staffroom. One appraiser pointed out to us after an appraisal interview:

> A I've been here a long time and I know my colleagues' views reasonably well, so I mean I was quite deliberately reflecting opinions from the staffroom.

Alternatively teachers themselves might use whatever they have heard from staff conversation as a form of evidence. The extract below, taken from an appraisal interview, is interesting in that the appraiser's experience of the person concerned did not bear out the judgment made:

> A In your answer to the question [i.e., included in the pre-interview questionnaire] 'in what way may illness, fatigue, stress or other problems have affected your relationships with other staff' you say, 'These stresses make me abrupt and difficult, but I'm working on it.' I have to say I've never found you abrupt and difficult, so I mean what makes you think that people think you are? Have you any objective evidence of this?
>
> T I think I've had one or two comments. I can't remember time, place, person or anything. Some slight, almost indirect references to my being fairly abrupt about this, that or the other or saying something or exchanging comments and then walking out.

In this case the appraiser's conclusion is positive but information such as this can be viewed as reliable and objective. Unless some systematic check on its accuracy is made it probably ought not to be used, as it may present a distorted view of the teacher concerned. Consider the next extract for example. One wonders what this teacher means by 'everybody' and how the conclusion was arrived at:

> I would defend myself, if defence is necessary, by saying of my form at the moment, my third year class as they are at present, everybody speaks very highly of them, almost everybody speaks very highly of them. I do think a lot of their good behaviour, that the favourable impression that they create, is due to the hard work that I put in with them in the first year.

Another problem with a reliance on opinions culled in an ad hoc manner is that it seems to be rare for teachers to comment on the good things about their colleagues, the aspects which are running smoothly and therefore presenting few problems. Thus perhaps teachers automatically adopt a view that performance is effective if nobody comments negatively on it. Below is the view of a Headteacher:

> I imagine that, if one's administration was inefficient, staff would be the people who would bear the main brunt of that and would quickly have something to say about it. I think when the administration in the school is smooth, nobody thinks about it and yet if it were going wrong . . . there would be a tendency for people to overlook the things which are okay and be acutely conscious of the things which are negative.

One systematic way of consulting individuals is to use appraisal interviews with one teacher to seek information for use in later ones about others. The Headteacher in the extract below had tried this strategy in two ways:

> I've tried two ways to approach the review. The first method was to see the lower graded colleagues in the faculty first and the more senior colleagues

later so that I could pick up, as it were, points as I went through you see and then be able to relate that to the more senior colleagues. I've also tried it the other way round, starting off with the senior colleagues, who have a different perception again and see them early in the review and then to pick up the junior colleagues later on.

Rarely it seems do appraisers draw on the views of 'outsiders' to the school, the exception being Headteacher appraisal (which is dealt with separately in Chapter 8). Here, however, are two examples in which Headteachers cited outsider evidence to support their view that school policies were effective:

HT1 I can only say that the reaction I get constantly from outsiders is what a happy, relaxed, ordered society the school is.

HT2 I like to think in fact that it is a successful school. It's certainly in big demand with parents.

Of course, outsiders rarely have access to detailed information about the workings of a school. Even LEA Administrators and Advisers are rarely possessed of an intimate knowledge. Thus, as the Head in the extract below pointed out, the assumption may be that if there are few problems and few complaints received, a school is running well. However, the mere lack of negative comments and information does not necessarily mean that a school is a good one:

HT The Divisional Education Officer, he knows how many complaints have been made to division about the school by parents and so on. I suppose any staff crisis would go up to him so there's a certain perhaps negative feedback there. If not much of that is coming through the chances are the school's running okay and the Head's doing his job and of course all it may mean is you're running a dead school, there's no conflict, there's no creativity . . .

Pupils' opinions

A controversial issue is whether pupils' views should be included as indicators of the quality of teachers' 'input'. In none of the case study schools was this attempted, although the College of Further Education encouraged lecturers to use a questionnaire for obtaining feedback from students. This was entirely voluntary, however. Obviously the younger the pupils, the less capable they are of articulating a view as to the effectiveness of their teachers. When we raised the notion of soliciting pupils' views for use in conjunction with the appraisal of their teachers, the response in the case study schools was generally one of emphatic opposition.

The Use of Existing Documents and Information

Another source of evidence for use in appraisals is existing school documentation and information routinely available. Much information already exists which can be made use of in appraisal of teachers. This includes: policy documents, syllabuses, outlines or schemes of work, samples of pupils' work, mark books (examination results and other assessment data have already been dealt with), samples of teacher-made curriculum materials, the application of new technology to teaching and the results of any surveys or information collected within school for other purposes.

Obviously any such information has to be considered carefully, since the indicatioans of performance quality might well be doubtful. Willingness to apply new technology to teaching, for example, has to be considered in the context of what is available and how practical it is to use. Some items, such as videos, are in heavy demand, whilst others, such as computers, may be too expensive to purchase in sufficient quantity for easy use. Furthermore, the use of such technical 'aids to teaching' may require differing amounts of in-service training, which may or may not have been offered. The use of materials and equipment may thus reflect more on whole school policies than the performance of the individual.

Some kinds of routine information, however, do reflect strongly on teachers themselves. The actual work completed by pupils is one example. In some of the schools we studied, appraisers looked at examples of the work pupils had done prior to appraising teachers. One Head of department commented:

> You know pretty well after looking at a few exercise books and so on and you can appraise them pretty well that way.

An examination of work done does provide evidence additional to and perhaps in conflict with that coming from the observation of the lesson itself. Lessons may appear not to be going very well and yet the work completed by pupils might be quite good, as one teacher pointed out when being appraised:

> T I would say, for instance, that I haven't done very well this year with that 4th-year group that I've got, and yet I look at their folders and they don't look too bad and I 've got the same old normal curve of distribution of the grades.

Another source of existing information that can be drawn on is any kind of report produced by County Advisers or Inspectors, although schools do not always respect what Advisers have to say:

> T We did have a very favourable Adviser's report . . .

> A Yes, except that it was the Advisers rather than the . . . It was a bit . . . superficial, wasn't it?

Much more highly regarded it seems is a report from HMI:

> A Well, you've got a glowing report from HMI on a couple of lessons that they viewed.

The Observation of Teachers

Perhaps the most talked about source of evidence for use in appraising teachers is lesson observation. A review of the literature (see Chapter1) reveals that there is no universal agreement about the behavioural criteria of successful teaching, that what succeeds varies in relation to context and that the criteria which have been used in making judgments have therefore tended to reflect particular views of teaching as an activity. Despite this uncertainty, the inclusion of formal observation in appraisal processes has been advocated in the White Papers *Teaching Quality* (DES, 1983) and *Better Schools* (DES, 1985a), in the HMI report on evaluation in schools (DES, 1985b) and in the Suffolk report (1985). The latter document makes the point that:

> Most teaching and much learning take place in classrooms so, if the effectiveness of the teaching and learning process is to be appraised, classroom observation will offer the most practical procedure for collecting data about teacher performance. (Suffolk Education Department, 1985, p. 5.)

This is not just an offical view. From our conversations with case study teachers, there seemed to be a widely held view that the appraisal of teachers is incomplete without some form of observation. This view is exemplified in the following comment by a Head;

> How can you formulate ideas of your staff if you never watch them teach?

However, there was less than total agreement among the teachers as to whether formal and deliberate observation should be part of a teacher appraisal scheme and, if so, how it might best be undertaken. Few of the schemes identified in our *Review and Register* include such observation but in our case study programme we deliberately included some which were tackling it. Although, at the time of our visits, industrial action placed a severe constraint on the carrying out of observation in schools, some managed to continue in a limited fashion. Moreover, we were able to talk to staff about their views on the use and validity of observation techniques in appraisal even if they were not themselves being observed or undertaking observation.

It seemed to us that school ethos was a very influential factor in determining whether teachers favoured observation, and whether it was possible for initiators of appraisal schemes to introduce it as part of a scheme. Much seemed to depend on existing practice and whether it was conducive to the introduction of formal observation or not. In some schools a degree of inter-teacher observation occurs as part of regular practice (i.e., team teaching), whereas in others to be observed by a collegue whilst at work with a class was rare indeed. Some of the teachers interviewed claimed that in their teaching career there were few if any occasions when they had been observed, once their initial training was completed:

> T1 When I think back — I've been teaching twenty years — I can't ever remember being watched teaching, except when people have come to watch more as a demonstration, with me setting an example, not coming to watch to see if I was doing it right.

T2 There's nobody coming into my classroom looking at my teaching. I haven't discussed it with any Head of department.

R He has never observed you at work?

T2 No. I don't think I've actually been observed in a lesson for quite a long time, I can't remember the last time.

Several teachers who were unused to being observed claimed that they would find formal observation of their lessons to be a threatening prospect:

T1 If you had formal observation of performance I think that would be threatening.

T2 I think people would probably feel threatened if that [i.e., observation] was suggested. It would smack of school practice and inspection and I think that would probably upset people.

T3 My dissatisfaction largely stems from the fact that, like anyone else, I'm nervous of being watched when I'm doing something and I think it's more a case of simply that reaction rather than any more serious concern.

T4 I would hate to be watched formally. Some people might not mind: some people might think it is a good thing. I find that if I've got someone else in the classroom, my approach is very stilted. I am conscious that someone is there all the time.

T5 I don't know whether it should be part of appraisal necessarily, because some people feel very threatened by the presence of a stranger in the room.

Other teachers were more open to the prospect of formal observation as part of appraisal because they were familiar with observation taking place already:

R Observation of teachers at work — how would you view that?

T Well, I view that differently from most other people because I'm heavily involved in in-service training. I've lots of teachers in my class all the time, and I spend a lot of time in other people's classes, so it's just meat and drink to me . . .

T2 I've had people coming in and out all the time. The Head comes in to see a pupil or deputy Head might come in, the Head of the department's always coming in to talk to me. So they have plenty of opportunity to experience the atmosphere in my lessons . . . without actually seeing what's happening *all* the time!

R Do you think formal observation ideally should be part of appraisal?

T I'm very lucky in a way. Because we team teach, there's a tremendous amount of observation going on already: me and two other people in the classroom at the same time and all aware of each other's approaches.

Some of those against the inclusion of formal observation of teachers in an appraisal scheme tended to take the view that enough observation was taking place informally and therefore there would be little gain in instituting a more formal process:

R What about more formal observation?

T1 I think enough goes on informally anyway. The Head of faculty pops in enough.

T2 You can pick up a great deal anyway without having to do it formally and set aside a time. I think I know X well enough, or anyone well enough who is in that position, through just wandering into the lesson, listening to things he says and things like that. (Head of faculty)

T3 Oh you'd really put the cat among the pigeons if you're suggesting that. Actually X [the Head] knows a lot that's going on in the classroom, he's aware, I think, of what is going on.

T4 He doesn't come and observe, but I don't think that he misses much.

R So you think he's sufficiently in touch, generally?

T4 Oh I'm sure, yes.

R Not to need a formal kind of approach?

T4 No I don't think so, I like his way.

T5 He [i.e., the Head of department] would be able to listen to how I teach because in Biology there's a Prep. Room next door to the Laboratory and you can hear every word the teacher is saying and you can tell from noise level or the type of noise level whether the pupils are interested or are playing up. It's not difficult to tell.

R Do you think there needs to be a formal observation of performance in appraisal?

T6 I think it's essential there must be, yes. I'm very lucky in that I'm a scientist and we can always find excuses for going into each others' labs.

On the other hand, some teachers argued that 'popping in and out of the classroom' was an inadequate basis for appraising teachers.

T1 He [the Headteacher] can see how I relate to other people, the children generally, within the school but he doesn't have the opportunity to see how I teach. He does pop in but really that's not enough.

T2 How can the man judge if he just passes by my classroom?

T3 The argument in favour of it is that perhaps too many people are judged on the basis of noise level by somebody just strolling past . . .

Despite such views, the tendency in the case study schools was for there to be either no observation of teachers by appraisers or for observation to take place on an ad hoc and unsystematic basis. There was, however, a move in some of the schools towards introducing systematic and formal observation. This was sometimes in response to comments from staff themselves. For example, in one school a Head of department did an appraisal of himself by issuing a questionnaire to members of his department. A prevailing view of staff was that he didn't get into lessons enough to observe them teach. He has since begun doing more observation of lessons.

Where observation is not taking place at all one consequence is that in appraisal interviews the actual teaching is not discussed.

> T1 At present we don't talk about the teaching part of it in interviews because it would be rather pointless: no one ever sees us doing it.

> T2 We don't talk about the teaching. The Head of faculty hasn't really observed — only popped in now and then.

One Headteacher, however, was of the opinion that in order to talk about teaching techniques, observation was not essential. What was important in his view was provoking thought to enable teachers to evaluate themselves:

> HT If I as an appraiser am acting as a facilitator in helping the member of staff to appraise him or herself, then obviously the skill that I then pursue, I hope, is to be able to direct that person's thinking towards issues identifying classroom organization and management, teaching styles and so on, but that doesn't necessarily mean me actually seeing the person in operation does it? That's asking the person to evaluate themself.

Views about the purposes of observation

This raises the question of what purpose classroom observation is intended to serve. There seem to be two purposes for observing teachers in existing schemes. One is to enable the appraiser to reach a judgment about the person being appraised, whilst the other is the sharing of ideas in order to improve practice. Whilst observation of lessons is one way in which appraisers can gain evidence about the teaching activities of staff for whom they are responsible, most of teachers interviewed, including Headteachers, claimed that the purpose of undertaking observation was to share ideas:

> T1 The purposes of the observation is seeing different people in action and seeing different approaches. (Headteacher)

> T2 I intend to introduce observation in pairs but on the basis of gaining insights rather than judging. (Head of faculty)

The view that observation should be undertaken for the purpose of sharing ideas about how to teach was one that teachers themselves seemed to accept most readily. If this is to be the sole purpose of observation then there is no reason why it should follow a hierarchical pattern. Indeed observation could operate at any level. Some teachers saw the advantage in senior staff being observed.

> T I think there should be a two-way process in observation. I don't think it should be just a question of somebody senior observing. I think there ought to be the opportunity for teachers to observe those senior to them teaching. I would like the opportunity to be able to observe my Head of department teaching, for instance. Not that we can directly copy another teacher but you can still learn from their techniques. (Scale 2 teacher)

Many teachers stressed that the main value of observation was obtaining feedback from colleagues about their teaching. Even criticism was welcomed:

> T1 I did feel in a way that it would be quite nice to know that somebody was watching me. I know this is a very unusual thing for people to say but I might actually not be doing a terribly good job and nobody would be in a position to tell me.

> T2 More feedback would be good — it would be nice to know what other teachers feel about you . . .

In such circumstances the role of the person conducting the appraisal is seen as a supportive and constructive one. Some appraisers realized that their staff were willing to accept criticism of their lessons, providing it was constructive:

> A The vast majority of colleagues can and do accept what I've got to say in guiding, or tutoring or giving them advice and in fact they're quite disappointed if I don't make critical suggestions, constructive suggestions . . . . (Senior teacher)

The giving of praise to encourage and motivate and as a means of reinforcing good practice was characteristic of a number of appraisal interviews. Below is an example of an appraiser's comments about lessons observed, made during an interview with a scale 1 teacher:

> A I was impressed, observing your lessons, I thought you were exceptionally good. I think it's good to find you've put improving and constant development of teaching, as an aim. I think that's marvellous, I think it's also good that it's paid off.

Procedures for observing teachers

In institutions which included observation in their scheme, a wide variety of different procedures had been adopted and such procedures tended to be very flexible. The

Headteacher of one school in particular delegated observation to Heads of faculties and encouraged a variety of approaches to be tried out. The result was that each faculty set it up in a different way. The Headteacher concerned explained his policy as follows:

> HT The Heads of faculty, who have a fundamental role in our system now dele-
> gated to them, are this term working on observation techniques.... I
> haven't set them any guidelines. I don't think there are guidelines for every
> subject observation and what I've done is simply to say to them, 'I want you
> to come back to me at the end of term to see your successes and failures in
> terms of observation and we will then come up with the best of the practice
> that we've experienced this term, in terms of how to observe and what we're
> looking for.'

In conducting observation, certain procedural decisions need to be made, the main ones being: how much observation would be undertaken in order that a teacher's 'normal' style and standard could be discerned; what should be included in the 'agenda' of teacher-behaviour to be observed? should those being observed be consulted in advance? what role should the observer adopt in the classroom? should feedback be given and if so what kind? Interviews with teachers highlighted some of the diversity in practice.

How much observation

The time appraisers spent undertaking observation varied considerably. Whilst some just observed one or two lessons, others did a great deal. Here are comments from two teachers who had rather different experiences of being observed:

> T I was observed taking an English lesson and I was observed when I was trying
> to teach the use of the library. It was a very short lesson, that was partly why I
> was aggrieved, the lesson was very short. I use the library because children
> want to read the fiction books. I used to use it for half an hour or so. By the
> time the children got in and by the time they'd found a book and you'd
> issued it out etc., half an hour was gone so it really was only time for
> changing a library book in some cases and if you really wanted to do using a
> library, the half an hour really wasn't long enough to really get on with
> doing something. I have really been judged on this!
>
> T2 I think it was about two or three days that the Head was with me virtually
> every minute. Some nights I thought he was going to come home with me
> because every time I turned round he would be there.

As well as having different experiences of duration, teachers opinions also differed as to what was an appropriate amount of time to be observed and of the range of activities which should be included:

T1 I think you'd probably get as good an impression as you could if you went in for one double lesson, with one group.

T2 I would have liked the Head to have been part of the teaching activities, to be involved in the teaching activities on at least four different occasions, four different sets of children and I would like the Head to be present at curriculum meetings to see how my role in that respect is developing.

Time is needed not only for conducting the observation but also in order to give feedback to the member of staff concerned, if that is the intention. This increases the total amount of time needed considerably, as the teachers quoted below noted:

A1 Every lesson I observed we then had something like an hour's debriefing and talking.

A2 So you're really multiplying the time by two, that's a valid point, isn't it, that if you are observing the time it takes is twice as long as you observe really?

A3 There is no way round it, I don't think. One of the problems is you can't always do it straight afterwards, but you have to work it within the day, so it would involve seeing people at lunchtime or after school.

T I think I was one of the first that had the individual appraisals, and it was observation of several lessons by the Headmaster, then a full afternoon's appraisal chat and then a debrief which took about an hour and a half, and a written report.

In order to reduce the time taken observing lessons, one strategy suggested by some teachers was to have several brief visits to the classroom rather than one observation of a lengthy period:

T1 The nature of how it's conducted is the key issue and personally I would prefer to have thirty visits of one minute than one visit of thirty minutes because the range of approaches would not be evident [in the one visit] and I think that one would have a much more clearer picture. Certainly I would feel threatened into trying to produce my idea of a perfect situation in a half hour period, which would not reflect the rest of the year.

T2 I wouldn't have any objections to being observed in a teaching situation. I don't know that prior to your appraisal interview would be the way, though. Perhaps a discreet way of doing it would be throughout the year; occasionally during the year, so he [the Head] gets an overall picture.

What should be observed

A crucial question to ask is what appraisers are going to focus upon when observing lessons. Should it be a general view of how that teacher works or is there to be a specific focus. In either case should teachers be told what it is? Some teachers did seem to be rather in the dark as to what was being looked at, whilst others had been consulted:

> R Did you not know what they were going to look at?

> T1 No, presumably they were coming in to observe how you started the lesson, your lesson content, the amount of interaction, or whatever. I don't know: it was just a general lesson observation.

> T2 We did agree sort of general ground rules in what we would be looking at, I think. To see what kind of teacher you are, what methods you use, how you relate to the children as well as the kind of knowledge you are trying to transfer.

> T3 The formal structure of lesson observation is agreed between the parties concerned so that the lesson observation is purposeful and is actually relating to a particular aspect of teaching methodology or whatever it might be.

There was also a concern among some teachers that there would be an idiosyncratic or 'hidden agenda' of what was being observed (echoing the conclusions in the literature about criteria reflecting particular views of teaching), or that they would be appraised according to very crude criteria.

Prior notice

Another procedural matter is whether any notice is given prior to observation. Some teachers had appraisers simply turn up without any advance notice. Others were given notice, but not always much in advance. Below are comments from two teachers:

> T1 We were told maybe ten minutes before that a particular person was coming in to see our lesson, and was that all right?

> T2 The deputy Head turned up for two lessons unannounced. I think it would have been nice to have been told.

The role of the observer

Observers also adopted different roles in the classroom. Not all of them just observed:

> T The person would just come in and literally sit at the back of the classroom and watch and then if the kids were working, in my particular case it was the deputy Head, he got on and worked with the kids too.

Feedback

Finally, procedures differed in terms of the feedback given. As we have seen already, feedback was not always given immediately after the lesson observed. Some teachers had to wait until they had their appraisal interview to hear what comments the appraiser had to make:

> T He wrote down what he thought about the lesson, He didn't tell me what he thought until I actually had the interview.

Reliability and Validity

Whatever the purpose of observation, one has to consider how far procedures for observation are successful in producing reliable and valid information about classroom practice. Of course some strategies might be more effective than others in this respect. We have considered the question of whether teachers are given advance notice of observation and whilst it might be considered fairer to give teachers adequate notice of when the observer would be visiting classes, there is also the possibility that teachers will take special care to prepare a 'good' lesson. This raises a question about how valid such observation would be, since if the observer were not to give advance notice, there would be a greater possibilty of seeing normal practice.

The following comments are from teachers who were of the view that, if notice was given by observers, it would affect the nature of the lessons considerably:

> T1 Once you say, 'Oh I'm coming in to watch you because I'm going to do an appraisal of you', well, then you think 'Better do something special!' and you're not your natural self.

> T2 We can all be brilliant when we're given notice. I mean, we all know what to do and what we should be doing. I'll be the first to admit I'm not doing it in every lesson! It's like when they say there's a Governor coming into school or we're having an Inspector coming into school, it's amazing how the walls seem to get covered up and the work's on display. But it's not like that every day . . . !

> T3 I wouldn't want to be told when, because it would be artificial.

Other teachers argued that, whether or not advance notice is given, the situation in the classroom changes immediately the observer enters the room:

> T1 It doesn't matter who it is, whether it's the Head or anyone else, I'm not the same person.

> T2 In many ways it was a kind of false situation because it was a bit like on teaching practice, you were being observed, notes taken, so you weren't projecting yourself like you normally would, you weren't as relaxed as you

normally are and I think perhaps the lesson didn't go the way that maybe it should have done. So you were not teaching in the normal way, the pupils were different. So I wouldn't say what was observed was typical.

T3 One almost feels that one should be teaching to please the person who is in. And that's one of the dangers when they are there. So if it is a traditionalist, you almost feel as if you should have the desks facing the front.

Not only does the presence of an observer affect the teacher's behaviour, the pupils too might behave differently. Here are contrasting experiences;

T1 I don't think you can honestly have your mind a hundred per cent on your topic and your lesson when you have got a senior management person present. They're going to walk in and sit at the back of your room and write notes. It isn't typical for the pupils. The pupils, especially those of lower ability, something like that distracts them totally. They want to talk to them [i.e., the observer] all the time, they're not concentrating, they want to show off.

A I think the thing which interested me actually, was that the pupils seemed to be unaffected by it, you know. I was creeping in through doors, rolling up into a ball in the back there just to observe things and the pupils just went on.

In some cases observers themselves tried to allow for the effects of their presence on lessons. There were instances, for example, where those conducting the observation believed that certain of their staff 'rose to the occasion' when being observed. The discussion below, between a Headteacher and a senior member of staff (who had conducted observation) relates to this problem:

A Yes. Certain people in those lessons were on their best behaviour and . . .

HT Performed.

A . . . out came overhead projectors and it was a strange coincidence to me that — —'s lesson was a lesson on study skills, on how to use your materials to revise and I thought, 'Well that's what I wrote down before . . . maybe he's doing it every lesson!'

HT Well it means that it's got to be a more spaced-out and regular check, hasn't it? The danger of course is that once they've got to know all the hoops that they've got to jump through, they just jump through them every time you appear, which is what you are hinting at.

A Well I think everybody does that, don't they, to a certain extent.

This experience was commented on in other cases too:

HT He's the sort of person who performs when somebody's there. I think that might be regarded as being realistic rather than cynical.

T Well there's one simple solution to that, the Head of department should turn up unannounced from time to time.

HT Well he's seen the worst, he has seen things being thrown out of windows whilst he's been in the room.

The last comment suggests that whilst it was believed that some teachers 'rise to the occasion' when being observed, the opposite was considered to occur in other cases: that as a consequence of being observed some teachers 'went to pieces':

HT We had the Advisers in to see her and she made such a palaver and fuss about it when she knew the Adviser was coming in that she made a complete hash of the lessons, she was so nervous. It wasn't a true reflection at all of her normal teaching. I think when you make these artificial situations, you immediately change the situation, don't you.

This raises the issue of whether being systematically observed is a familiar enough experience for most teachers for them to behave even reasonably close to normal. The tendency for teachers to adopt an approach which they believe the observer favours has been commented on. However, if teachers become familiar enough with having observers in the classroom they may become confident enough to adopt their own approach:

T The Head's been in one lesson and I've been interested in that I haven't changed as much as I thought I would have changed. I think last year or the year before, if he came in and I was conscious that he was coming in, I would have been a lot more traditional and I would have felt constrained. It would have been a talk for ten minutes and then give them a handout because I then feel, 'Oh well they're working.' But I don't worry too much about that now because I feel a lot more confident in the classroom teaching anyway. So it depends if people are prepared to be themselves.

A further issue relates to observer bias. Even if what is observed is a reasonably accurate reflection of a teacher's usual performance in the classroom, it may be interpreted in terms of prejudice either in favour of or against the teacher concerned:

T It depends on the boss [Head] and whether you get on with him. Those that don't get on with him think, oh what's he going to moan about now.

The above viewpoint reflects a certain amount of cynicism about the validity of formal observation in appraisal. Merely including observation in appraisal does not guarantee objectivity. Whilst this needs to be recognized, there is still the question of whether it is acceptable for an appraiser *not* to have conducted any direct and deliberate observation of that person's teaching.

As a final point we should say that we have concentrated here on the observation of *teaching*. In the case of senior staff it is accepted that teaching duties may comprise only a proportion of their job. For this reason we look into the question of appraising a senior management team in Chapter 10.

Conclusions

Four sources of evidence for use in the appraisal of teachers have been discussed in this chapter: indicators of outcomes and input; consultation with third parties; use of school documents and routine information; and systematic classroom observation. We have illustrated these with the views of staff in the case study establishments, noting the advantages as well as the pitfalls involved.

In the case study schools, much appraisal activity seems to draw on nebulous and sometimes even questionable evidence, and where clear-cut evidence is available its implications in terms of teacher performance tend to be unclear. However, at least these institutions were attempting to grapple with this difficult problem so that appraisal is based on something more than mere opinion. Clearly the effective use of evidence is likely to be one of the issues that will need to be addressed before any more widely applicable model for teacher appraisal meets with widespread acceptance. In saying this we should point out that such strategies in use in the case study schools represent what is in many respects at the forefront of emerging practice. Any move for more systematic ways of applying evidence in appraisal needs to take account of what *is* happening in schools rather that what *should* be happening. It is only by building on what schools have achieved so far that realistic strategies for making use of evidence in the appraisal of teachers can be applied successfully.

Chapter 8

Involvement in Appraisal

Introduction

In the last chapter we looked at the range of different matters that had been taken into account in the appraisal of the teachers in the case study institutions. We now turn to the issue of who had been involved and their views concerning involvement. This will include discussion of the extent to which such involvement is coerced. We shall also consider the issue of skills required by appraisers in order to carry out appraisals. This will lead on to a discussion of the delegation of appraisal in large schools and the implications for appraisal and for the institution of the different levels at which it might operate.

The Extent of Staff Involvement in Appraisal

In schools where a system of staff appraisal has been set up which is compulsory, all staff are in some sense 'involved' in being appraised. The extent to which individuals perceive that they are actively involved however varies. Whilst for some staff the annual appraisal interview can be a brief and superficial exercise, others might take a very active part in the preparation for the interview, in deciding the agenda, in conducting the interview itself and in following it up (see Chapter 6).

Many schools however operate voluntary schemes of appraisal and thus the extent to which teachers wish to be involved in the process is a matter for them to decide, at least in principle. Some opt out (or do not opt in, as the case may be) of having an appraisal and there are many reasons for this, such as suspicion as to what the scheme is about and scepticism as to whether it would have any positive outcome. When a scheme is first set up, some staff prefer to wait and see what happens before rushing to be involved. One teacher put it thus:

> I'm just ignoring it because I've decided that at this present time I'd like to see the way it's going.

In practice, however, it seems that no scheme is ever truly voluntary. If it is left entirely to individual members of staff to decide whether to have an appraisal or not their choice is influenced by what other staff opt to do. When one teacher was asked why he decided to have an appraisal he said:

T I think there's possibly two reasons that come to mind immediately. The first one is the fact that everybody else seems to be doing it . . .

So if everybody chooses to have an appraisal anyone who decides not to becomes the 'odd one out'. Once a certain level of staff involvement is reached then opting out becomes difficult. The following comment endorses this:

T About a quarter to a half of staff have opted in to the scheme. If a voluntary scheme reaches a certain level it can become the accepted thing.

It is questionable whether something which is 'an accepted thing' is really voluntary. With regard to appraisal schemes, the idea that voluntary amounts to 'free to choose' is therefore something that cannot always be assumed. Pressures exerted by a majority over a minority, however, do not only apply in the case of staff deciding whether to opt in to an appraisal scheme. It can work the other way with the result that staff who want to have an appraisal decide not to because of what others might think or say. The following comment by a teacher relates to those few who opted in to one particular school scheme:

T Some people are seen to have been 'done' and to have had all sorts of reasons for doing it. Some staff are quite cynical about it.

In this case the decision to be appraised is seen to be based on ulterior motives, laying the participating teachers open to innuendo.

The weight of staff opinion is at its greatest where senior management adopts a neutral 'take it or leave it' stance towards a voluntary scheme. However, it is difficult for a senior management team to be entirely neutral in this respect. If voluntary implies an active decision on the part of staff to opt in to a scheme, then opting out is a passive act and is consequently a very easy one. If, however, staff are placed in a position where they are 'invited' to have an appraisal, then opting out is much more difficult. Subtle pressures operate on teachers to opt in as described by one teacher:

T Well I feel torn, I ought to go out of politeness really. It seems a bit of a personal rejection.

R Oh I see, it's set up as more of a scheme that you opt out of rather than opt in to.

T Well, I think people feel that not to be involved suggests that the person who's doing it is not doing it effectively and I think it's likely that people are going to feel embarrassed about that, and keep going to spare the feelings of the person who's doing the appraisal and out of courtesy rather than any sense that they're getting anything out of it.

In many cases it seems that teachers became involved simply because they were asked. In particular it is difficult to refuse such a request of a Headteacher. When we asked staff in one school with a voluntary scheme why they opted in, many replied simply that the Headteacher had asked them to. Here are three examples:

> R Why did you decide to opt in to the scheme?

> T1 The Head approached me and asked if I would be willing to do it, and we fixed a time and had two sessions.

> T2 Because the Headmaster asked me. It was just at the time when the appraisal scheme had reached a certain stage and he realized that not much had been done and so he thought he'd better appraise one or two more people and so he asked me to take part, that's why.

> T3 I was approached by the Head to see if I was interested in having a chat with him under appraisal guidelines.

If an individual approach is made in this way teachers find it difficult to say no:

> T It was presented in such a way that in some ways you couldn't say no I won't take part in an appraisal

An element of persuasion might also be necessary:

> T We were given the chance to refuse to be observed or interviewed if we wanted that.

> R So it was voluntary by the sense of being able to opt out?

> T Yes but I mean obviously you can't really opt out, in fact I'd been persuaded not to.

Those who find 'persuasion' a little too strong can resort to 'encouragement' instead, a term used by the appraiser below:

> A I encouraged teachers to take part because I felt it was constructive, and I feel that's the important part about it. (Head of faculty — Appraiser)

Perhaps the most interesting case from all our interviews with teachers is the one of the teacher who was appraised without even knowing it! In her own words:

> T What happened was I went to see the Head to say I'm applying for this job. He said, 'Would you like to come and have a chat about what you're applying for, you know, what you think your strengths are.' I said, 'Fine I don't mind at all' so we set a time. Now he didn't mention assessments or anything you see at that point, to me it was a case of I'm going to have a chat with the Head and I didn't think anything of it. At the end of the chat he said well do you realize this is your appraisal.

If such strategies need to be employed to entrap teachers into taking part in an appraisal, one wonders whether it might in fact be better to have a compulsory scheme.

The philosophy underlying a voluntary system is that staff can arrive at their own decision as to whether having an appraisal would be advantageous or not. Yet in order to make a reasonably informed decision staff need to know what appraisal entails. The fact that most staff were unsure as to what their scheme amounted to made an informed decision impossible. In fact, staff could not really decide whether an appraisal would be advantageous until they had had one. Many staff thus opted in partly to satisfy their curiosity about the scheme:

> T It's a new system, I wanted to be part of that new process to know what it was about, otherwise you're on the sidelines, not knowing what's going on.

Those not opting in might well have opinions about what the advantages and disadvantages of the scheme are but unless they actually experience an appraisal then they themselves are open to the accusation that they do not properly understand the nature of the scheme. In one case it seemed that a teacher with a negative attitude to appraisal opted in purely in order to validate his preconceptions. This was the view of one member of staff who described the motives of the teacher concerned:

> T One teacher who has been negative about it is opting in on the grounds that he wasn't allowing himself to find out the disadvantages of the scheme, i.e., he wants to try it for negative reasons.

Teachers as initiators

Thus far we have reviewed teachers' involvement as a matter of responses, whether willing or otherwise. In one of the case study schools, however, the actual development of the scheme had been undertaken by a staff committee, thus for some teachers involvement amounted to having a part in deciding the nature of the scheme and acting as 'guinea pigs' in the piloting stage. Staff who had been involved in this way tended to see the scheme in a different light and for them it was not a case of wanting to opt out:

> T I was an original member of the committee and was present at most of the meetings. I was one of the three members of the sub-committee that did some work on the initial questionnaire and after that I was one of the first to be appraised: a guinea pig, as it were.
>
> R So your perspective of it is likely to be different from most of the staff in that you helped to shape it?
>
> T Yes, oh yes I have a definite bias in that I was both interested in and aware of what was going on.
>
> R Also I suppose you'd then have been in a difficult position to opt out?
>
> T Well, much would depend on how stong-minded one was I think. I do not feel any urge to opt out of the system so it's not so much a question of

wanting to opt out, or the feeling that I can't opt out. It's simply not wishing to opt out.

In the case of the scheme which enabled teachers to choose who would be their appraiser(s), they could also find themselves being involved on both sides of the 'appraisal divide'. There were even cases where staff who themselves had opted out of having an appraisal were called on to take part in conducting appraisals. In such circumstances they might well find it difficult to refuse:

T I was actually asked if I would go down and be on somebody's appraisal panel, which is not . . .

R To take part in an appraisal interview?

T Yes, but that person was quite aware that I wasn't too keen on the whole situation. I made it quite clear to the lady that I felt like that and she said, 'That's why I want you to be there'!

The Skills of Appraisal

It seems that in the case study schools more thought has been given to who should conduct appraisals than to what kind of skills, knowledge or other attributes an appraiser should ideally have. The experience of some teachers, however, suggests that it is not sufficient simply to allocate to someone the role of appraiser. No matter how senior their position or what credibility they have with staff (matters discussed in Chapter 6), they may not possess the skills which make them good appraisers. In the opinion of many teachers the success of an appraisal depends very much on these skills. Here is one such view:

T I think the appraisal is only as good as your appraiser, quite honestly. Obviously your response is important but they're the ones who are leading it all. They are the one who's holding it together and I think their role is crucial.

There were certainly cases where staff claimed that their appraiser did not possess the skills they considered to be necessary:

T It comes down to the Head of faculty who is well-meaning, but who doesn't have the management skills.

Most appraisers in the case study schools had had little or no training in the techniques of undertaking appraisal interviews. The fact that such training is necessary was acknowledged by both those being appraised and those responsible for conducting appraisals:

A1 Because we are Heads of faculties, that doesn't mean to say that we're particularly skilled for appraisal, and I would agree that all managers, which we are, need training and need to be trained into these skills regardless of our background. (Head of faculty)

A2 I haven't actually been asked to be an appraiser for anybody and I haven't spent any time concerning myself with what would happen if I was, but I am aware of the fact that I have a lack of knowledge in this respect. (Head of department)

A3 Our Head of faculty isn't really able to do that sort of thing: he hasn't had any training. (Scale 2 teacher)

In response to comments such as these Headteachers in several of the schools where a delegated system of appraisal had been set up had come to appreciate the need for some kind of training for the appraisers. Unfortunately this was done as an after-thought in most cases:

R Did the staff receive any training in interviewing and other appraisal tech-niques before they embarked on this?

HT No, none at all and we are looking at this at the moment, in fact. We have just written a handbook for appraisers but we have only just got it out and it's still in draft form.

However, to introduce a course of training once staff are well established in the role of appraiser can lead to problems. In such circumstances the suggestion that training is necessary can be seen as criticism. If appraisers consider that they are doing their job successfully they may well ask why they should suddenly need training. In one school in particular the Heads of faculties seem to have responded negatively to the request that they have some formal training in appraisal. In the words of one member of staff:

The issue of training led to a disagreement, the Heads of faculties didn't like the view that they needed training.

Whilst the need for training for appraisers was accepted by most of the Head-teachers concerned, one in particular was quick to stress that it was no substitute for experience:

HT This week I'm doing a session on appraisal interviewing with senior staff, where I've got a video which I'm showing them and we've got to get that in sometime between 9.00 a.m. and 4.00 p.m. But training is no substitute for experience. What I'm saying is that whether you're on the receiving end or the giving end it's a bit like swimming: until you get in the water you don't appreciate the problems. I do feel that an important part of training for interviewing for appraisal is experiencing it, whichever side of the fence you are on.

There are now many courses on offer to teach skills for staff appraisal. Most of these courses are concerned with appraisal interviewing, for example the one-day courses run by the Industrial Society on appraisal interviewing skills. It is not our intention to review such courses here but to comment on the extent to which the presence or absence of skills of appraisal seemed to be evident in the case study schools. Few teachers would dispute that certain skills are a necessary prerequisite for a successful appraisal interview. Where interviewers were perceived to be lacking in such skills, appraisals tended to be viewed as unproductive. In some cases, because of poor interviewing technique, there was a breakdown in communication in appraisals. Consider for example this extract from an appraisal interview in one of the case study schools. The person speaking is the appraiser:

> A Are there any comments about the impact you feel of any of those courses and in particular things you feel have spilled over into your own work and position. I'm thinking, for example, that I see a link here that your own anticipation of promotion into greater responsibility within primary education, which I see as a wholly realistic aim on your part and one that you certainly should be actively pursuing, but maybe it's relationship with management courses for I wonder what you would see as the value of those and involvement?

It is easy to be critical of appraisers, and in any case extracts from speech do not always make sense as text, but this 'question' is typical of the sort which teachers find hard to respond to (and which we heard all too often!). In effect the appraiser is asking what impact in-service training courses have had for the teacher concerned, but the question is very wordy and is neither clear nor specific. It begins as a very broad question, then digresses into an opinion and ends with a specific focus on particular types of courses. The teacher appraised said at the end of the interview:

> T Sometimes I found it difficult interpreting the question and deciding what responses was required from me.

One of the key messages in most appraisal interviewing skills courses is that it is important for appraisers to make sure that they ask clear and straightforward questions. From a consideration of our transcripts of appraisal interviews it seems that this is easier said than done! There was also a tendency in some of the interviews we observed for appraisers to monopolize the conversation. Yet when asked what makes a good appraiser many teachers claimed that it was someone who is a good listener. The ability to make criticism in a tactful and constructive way was also seen to be an important skill. One teacher said in his appraisal:

> T Anything which came across as critisism was done in such a manner to make it not sound like a criticism.

Comments made by teachers who had been appraised suggest that it is also very important for an appraiser to have adequate knowledge of the person they are appraising. Many of the teachers who described their appraisal as 'disappointing' commented on the appraiser's lack of knowledge about them, a matter which we considered in the last chapter.

> T1 I think the process has been, in the faculty I'm in, rather a disappointment for people and, not just speaking for myself particularly, but generally people feel that the Head of faculty doesn't know enough about them as individuals or for whatever reason feel all that much interest in the development of their careers.

> T2 One of the things that I feel that the Head of department's not too good at is actually knowing what's going on at an intimate sort of shopfloor level.

> T3 How can the Headmaster in a school this size judge me in my classroom? He can see how I relate to other people, the children generally, within the school but he doesn't have the opportunity to see how I teach. He does pop in but really that's not enough.

Who Should Appraise Whom?

This question of appraiser knowledge has implications for who should appraise whom in the school hierarchy. The teachers quoted in the extracts above were arguing in favour of being appraised by someone who has a close knowledge of their everyday activities, that is somebody who works closely with them. Some teachers on the other hand saw this as a disadvantage:

> T1 There are advantages in the person being a little bit outside the team. If it was my team leader asking me all those questions — there are things that I might want to say about him for example, which I obviously can't say to him, whereas going to someone more senior than him there are things that one can say about almost anybody, reasonably candidly.

> T2 What some people want to talk about in their interview is the Head of department. There is a problem if the person who appraises them is the Head of department!

Thus, some teachers wished to be appraised by someone who was distanced enough for one to be able to speak candidly about their immediate superiors. Others argued that it was part of a Headteacher's job to know members of staff well enough to be able to appraise them and write references for them.

> T In any school, the Head's probably one of the few people that have a job role written out and one part of that is to know the staff and to work with them and I think that is his job really. He should be in the position to write me a fair reference when I leave and to do an appraisal.

Some appraisers also claimed that they found it very difficult to appraise those staff with whom they were regularly in close contact. They found it difficult to stand back sufficiently to get an objective enough view. One Headteacher said this of appraising the deputies:

> HT I should say that, given the way the Deputies work with me, these interviews are the most difficult and one of them said it was the most artificial of all the appraisals. (so) I gave the Deputies an opportunity for an outsider appraisal.

It was interesting that, in the school where staff could choose appraisers, in the majority of cases the Headteacher tended to be chosen, on the grounds that he was the major gate-keeper of their professional futures (thus implicitly stressing the career development role of appraisal). But this was not always the case and those staff who chose other appraisers tended to point to the Headteacher's lack of knowledge of their work as one reason:

> T The two teachers I selected have had more of a knowledge of my role as deputy Head of House than the Headmaster.

Appraisal and Gender

As well as having sufficient knowledge about the person appraised, some staff believed that the appraiser should ideally be a member of staff with whom the appraisee can identify. A person who is too distanced from the appraisee might be unable to empathize with their particular predicament. Moreover they may be at opposite ends of a spectrum of opinion which makes communication very difficult. The issue of gender is important in this respect because in the case study schools virtually all the appraisers were male. In that appraisers tend to be Headteachers or senior staff and that there is a disproportionate number of males in senior positions within the Education Service, it is likely that in most schools teachers will be appraised by a male member of staff. This still tends to be the case in schools where the majority of staff are female as was the case with two of our case study schools.

The right to choose the gender of the appraiser was an issue some staff considered to be important. One female teacher argued;

> T I think it's a pity that when a staff development system is set up, especially when so much of the previous bitterness had been about women's careers, that women find that they are expected to go to a Head of faculty, who's a man, and talk about their career. Just at some point it would be nice for experienced women teachers to talk to a woman about the development of their career, because it does affect it, there's no doubt that it does make a difference and that with the best will in the world, the most sympathetic men involved in the staff development machinery cannot as clearly understand the points that a woman is trying to make.

The kind of bias experienced by female staff from male appraisers is typified in this extract:

> T Women don't mention their children. You're told as soon as you come through the door, don't say anything about your kids . . .

Again, when staff were given a choice of appraisers women tended to feature in choices. Some teachers were chosen on the grounds of their gender, as evidenced below:

> A I was asked in because she wanted a woman, she wanted a senior woman on the panel and so she asked for me in that role.

Involving Outsiders

The question of whether persons outside the school should be involved in the appraisal of teachers is also a controversial issue. The threat of being 'inspected' by someone from the LEA or from HMI was something many staff wished to avoid. Not only was this because of the possibility that such outsider involvement would have tended to stress accountability as an aspect of appraisal, but also, again, because of a probable lack of knowledge on the part of the person doing the appraising. Some teachers were concerned that an outsider might not know them very well and what they might observe briefly could be untypical. The issue of the typicality of lessons observed was discussed in the previous chapter, when it was seen as a problem even with 'insiders'. Here is a comment from one such teacher:

> T Now I wonder if I'd like to be appraised by someone who didn't know me. I mean they might just get a couple of lessons that were funny, strange lessons and make a judgment from that. Whereas someone who knows the work you've built up over the years can see things in a different way.

Teachers who were in close contact with particular LEA Advisers, however, are perhaps in a different position. Some teachers were in favour of certain Advisers being involved because the Adviser concerned could present a valuable perspective as a fellow professional and an expert in a particular subject area. However, only in the case of Headteacher appraisal (see Chapter 9) were such outsiders actually used in any of the case study schools. This was because of a concern among initiators of schemes that they be kept part of internal management and not in any way become connected with any LEA or national scheme. That Advisers were kept out was something some staff found disappointing. One teacher who wanted his subject Adviser to be involved in his appraisal made the following remark:

> T The other person I suggested was the Science Adviser in the County, who I have a lot to do with and the Headmaster didn't bother to get him in. He didn't want an outsider in.

The involvement of the laity, such as parents, did not occur, even in Headteacher appraisal, in any of the schools. One Headteacher claimed that the issue was a 'mine-field' and for that reason wished to avoid even suggesting it as a possibility:

> HT I think to get parents involved in staff appraisal is a minefield at the moment and for the foreseeable future . . .

The Use of More Than One Appraiser

Opinions as to who is the single best person to appraise whomever in the school hier-archy seem to vary. Whilst some teachers argued that the appraiser should be someone in close contact with the person they appraise and have knowledge of their everyday performance, others argued that the appraiser is best a more distanced and objective member of staff, a 'grandfather' in the hierarchy. Since no one person can be both in close contact with a member of staff and at the same time distanced, the solution could be to have more than one appraiser. The idea of being appraised by a 'panel' is something which many teachers would see as even more threatening than having one appraiser, yet it is interesting that in the school which allowed free choice of appraisers, many staff did in fact choose more than one appraiser and there was an increasing tendency for this to happen.

The advantages of having more than one appraiser are obvious when we consider many of the comments made by teachers about the purposes of appraisal. If appraisal allows teachers to obtain feedback, then the more staff that are brought in the more varied the feedback they can receive. Furthermore a variety of perspectives can be offered and this reduces bias. Many teachers did want to have a variety of different viewpoints on their performance. One such teacher claimed:

> T I felt it was better to have the several appraisers this year. I just wanted a different perspective on my work from somebody in authority.

As well as offering different perspectives on the performance of the person ap-praised, the use of a panel of appraisers also enables more evidence to be brought to bear, being a form of the 'third party' consultation process discussed in Chapter 7. The appraisal therefore is no longer limited by the knowledge any one particular ap-praiser has about the person concerned.

However, the setting up of an appraisal panel can be difficult. Time needs to be set aside when all parties can be present and this can be almost impossible if the ap-praisal takes place in school time. The consequence is that in practice teachers in this school did not always get the people they wanted to take part in their appraisal. In terms of time taken, then, appraisal by a panel is very costly — something we will consider in Chapter 13.

Conclusions

The question of what is entailed in being involved in appraisal has been considered in this chapter. It was first of all noted that the staff are involved in appraisal to differing degrees and in a voluntary scheme they may opt out altogether. This led on to a consideration of the subtle ways in which involvement in appraisal might be coerced. Teachers may well experience pressure to opt in or out of a scheme by fellow staff or by their seniors. An invitation to have an appraisal may be difficult to turn down without incurring rancour. Certainly there were staff in the case study schools who claimed that they did feel pressurized one way or the other and this raises the whole question of what is meant by 'voluntary' in the context of an appraisal scheme. It certainly means something very different where individuals choose whether they wish to opt in to a scheme as opposed to where they have to opt out.

We also considered staff involvement in conducting appraisals. Many of the larger schools selected for case study have delegated systems of appraisal and staff other than the Headteacher have a role as appraisers. Here an emerging issue seemed to be the skills needed in order to carry out a successful appraisal. Several teachers believed that their appraisers lacked important skills and as a consequence their appraisals had been far less useful than they might have been. This raises the issue of training in appraisal techniques. It was apparent that in most of the case study schools those responsible for conducting appraisals had received little or no training. A related issue is that of appraiser knowledge. Some teachers complained that the person conducting their appraisal had insufficient knowledge of their performance. Some appraisers were criticized as being too distant or out of touch. This raises the question of who should appraise whom within the school hierarchy. This is not an easy question because as well as teachers who perceived their appraiser as being too distant and lacking knowledge about their day-to-day performance, there were also cases where teachers saw their appraiser to be too close to their everyday work situation to be able to offer an objective enough viewpoint. Since an appraiser cannot be both an insider and an outsider we concluded by looking at the notion of appraisal by a panel of staff — a practice which was increasingly taking place in one case study school. This approach may well overcome many of the problems inherent in vesting the conducting of the appraisal in any one person, but it is very costly in terms of time and may be difficult to administer.

Chapter 9

The Appraisal of Headteachers

Introduction

In the last chapter we dealt with the issue of which staff in schools should be appraised and who might be the best persons to do it. Because of its importance and the problems attaching to it, however, we have left the appraisal of Headteachers to be considered in its own right. In this chapter, the appraisals of three Headteachers and the Principal of a College of Further Education are described and discussed in the light of the current debate about how the appraisal of such 'captains of institutions' might best be undertaken.

Whilst there has been much debate about how Headteacher appraisal might be undertaken, it seems to have been almost universally accepted that Headteachers should be appraised as part of a school's appraisal scheme. A recent HMI report on appraisal in schools asserted that:

> More attention needs to be given to the appraisal of middle managers (Heads of department, for example) in schools, and even more to the appraisal of deputies and Heads. For schemes to be fully effective they should include all staff and be seen to do so. Difficulties are not confined to teachers at the most junior levels. (DES 1985b, paragraph 148)

However, what evidence exists so far on school appraisal schemes suggests that whilst Headteachers are likely to play a key role as appraisers, they are not often appraised themselves. A survey of 233 comprehensive schools in seven southern LEAs (James and Newman 1985) revealed that very few school schemes included the appraisal of the Headteacher. In requesting information for the first edition of our *Review and Register* (Turner and Clift 1985) we did not explicitly seek information about Headteacher appraisal. Nevertheless, in some cases information about this was given, supporting the conclusion of the above survey that Headteacher appraisal was a rare event. For our second register (Turner and Clift 1987) we specifically asked respondents for information about Headteacher appraisal and the indications were that an increasing number of schools were experimenting in this direction.

The Headteachers Studied

We decided to make the study of Headteacher appraisal a part of our case study programme. The Headteacher of one of the schools (secondary comprehensive) had a well-established approach which we were able to study. In two of the other schools (a primary and a secondary comprehensive), experimental or pilot schemes were just being put into practice and we were invited to observe these also. Finally, indirectly we heard about a College of Further Education where the appraisal of the Principal had emerged as part of a network of review processes. This college was not part of our case study sample, but we were given permission to observe the process as a 'one-off' exercise.

The four appraisals followed different patterns. All three of the Headteachers chose to have an LEA Adviser (inspector) conduct their appraisal. In one case an LEA administrator provided backing to the adviser. In another, the deputy Head, who was also a teacher-governor, provided backing. In the third school, the Head had a second appraisal, this time with a panel of teachers from his school. The college Principal was appraised by his Vice-Principal. Thus there was a balance in these appraisals between outsider and insider presence.

Who Appraises the Head?

Despite apparent agreement that Headteachers need to be appraised, there is contention as to by whom. The research team set up by Suffolk Education Department looked into this question and concluded that:

> If the appraisal of Headteachers is to be developmental and constructive then the Headteacher's 'line-manager' must be clearly defined. 'Line managers' are expected to be people who know the subordinate's work well and who are also intimately acquainted with the context in which that work is carried out.

The team went on to say:

> In order to know the work of the Head, the appraiser should be experienced in the task of Headship. (Suffolk Education Department, 1985)

The Suffolk team advocated that LEAs should create a post of a promoted Head who would be responsible for undertaking the appraisal of Headteachers in the LEA. However, at present such posts do not exist and few LEAs have Advisers who are experienced in Headship, particularly of large secondary schools. This fact has been recognized by the Committee of Heads of Educational Institutions (CHEI) who have proposed that a national body of appraisers of Headteachers be set up responsible to the Chief Inspector (see Glazier, Campling, Miles, Snape and Swallow, 1986).

Given the present situation the nearest alternative to these suggestions would be for either one of an LEA Advisory team or for one of HMI to act as appraiser. The advantage of having a local Adviser/Inspector, even if that person had no experience of Headship, would be:

1   The appraiser would have considerable knowledge of the LEA in which the school is situated.

2   He or she would also be able to make some comparison with other Heads and other schools in the same LEA.

3   From previous work the appraiser should have some knowledge about the school and its history.

However, the CHEI strongly advocates that the person who appraises the Head be *independent* from the LEA concerned. They rejected the use of local Advisers/Inspectors for a number of reasons:

> Direct appraisal of Heads by local authority officers or advisers has to be ruled out, not only on grounds of credibility but also because it would confuse organisational relationships and damage the professional independence of Heads. (Glazier *et al.*, 1986).

None of the Heads that we studied who chose local Advisers accepted this viewpoint, although the question of credibility still arose. Only in the case of the primary Headteacher did the appraiser have experience of (Primary) Headship. It is to be expected that Advisers with the experience of running secondary schools are unlikely to exist in most LEAs given that Advisers are seldom senior in status (or salary) to secondary Headteachers. This poses another question: how far do current experiments in terms of Headteacher appraisal amount to peer appraisal or even subordinate appraisal? The choice of a deputy Head, a Vice-Principal and a panel of staff, represent attempts to use subordinates. However, even where Advisers and officers were used the situation is more akin to peer appraisal than appraisal by one's appropriate line manager. We saw no case of a Headteacher going direct to the CEO, for example.

Methods Adopted for Headteacher Appraisal

In all four cases the chief method adopted for the appraisal consisted of an appraisal interview. In three cases this was based on a questionnaire or *pro forma*, whilst that of the College Principal was based on a detailed job description. The interviews varied in length from one hour to two hours and in one case two separate sessions were held. In this appraisal there was even a further session to discuss the report and reflect on the process.

In that a Head is ultimately responsible for all aspects of a school there is a sense in which a Headteacher's appraisal amounts to an appraisal of the school itself. This is especially the case when a Head has been incumbent for some considerable time, as was the case in all but one of the institutions in question. An immediate problem in such an appraisal concerns the extent to which any Head can be called to account for aspects of school life which are delegated to colleagues, especially those involved in aspects of administration and management. Although in theory a Head is accountable for all aspects of a school, any realistic appraisal of a Head's work needs to take into account problems which might reflect the shortcomings of his/her colleagues.

In two cases the Headteacher's appraisal was based on an adaptation of the *pro forma* already adopted for the appraisal of other staff in the school. The adaptation of it was considered to be necessary in both cases to enable it to deal more specifically with the Head's role. In one case this adaptation was undertaken by the two appraisers — the Adviser and Deputy Head — whilst in the other the Head himself played a major part in redesigning the *pro forma*. These forms or *pro formae* differed in how specific they were. In one case a four-page checklist was developed whilst in another case there was a much shorter list covering a very broad agenda.

In terms of selecting an agenda, what to include and not include created something of a problem for some appraisers. If the appraiser was a subordinate, he or she found it difficult to decide which aspects of the role of a Headteacher to emphasize in the appraisal. This was noted by one of the appraisers concerned:

> The problem was what questions do you ask a Headmaster in an appraisal. Suppose you are a member of staff and you are given the task of interviewing the Head about certain areas, what areas do you ask him about? Do you ask him those areas that are of concern to you as a member of the staff or those which concern his role as an authority figure in the school, in relations with the kids, or other members of staff, or do you talk about what he does outside the school with the Local Authority, with parents, with other Heads, teachers' organizations, whatever? In the end we listed quite a large number of possibilities and only when we actually got down to it concentrated on a small area but we drew up a very considerable list. I got the feeling that he would prefer when being appraised by his staff to talk about his role in the school rather than outside the school and I think that is the way it has developed.

The Head who had played no part in designing the form used in his appraisal was least satisfied with what was contained within it:

> HT I was asked what I thought about what went on in the form before it went ahead. I think it needs working on, I don't think it is the most ideal for a Head's appraisal. I think there are too many issues which lack clarity, which is true of the other form we had for all members of staff.
>
> I think it's just a question of terminology and understanding, even the area 'do you see any areas for improvement in personal relationships'. It might be seen as a contentious one but I just think it may be the phraseology of the questions. You see coming back to that one, I could have answered no or yes and that would have been the end of the issue, it's a closed question.

In only one of the four appraisals was there any systematic attempt to consult other staff prior to the interview. Here, the deputy Head spoke to a number of teachers the week before the appraisal interview. However, in another case an appraiser drew on staff perceptions in an unsystematic way:

> I was Chairman of the Common Room for a time, I've been here a long time and I know my colleagues' views reasonably well, so I was quite deliberately reflecting opinions from the staffroom. I wasn't doing it just because it happened to be an interest of mine, I wasn't pursuing something unnecessarily, it had been something that was genuinely raised. So I mean in all the questions I drew up I was basing them on all things that I'd discussed and heard discussed by the staff.

In another case the deputy Head drew throughout the interview on prior consultation with staff. For example:

> I think we all agree that you handle the discipline of individual children, especially the junior children, very, very well. I do wonder at times whether you're perhaps firm enough with some of the little ones that are brought to you because they're only brought to you as a last resort, they're little so and so's and I wonder sometimes . . . I think other members of staff would like . . . this is a difficult year again, but I think members of staff would like to see you more in evidence during lunch hours.

Perhaps the most effective way in which staff opinion was brought into a Headteacher appraisal was the case where the Headteacher was appraised by a panel of internal staff. By virtue of the number of people involved a balanced view was more readily attainable. There were even instances when members of staff defended the Headteacher against criticisms:

> T One of the things that staff tend to say about the Head is that he is too remote from the classroom situation . . . In fact one of the staff responded first and leapt to his defense saying that in fact he did teach some English and I mean he does in a crisis situation go into the classroom.

Observation of the Headteacher was not conducted in any of the appraisals in a formal sense. It should be noted, though, that the deputies involved had considerable experience in working alongside the Head. In one school two Advisers made an initial visit to the school prior to the appraisal interview. They made a report on these visits and then met to decide the salient issues for the appraisal. However, the observation was of the school in general, rather than the Headteacher specifically, and in this sense was much more an appraisal of the whole school.

One of the Headteachers was doubtful as to the value of observation as part of an appraisal of a Headteacher.

I think that's a bit like a Head going into a class to see how a teacher performs. An interview with a member of staff, parents, or a pupil on sensitive issues, obviously with an observer sitting there is not going to be a real situation.

When I took up the issue of the need for evidence and knowledge of the person at work this Headteacher did concede that, imperfect as it is, there is in fact no substitute for observation. However he went on to say:

I think the question is how many people — advisers, inspectors, education officers — really have much intimate working idea of what constitutes a Head's day. The further problem of course, even in observation, is what is a Head's day, because one day can differ enormously from another.

The Choice of Appraisers

Perhaps the main difference between the Headteacher appraisals studied and those of other staff was that in each case the appraisers were chosen by the Heads concerned. Only in one of the case study schools did other staff have any choice over who would be their appraiser. However, given the fact that there is much less agreement over who should conduct Headteacher appraisal, it would be useful to examine the rationale behind the particular choices made by the four Heads concerned.

For one of the Heads the appraisal by an LEA Adviser was just one of a series of experiments with different appraisers. It was a pilot exercise aimed to throw light on some of the advantages and disadvantages of a Head being appraised by an Adviser. The Head explained the rationale behind it as follows:

HT   It was partly experimental because when I began I thought I would have a session with a number of different people like the Divisional Education Officer, Adviser, fellow Head — who happened to be deputy Head at this school many years ago — possibly a Governor and possibly a parent. I had those five people in mind.

For another Head the choice related to a process of evaluation of the whole school within the context of the LEA and hence the choice of an LEA Officer and Adviser. The session was actually termed a debriefing. Similarly the appraisal of the College Principal has to be seen in the context of a role shared with the Vice-Principal, and the appraisal has as its purpose review and planning within the college.

In the fourth case the Headteacher concerned believed that two dimensions were necessary, one being the input from outside the school but within the LEA context, in this case an Adviser with experience of Headship, the other being an input from someone with considerable knowledge of the school and able to offer an extension of the Governor role. This was the deputy Head who was a school Governor.

Whilst these are the basic reasons for the choices made, it seems that in some cases a particular individual was chosen from within a body of appropriate personnel for personal reasons. In the case of the Advisers chosen this amounted to someone who had credibility and who already had a working relationship with the Head. One Adviser pointed out after the appraisal had taken place:

> We have got very good rapport so we were quite at ease and there was no suggestion that anything I said or anything he said would be taken in the wrong way so I think there was no problem there.

It is perhaps the issue of relationships which underlies the position taken by the CHEI noted earlier. The concern shown by Heads might have more to do with the question of which particular Advisers will be brought in to undertake an appraisal. In the case study schools the Headteachers readily accepted there were probably other Advisers within the same LEA about whom they would perhaps have very strong misgivings. Some Headteachers may feel this way about all the Advisers in their LEA. But whatever the objections about particular individuals, we have a situation no different from that of a teacher within a school who does not consider that their appraiser has credibility. Why should it be different for Headteachers, and if they are to exercise choice over who conducts their appraisal within the Advisory team are they not open to the criticism that such appraisals will end up as cosy and informal chats with their friends on the Advisory team? This is an important point to bear in mind if part of the aim of the Headteacher in having an appraisal is to make it clear that they are themselves being subjected to the same process as other staff.

The Appraisal Interviews

All four appraisal interviews followed a broadly similar pattern in the sense that the appraiser worked within a specified agenda and the bulk of what was said consisted of the Headteacher explaining, sometimes at great length, the rationale behind particular decisions, policies and institutional arrangements.

Some of the interviewers confined themselves almost entirely to asking the questions which were provided on the *pro forma*, whilst others followed up a lot of the points with further questions. The incidence of such probing seemed to reflect not the status of the person but how familiar they were with the process of appraising and the nature of the relationship they had with the Head. At least two appraisers seemed to be reluctant to take the initiative in the appraisals. One in particular seemed to place control of the process into the hands of the Headteacher himself with comments such as the following:

> A Right, do you feel that's all you want to say at the moment on curriculum?

and

> If you are satisfied we can go on to . . .

In asking the Headteacher whether he was satisfied whether a particular area had been adequately covered, the appraiser here seemed to be transferring decisions about the control of the interview to the person being appraised. When additional questions were asked by the appraiser they were geared to clarification of a point or to establish the rationale behind a particular policy. Criticisms were not made at all in this appraisal although there were one or two instances where the Head's response was questioned. In the other appraisals criticisms were sometimes implied in the questions asked or were made directly. One appraiser pointed out that the appraisal in which he was involved was 'judgmentally' oriented in many respects:

A(T) It was judgmentally orientated because I had chosen the questions and I chose the questions because there were certain things that I thought he should discuss with staff and should in a sense have a philosophy about and although I've known him a long time now, and I probably knew the answers, I thought also it would be interesting for him actually to give a formal statement about these particular questions. I mean I wasn't in a sense criticizing, I was giving him the opportunity to talk about things that I knew caused some comment, not disquiet — that would be putting it too strongly — certainly comment amongst other staff. So I was trying to be both in the shoes of any other member of staff and putting questions that particularly interested me as well.

R Could you offer an example?

A(T) Well this came up, I think I might have been condemned for having raised it at all but one of the things that staff tend to say about the Head is that he is too remote from the classroom situation, he doesn't get into the classroom enough, he doesn't have a formal timetable, he doesn't have an accurate knowledge of the realities of the classroom — that sort of thing. So I phrased the question in as neutral a way as I could to bring about some discussion of that and how he felt he could assess a teacher on classroom performance when he was rather removed from classroom practices and so on. So I mean yes it was judgmental in that sense.

Of course the above points raise the question of the purpose of the appraisal and the extent to which the Headteacher is being called to account for his or her actions. Furthermore, there is the question of what role should be adopted by the appraiser. Is it one of making criticisms and judgments on performance or is the interview rather a means of provoking thought, communicating ideas and mutual problem solving?

In the appraisals observed this did not always appear to have been fully thought through and agreed in advance. It seemed that in at least one case the appraiser and appraisee had perceived the appraisal in different ways. In the appraisals which were experimental, different perceptions were to some extent inevitable given that it was done on a 'try it and see' basis.

Differences in perceptions seemed to relate to the question of how far the appraisal is geared to self-appraisal rather than the making of judgments. In one case the appraiser saw himself as the facilitator of the Head's self-evaluation:

> R Were you trying to facilitate the process of self-evaluation or were you trying to offer your own evaluation?
>
> A Very much the former — trying to facilitate a process. When I came at the end to write down what I thought about the exercise, I found that in terms of evaluating the school, I didn't have a great deal to say that was different from the sort of things the Head had said by virtue of the nature of the exercise.

The Headteacher on the other hand seemd to view the exercise more in terms of the appraiser taking a critical approach:

> HT A certain lack of challenge in the actual interview was perhaps disappointing. I think the end result was good for me. One is honest as far as one sees oneself but one of the values of appraisal must be getting an objective view of oneself. Being subjectively honest I don't think is necessarily the answer. I think it must have the dimension of allowing me to see myself performing as others see me performing.

The lack of challenge experienced by the Head in this appraisal, although to him something of a disappointment, can be seen as an inevitable result given the methodology of the appraisal and the limited knowledge of the Adviser. The latter pointed out that it was the first time he had been called on to undertake such an exercise and, moreover, that there were perforce areas of the Head's activity that he was unable to offer any appraisal of:

> I felt when talking to him there were large areas of his activity relating to school management, to dealing with non-teaching staff, negotiations with unions, a lot of the non-teaching activity of the Head I had very little direct knowledge of it and so didn't pursue questions on it.

This brings the discussion back to the issue of the limitations of an appraisal of a Head by a subject Adviser who has had no experience of Headship. Nevertheless similar limitations were recognized by the Headteacher concerned in potential appraisals with many of the other people he had proposed as possible candidates for a Headteacher appraisal — the Governors, the Divisional Education Officer and a parent. He claimed that:

> HT I'm not sure how far there would be genuine dialogue — based on knowledge on both sides — and I don't quite see the solution to this.

So to a very large extent the agenda of these appraisals — or the extent to which certain aspects of the agenda were pursued — reflected the knowledge and experience of the persons conducting the appraisal. The consequence of choosing certain individuals therefore, is likely to be one of limiting the agenda in some way.

This is even more likely where the appraiser is a subordinate. As well as perhaps not having adequate knowledge of the whole job, they would also be a rather un-fitting person to discuss the Headteacher's career development. In the case of the appraisal of the Principal by a Vice-Principal the issue of career development was left out of the appraisal altogether. Clearly it was not seen to be an appropriate part of that particular exercise.

There are also problems with subordinate appraisal in the sense that traditional roles have to be reversed to some extent. It may well be that the appraiser finds this difficult. Obviously much depends on what the purpose of the appraisal is and whether that is fully understood by the parties concerned:

R   Can I pursue that issue of the difficulties of being an appraiser with somebody who is senior. What do you see as the problem with it?

A(T1)   Well I think the problem really is that you don't really think it is your place to ask these questions or to suggest the areas for discussion to somebody with more experience and more authority than you. I think you've got to agree beforehand with both appraiser and appraisee what it is you're looking at and what effects you hope it will have. If the person who is senior to you is looking for, if you like, confirmation that his policies or her policies are the right ones, then there's not very much point in doing it through an appraisal situation. It begs the question exactly what appraisal is all about when you reverse the roles like that and I suppose that it is a sort of joint effort to improve performance rather than a session where you are actually dotting the 'i's of something that has been done or going over the reasons why whatever it is has failed.

A(T2)   In a sense I felt that appraising the Headmaster I was being rather cheeky in asking some of the questions or introducing areas for discussion that we did but so long as the person being appraised is prepared to accept that and obviously he was, it didn't really cause any great difficulty.

The Agenda for Headteacher Appraisal Interviews

We have noted that the *pro formae* used in the Headteachers' appraisals studied differed somewhat. Differences in what was discussed were also a consequence of the choice of different appraisers. Thus, it was unlikely for the subject of staff relationships and the performance of staff within the school to be discussed when insiders were brought into the appraisal interview. However, where Advisers were used on their own, there was discussion of staff performance. Even the issue of incompetent members of staff was raised on one interview. Below is a comment made by an Adviser during that appraisal interview.

I can think of some members of the Science Department, not only was it necessary to change their attitudes but also their basic classroom practice. Their craft wasn't up to the necessary standard.

Another area of discussion (perhaps less appropriate to the appraisal of a Head-teacher) was the potential of certain members of staff and the likelihood of their being promoted within the LEA. In one such appraisal a Headteacher and Adviser discussed at great length the chances of one of the deputies of gaining a Headship.

One interesting aspect of deciding the agenda was what happens where matters of policy produce disagreements, either within the school or between the Head-teacher concerned and the LEA. Sometimes Headteachers were unable to respond directly to questions asked because they involved the making of value judgments.

A   Would you like to go to the disciplinarian aspect?

HT   Yes. I find this such a contentious issue because whereas one can define management and organization probably in more precise terms, one gets into a far more subjective and emotive issue when you start to talk about discipline and I've therefore got to, not to comment so much about myself as a disciplinarian but more about what I mean by discipline. Now if for example this question or point is prompted by somebody who perceives education as being ruled by a rod of iron, by somebody who wished to see a return to corporal punishment within school then I suspect I would be seen as a soft disciplinarian. If on the other hand it were prompted by somebody who perceives a very *laissez-faire* school based on a relatively free attitude of discipline, I suspect I would be seen maybe as a firmer disciplinarian. So I find that it's very difficult to respond to that so I've got to define really my own feeling on discipline and I really would accept neither.

As with subordinate members of staff, Headteachers could use the opportunity of the appraisal for special pleading or the airing of grievances. The presence of an Adviser or officer from the LEA thus presents an opportunity to challenge LEA policies. In one case, for example, a Headteacher voiced his protests about the LEA's policy to abolish school sixth forms in favour of a sixth-form college.

Evidence Used in Headteacher Appraisals

In these appraisals of institutional Heads, where evidence was used it tended to be about matters relating to the institution as a whole rather than the individual's performance. Nevertheless, as we said at the beginning of this chapter, it is difficult to divorce one from the other.

The kinds of evidence Heads did cite were comments from outsiders, parents and the like, and the reports of Advisers and Inspectors, both LEA and HMI. The views of the Governors were rarely mentioned and indeed one omission throughout these appraisals was any systematic involvement of lay Governors. It is important to point out that the use of Advisers meant that there was an outsider view which in some appraisals provided an important dimension. Below is a comment from an LEA Adviser to pastoral care made during an appraisal interview:

> A Can I say as an outsider I must admit that I would agree with you entirely that whenever I come into the school it is ordered. Rarely does one pick up on disorderly things — children racing down corridors, untidy places and so on so I would go along certainly from an outsider's point of view I think that the discipline within the school is superb, as I see it and I think that needs saying from an outsider.

Records Kept on Headteacher Appraisals

In only one of the appraisals studied was a report presented afterwards. This was in the case of an appraisal by an Adviser. The Adviser wrote up the report and it was discussed in a follow-up session. This report praised the general functioning of the school, but criticisms were made about the curriculum and the extent of governor involvement in the school.

In one or two places in the report, evidence was brought in to back up a particular judgment. For example, the view that the school is popular and successful was supported by reference to the fact that there is high parental demand for places at the time of secondary transfer. In the main, the report represented a distillation of the Head's own comments made during the interviews. The Adviser in fact recognized this to be a consequence of the methodological limitations of the appraisal as it was undertaken and in the report he included the following paragraph:

> Seeking to appraise the performance of a Headteacher solely by means of a questionnaire is — with the benefit of hindsight — likely to evoke an uncontentious response from an outside appraiser. This is not to say, however, that the Head's responses in interview were anything less than frank and thoughtful. A questionnaire provides no chance to ascertain whether or not there is any mismatch of perceptions about the Head's performance and methods.

We took up this issue with the Adviser afterwards and he made the following point:

> I think when I sat back a little and reflected on the information I had obtained, the sort of things that we had discussed, I felt very strongly that by definition I was getting his perception of how he operated and that in any scheme of appraisal that is meant to be free standing you have obviously got to have more than one perspective to offer.

This point was discussed in the session arranged for consideration of the report. Both parties agreed that in any future appraisal it would be useful for the appraiser to interview some of the other staff to see how far their perceptions agreed with the picture that had emerged during the appraisal.

Despite the inclusion of a session to discuss the report, this particular appraisal was overwhelmingly retrospective in nature. Although the appraiser made a list of some issues that could serve as a basis for future action, these potential targets emerged only as an afterthought. This is in marked contrast to the appraisal of the college Principal where planning ahead was a main function of the appraisal. In this case although a report was not written, the job description was modified to incorporate new developments. These would then be reviewed in a future appraisal interview.

The Value of Headteacher Appraisal

One advantage of including the Headteacher or Principal is the appearance of even-handedness which it lends to a school- or college-based scheme: sauce for the gander as well as the geese, as it were. Such inclusion may well increase the acceptability of the scheme to subordinates. Reflecting on the purposes of appraisal as seen by teachers (Chapter 11), however, it is apparent that they do not apply readily or totally to Headteachers. As conducted in the four cases reviewed, appraisal seems unlikely to have any major implications for these people's career development, either because the persons conducting the appraisal were unable to offer much in the way of advice or because the Headteacher or Principal concerned had no plans in this direction. It is likely for such posts to be the final rung in the career ladder and once a person has achieved it there is little prospect for development except perhaps to move to a larger school or college. In the four examples studied, career development was either not mentioned or little came out of it being discussed.

The main advantage in Headteacher and Principal appraisal, in the way in which it was carried out in the cases studied, seems to have been as a spur to self-appraisal. Even if little came about in terms of change and development, at least there was an opportunity to reflect on practice in a manner otherwise absent in a busy institution. The comments from Headteachers themselves bear this out:

HT1 It has made me clarify aims and objectives. It has posed questions as to the distribution of time, that I think probably came through very clearly from the appraisal. It is an issue which I was aware of but this really highlighted it, brought it out into the open. It may be that I'll come back and continue doing what I'm doing now but it definitely needs looking at and a clearer assessment of that, that has to come through more strongly. It has also raised issues of delegation, which again I was aware of obviously because of the very nature of the exercise of delegation to the two deputies that has taken place in the last few weeks after a lot of consultation with them.

HT2 It did make me think about issues very deeply and in certain cases issues which I would not have otherwise given consideration to.

Conclusions

Bearing in mind that most of these appraisals of Heads of institutions were experimental, we shall now turn to some of the main issues and present our own viewpoint on how the appraisal of Headteachers might best proceed.

It has been argued that a Head's appraisal should be undertaken by someone with past experience of Headship (Suffolk Education Department 1985). However, even if someone with considerable experience of Headship were able to act as appraiser, they would still require much background knowledge about the school itself and would need to know about how the Head carries out his duties. A deputy might have more knowledge in this respect but it is questionable how far he or she understands the nature of the whole job. A person in such a position would be likely to see the Head's role in terms of their own more limited concerns. In addition there would still be limitations on how much evidence as opposed to subjective opinion they could bring to bear. Certainly it would be difficult for a deputy to see a Head's activities in a wider context and beyond that particular school. This would of course depend on how many Heads they had worked with.

Given such considerations we would argue that the key issue in a Headteacher's appraisal is that of adopting an appropriate methodology. The appraiser, whoever it may be, needs to be able to base questions, criticisms and judgments upon concrete evidence, and this is best acquired from observation of the Head at work, interviews with other staff and appropriate documentary material, such as letters to parents, notices to staff and so on.

The appraisals described in this Chapter seem to have been most successful as processes of self-evaluation on the part of the Head, facilitated by the appraisers concerned. However, a self-evaluation can be facilitated by almost anyone who can provoke thought and self-criticism. In order to make judgments, sound evidence is essential, otherwise there is no basis upon which to resolve potential disagreements. A critical appraisal needs to be more than the presentation of an opinion. One has to bear in mind that it is only where both parties are in agreement over the facts that further developments can be fruitfully discussed and implemented.

We would conclude that a person without experience of Headship is a potentially valuable person to conduct the appraisal of Headteachers, but that such an appraisal needs to be based on more than an appraisal interview. Of course observation of a Head at work, interviews with other staff and use of documentary evidence all have their limitations and potential for distortion. They also make appraisal very costly in terms of time. But what is the alternative? Should we not be considering the best practical ways of conducting a Head's appraisal? On the one hand we should try to avoid a procedure that is too limited in scope and, on the other, try not to aim for the impossible.

Chapter 10

The Appraisal of a Senior Management Team

Introduction

Schemes for teacher appraisal represent an attempt to appraise individual teachers in schools. Schemes for school self-evaluation on the other hand have an institutional emphasis. Just as it became apparent in many schools that to appraise the institution as a whole carries implications for the individuals who work in it, the appraisal of individual teachers also raises questions about the institutional context in which they operate.

There have, however, been approaches to evaluation and appraisal in schools which to some extent bridge the gap between the individual and institutional levels. Perhaps the best example of such an approach is that of departmental review in secondary schools (see Clift *et al.* 1987). Such reviews acknowledge the fact that teachers do not operate in isolation, and emphasis is on how a team operates as a whole, not just on the strengths and weaknesses of individuals.

At a time when there is growing emphasis on the appraisal of Headteachers, little has been said about the role of the Head as a member of a management team, sharing responsibilities and working in collaboration with deputies. Clearly the larger a school is, the more important the delegation of responsibilities becomes. In a secondary school of over 1,000 pupils, collaboration over decision-making and the delegation of key responsibilities is virtually unavoidable. The more a Head does delegate important tasks to deputies the more it makes sense to appraise the senior management team (SMT) as a whole rather than the Head and each of the deputies separately. However, it should be stressed here that the purpose of such an appraisal is the effectiveness of the SMT as a unit and not the individual career development of the persons concerned.

The Case Study School: Previous Attempts at Management Appraisal

The school in which a management team appraisal was undertaken and evaluated is a twelve to eighteen urban comprehensive of over 1,400 pupils. It has had an appraisal scheme for six years and in that time much thought has been given to the issue of who appraises the appraisers — the SMT. Although the Head undertakes appraisal interviews with the deputies, there is no provision for an appraisal of the Head and it was felt by the team that an appraisal of themselves as managers needed to be undertaken.

Over the years several approaches to management team appraisal were tried out in the school, but all were perceived to be unsatisfactory: too limited in their implications and scope. All had involved the use of 'outsiders'. The first approach was an industrial consultancy. A person from industry was invited into the school and observed the SMT for three days. Whilst having the advantage of an outsider input and a management perspective from the industrial angle, the team thought that the feedback they were given was of limited value. Whilst it was useful in getting them to think about the way they held meetings, for instance, it was wholly lacking in educational terms.

The next approach involved two days' input from the LEA Advisory service. This offered the educational perspectives lacking in the first approach but the problem here was that the Advisers concerned had had no experience themselves of running a large comprehensive school and again were able to offer little feedback of any value in terms of the management of a large and complex institution. They had been full of praise for the SMT but the team had wanted a more critical approach.

In an attempt to combine what had emerged as the two essential elements, the last approach was to invite in Bertie Everard from the Institution of Education, London University and formerly of ICI, who observed for one day. Although the Head thought that a lot had come out of that, it was still not judged to be adequate and was not the approach the team wished to adopt for the future.

Other approaches had been considered but rejected. Peer appraisal, using a Head from another school in the same LEA, was rejected because of lack of time for people from other schools to undertake the work required. Appraisal by a panel of staff was considered but the objection raised to this was that the junior staff are generally unaware of many of the aspects of the job of the educational manager.

The Proposed Strategy

It was at a time when the SMT were still trying to resolve this problem that one of the deputies contacted us in response to our advertisement for information about school- and college-based appraisal schemes, for inclusion in our first *Review and Register*. He asked if the Open University might be able to help them with the problem of SMT appraisal. We discussed the request with our colleagues Professor Ron Glatter and Colin Riches from the University's Centre for Educational Policy and Management and they readily agreed to be involved. A meeting was set up with one of the deputies at the school to discuss the matter further.

At this initial meeting we tried to decide the role that we of the School of Education might best adopt in order to meet the needs of the SMT. As far as we were able to establish, there were no existing models for such an appraisal which would simply be adopted or adapted to suit the particular purpose. It was therefore decided to adopt an experimental approach which could then be evaluated and modified as necessary. Broadly it was agreed that we researchers would undertake a 'shadowing' study, observing each of the deputies at work and recording factual data. This data would then be presented to the SMT and to Ron Glatter and Colin Riches. Glatter and Riches would then discuss with the SMT the management implications of the data and consider the way forward both for the SMT as managers and for the development of an SMT appraisal system for the future.

Further meetings were then held to firm up the details. It was decided that each member of the SMT, the Head and the four deputies, would be 'shadowed' for two days. As a follow-up to this, we would interview each member of the team to explore their perceptions of their roles, to consider the typicality of the days observed and thus to provide an opportunity to place the data collected in a wider context.

Stress was placed upon the need for the exercise to be perceived as a trial of an approach for appraising the team as a body and not each individual separately. It was decided to try as far as possible to select for observation two contrasting days for each person and, because of the emphasis on management functions, days which included a minimum of teaching time, although some lessons would necessarily be observed as part of the days' events. After-school activities were to be included where feasible. The notes produced, both from the shadowing and from the follow-up interviews, were to be typed up and given back to each person for verification. Once this stage was completed all of the typed-up notes would be distributed to all members of the SMT and to Glatter and Riches in readiness for the follow-up meeting.

We also considered interviewing a selection of staff at different levels in the school hierarchy about their perceptions of the SMT. It was concluded, however, that the shadowing and follow-up interviews with the SMT were enough in themselves and that to some extent staff perceptions of the SMT would be evident from interaction between staff and members of the SMT. In any case it was felt that an SMT appraisal need not be the same every year and that the issue of staff perceptions might be something to include in a subsequent appraisal.

The time scheduled for the shadowing was the first part of spring term of 1986. It was noted that this would be a critical time of the year and that there would be many problems caused by Union action over the pay dispute. The team decided that it was important that the shadowing should be 'warts and all' and that they would try to go about their duties as far as possible as if the observation were not taking place. In terms of interaction with individuals, it was recognized that certain delicate matters might be affected by the presence of an observer and that in some cases the persons involved should be asked whether they objected to our presence. It is worthy of note that on no occasion was any objection raised.

Roles and Responsibilities

The SMT consists of:

Headteacher (HT)
First Deputy (DH1)

Second Deputy (DH2), responsible for Centre A;

Third Deputy (DH3), responsible for Sixth-Form Centre;

Fourth Deputy (DH4), responsible for Centre B.

Centres A and B are separate pastoral units of over 600 pupils each, contained within separate buildings. DH2 and DH4 thus have responsibility for running a centre of about the size of a small secondary school. The sixth form, of about 150 students, also occupies a separate building which it shares with the Department of Business Studies of the local College of Further Education and also contains a Youth Wing.

The faculty structure, however, operates on a whole-school basis. DH1 is principally a curriculum deputy, responsible for curriculum co-ordination. The other three deputies are allocated specific responsibility for general oversight of two faculties in addition to their Centre responsibilities. There are no Heads of years or houses in the school structure: instead the three deputies with responsibility for running centres each have an assistant and together work with the form tutors as a pastoral team. The assistants also share the responsibility for the two faculties with their superior. The assistants are part of a senior team: they have scale posts and a reduced teaching load. They are not, however, senior to Heads of faculties. The senior staff meeting is attended by fourteen: the Head and four deputies, the three assistants and six Heads of faculties. Due to Union action this extended management team was not meeting at the time of the shadowing.

The deputies are allocated other more specific responsibilities and are members of smaller teams which have their own regular meetings. Although each member of the SMT has a specific role outlined in their job description, the team tries to avoid strong demarcation and roles are shared wherever this proves to be advantageous.

The Shadowing

Notes taken during the ten days' shadowing amounted to some 150 pages of A4 sheets. It is not practicable to reproduce them here in their entirety, but in order to offer something of the flavour of those days, and to demonstrate the style of note-taking employed, here are the complete notes taken during the first half-hour of the second day that the Head (HT) was observed.

Shadowing of HT by GT: 4.2.86 (first half hour)

8.13 HT arrives and takes the milk to the staffroom.

8.15 He arrives in his office. He does a quick agenda for the Senior Management Team Meeting. He says it was agreed at a meeting last night. He talks to me.

8.23 He goes through a pile of papers, some are from the Governors Meeting, others are for this morning's meeting. He sorts them in order of priority.

8.26 He rings DH2, there is no answer. He rings a teacher about the cover situation who then passes DH2 on. He writes down on a pad which periods can't be covered; periods 2–6.

8.28 He goes to see DH4's assistant and discusses cover. There is a problem over period 6. He looks at the cover list and talks to two teachers and tells one teacher which group she will be covering.

8.33 He gets a cup of coffee and a teacher briefly sees him. It is the AMMA representative, who won't cover. He sees DH4 over what can be covered. A teacher approaches him with a query, a paper headed 'Southern Regional Exam Board', another teacher comes over. There is a group of four with DH4 chatting informally. The other two teachers depart. He continues talking with DH4 over the cover arrangements. DH4's assistant comes over and adds things to the cover list. He sees another teacher about exams. He then discusses the cover list with DH4.

8.43 He goes back to his office and rings DH2 to tell him what the cover situation is and which classes he will have to send home.

8.45 He rings his secretary and asks her to see him later because there are a fair number of letters to do. He sorts out some more papers. He looks at the text for his fifth form English lesson this afternoon and reads the papers for the Senior Management Team Meeting.

Members of the team were shadowed all the time that they were in school on the days concerned, including breaks and lunchtimes. 'On the spot' notes were taken as activities progressed. The notes were broken up according to the length of activities, or where breaks occurred such as telephone interruptions. There were several cases where the team as a whole, or several of the team, were observed interactively, such as at SMT meetings and the 'diary meeting' at which events over the coming week were announced. The bulk of the shadowing was undertaken by Glenn Turner. In order to provide a contrast and a degree of triangulation in terms of the process of observation, one of the ten days (day 1 with DH2) was observed by Phil Clift and we both took part in the follow-up interview with DH2. This gave an opportunity to discuss the implications of a different person doing the shadowing, and to what extent the data produced were influenced by the person undertaking the observation.

The Follow-up Interviews

As well as providing an opportunity to discuss the background, history and the rationale behind the events of the days shadowed, the follow-up interviews also enabled us to talk to members of the team about the value of the exercise and to consider the methodology.

Perhaps the greatest value to the individuals of being shadowed and the notes later presented to them is the raising of consciousness about their everyday activities. The advantage this has over self-evaluation or introspection is that those observed can be made aware of things they hadn't noticed and can see in detail a record of a day's activities, showing how much time is spent on particular tasks.

One of the things raised in the follow-up interviews, therefore, was the extent to which members of the team had been surprised by what had been reflected to them in the notes. The Head claimed that he had been 'amused and appalled' by reading about his own two days:

> HT   I was amused by some of the reactions that I'd made to people . . . [also] what amused, impressed really was how . . . it is an extremely difficult time and most of the time, according to that, we stayed sane and not too excessive, which is not actually a picture I have of myself . . . you know, it was a sort of coping circumstance. What appalled me, but it always does . . . was how many decisions I had to make and communicate instantly. I mean that is absolutely terrifying because although most of them were not world shattering and were not going to alter the life of anybody very much, they were all important particularly to the person receiving the decision.

DH2 claimed that the notes from the shadowing highlighted the fragmentary nature of his role and, again, the number of decisions that were made in a short time, seemingly with little consideration. However, both he and the Head stressed that such decisions are based on very considerable amassed knowledge and experience. DH2 also pointed out that a number of individual encounters made his role appear as a reactive one.

DH1 and DH3 said that they were not at all surprised by what they had read in the notes but DH4 made an interesting observation about some of the more routine events:

> DH4   It's interesting that there are instances in [the notes] that I don't necessarily recognize — that I'd dealt with so subconsciously that they'd not really registered with me and I couldn't for the life of me tell you what they were about.

The issue of the typicality of the days observed was raised. The Head pointed out that it was an untypical time, generally, given the effects of the industrial action and this was reflected in the days concerned. He claimed that much time was now spent dealing with 'urgent trivia' rather than important long-term matters and that the number of individual encounters had increased due to the lack of opportunity for interaction with large groups of staff at meetings. He also noted that much of his time was spent in 'front-line' pastoral duties, given that lunchtime supervision now had to be undertaken by the SMT. The deputies also claimed that this had happened, making it more difficult for them to act as the 'last resort' in pastoral matters.

Of the deputies, DH1 seemed to have been by far the most affected by the industrial action, to the extent that he was unable to undertake his role as specified — that of curriculum deputy — because curriculum development could not proceed. Due to this, his role had become, in his own words, an 'odd-job role', and he had ended up taking on self-contained jobs on a one-off basis — such as dealing with examination entries. The other three deputies were less affected by the action, since their major role was that of being in charge of a Centre. However, they too were affected by having to supervise the Centres at lunchtimes and having to cover lessons.

Thus the notion of a typical day was somewhat problematic for any of the SMT as it was hardly a typical time. However, the Head pointed out that even if events were to some extent untypical, the way he had reacted to things was probably not, and in that sense the data were a valid reflection of his managerial style.

Methodological Issues

The methodological implications of shadowing were discussed with the team. Our major concern was the extent to which our presence had affected what we were observing. Whilst not denying that there were some effects, the Head claimed that in his own case they were trivial.

Since the intention in producing the shadowing notes was to provide a descriptive account of the days' events, in the follow-up interviews opportunity was taken to ask how far the notes were neutrally descriptive rather than value laden. None of the team thought that the notes were value laden: there were just a few cases where they questioned the use of words, for example whether 'haranguing' a pupil was an appropriate description of what had taken place between DH2 and a late-comer.

Perhaps the main difficulty in a shadowing exercise is capturing the essence of tasks without having the necessary background information. Thus, much activity simply appears in the notes as 'enters something down on a pad' or whatever. It was particularly difficult to capture fully the clerical side of the roles and the notes taken seemed to trivialize activities. What is said at the other end of a telephone was always difficult to hear with the result that it was generally left out. Certain things — such as the thinking behind decisions — are simply not observable. The extent to which it is possible to capture the entirety of the role in a shadowing exercise was questioned by DH4:

> I'm not sure that the role as such you can reflect entirely in this sort of analysis. You are reflecting some elements of the time management and some elements of the strategies one uses, but they tend to be the obvious and the superficial ones . . .

Similar points were raised by DH1:

> I think they [the notes] were objective but I think they missed a very significant thing . . . for instance the actual content of some of the conversations and maybe a certain degree of humour or warmth in the interaction between myself and another person. There were one or two occasions for instance where I deliberately spoke to people to give them either encouragement or positive feedback and that's something that didn't come up . . . In the interactions I've had with staff, the benefits which might have come out of a particular way of interacting are never shown there at all.

This highlights the limitations inherent in undertaking a descriptive exercise which in its nature seeks to be as objective and value-free as possible. If the observer were to present in the data his or her own opinions about the effectiveness of particular strategies then there would be scope for discussion with the team about their aims and objectives and the extent to which they appeared to be achieving them. However, this places the observer in the simultaneous role of observer and evaluator and clearly one of the dangers would be that the observer might then distort the portrayal of events by presenting their own perspective. This was something we tried hard to avoid.

The Follow-up Meeting

At the meeting of 2 May, Ron Glatter and Colin Riches discussed with the SMT the management implications of the data gathered from the shadowing and interviews. We (researchers) were also present. The meeting was divided into two parts. The first was a discussion of the themes emerging from the data and what changes in arrangements the SMT might wish to make. The second part consisted of a discussion of what might be adopted as a system of appraisal for the SMT in the future.

The meeting was opened by Ron Glatter outlining the need to look at the data on individuals from the point of view of the management team as a whole. He suggested that they treat it as a kind of workshop session to identify problems and consider solutions. He and Colin Riches then identified three broad themes emerging from the data. These were:

1   The use of time

    proactive versus reactive;
    time for strategic and educational thinking;
    busywork versus meaningful work;
    the extent to which crises are created by the context.

2   Roles and Responsibilities

    distribution;
    coherence;
    responsibility for centres;
    the role of assistants;
    how to achieve consistency.

3   How Jobs Are Interpreted by Their Holders

    individual differences;
    paper shuffling versus individual interactions;
    staff development.

Much of the discussion centred around the issue of the use of time. The number of decisions made and the extent to which time was occupied in reactive tasks concerned the SMT greatly. DH2 noted that the team spent its time being reactive, dealing with 'busywork' and dealing with crises. Consequently it is extremely difficult to measure their success. Their job descriptions do not include the 'reactive' side of roles and in the light of the shadowing exercise, this was considered to be an omission. Glatter pointed out that there seemed to be three ways in which time is used: routine activities, dealing with crises and planning. DH3 claimed that the routine tasks get done because they have to be done, there is more crisis management than there ever used to be and therefore it is the creative planning that is pushed to one side. It was suggested by Glatter that they could devote certain meetings to the creative side of the job but DH2 argued that on the days set aside they would tend to end up being overtaken by a crisis and have to deal with it.

The nature and role of assistants to the deputies was brought up in this context. Riches suggested that the assistants could be used to deal with some of the constant flow of demands which intervene and disrupt meetings on so many occasions. How far decision-making could be delegated to the assistants was discussed. The Head claimed that things which are delegated keep coming back to the team, making it more time-consuming than doing it oneself in the first place. It was pointed out by DH2 that delegation can only work effectively if the philosophies of the school are clear and that during the action it has been difficult to have any discussion of the kind necessary for this. The question was raised as to how well defined the role of assistants is and Glatter argued that the lack of Heads of years means inevitably that pastoral decisions are pushed up to the level of the SMT. However, the system had been devised in this way in order to prevent important matters being kept at the level of middle management and not discussed by the SMT. DH4 argued the need for a proper system of accountability and feedback *vis-à-vis* the assistants so that they did not have to keep coming back to the deputies all the time.

Some time was given to the question of DH1's role and whether, given the teachers' industrial action, it required greater clarification. This was not resolved since it led on to the issue of 'territoriality'. It was pointed out that roles deliberately overlap so as to prevent them being perceived as an individual's territory. The reactive side of the SMT's function is shared in order to provide flexibility and an opportunity for subordinate members of staff to go to a member of the SMT of their own choosing. The Head saw this as an advantage but that it has a cost in that roles might not seem very clear to staff.

The second part of the meeting began with a brief review of the different approaches that the team had adopted in order to appraise their management functions. The extent to which SMT appraisal should take on board the perceptions of staff was then considered. The Head pointed out that staff tend to say what is wrong at the faculty level but not at the whole school level and in relation to himself. Riches asked if there was a body of staff from which they could gain critical feedback, and the possibility of setting up some kind of working party of staff to provide this was considered. DH2 stressed that staff saw appraisal in hierarchical terms and therefore expected SMT appraisal to be undertaken by persons senior to them, although precisely who this should be was not clear. It was noted that junior staff perceive there to be a very cosy set of relationships between the SMT and LEA Officers and Advisers and such people are not thought to be sufficiently removed to act as appraisers. The question of who is appropriate to undertake SMT appraisal thus remained unresolved. DH1 argued that staff have still not seen any data from SMT appraisals and it was agreed that something summarizing this particular appraisal ought to be circulated to staff.

Given that many ideas had been put forward as to the possible nature of future SMT appraisal, it was decided that members of the team needed to go away and think about them and then have another meeting to discuss the specific nature of a future approach. The view was expressed that the system did not have to operate in the same way every year and that each appraisal might adopt a different emphasis.

Conclusions

The aim of this part of the research was to evaluate an experimental model for the appraisal of an SMT in a large comprehensive school. We will now consider the effectiveness of the approach as a general strategy for management appraisal.

The first point is, how effective was the strategy in terms of the appraisal of a team? It could be argued, owing to the decision to shadow and observe the team as separate individuals, that the methods employed emphasized the roles undertaken by individuals as opposed to that of the team as a whole. However, in shadowing individuals there were many occasions where the SMT was observed interactively, such as at meetings. One cannot shadow a whole team collectively and, arguably, the extent to which an SMT operates as a team will be evident from the observation of its individual members. It is difficult, from this point of view, to see how the strategy could have been more oriented to a team perspective.

A second point to consider is how far the industrial action affected the nature of the exercise. It could be argued that the case study did not reflect the SMT as it would normally be operating since meetings and activities were not taking place, whilst the SMT was forced to take on a major role in alleviating the worst effects of the action. Nevertheless, one could argue that one of the best times to evaluate the performance of a team is when there are additional pressures and crises. Although one would expect to see the team in much more a reactive role, the effectiveness with which crises and unanticipated problems are dealt with is surely indicative of the quality of a team.

Another concern is the limitations in the research methodology. In this instance the perspectives of subordinate staff were not explored. In future this might well be included. A second limitation was the failure of the strategy to go beyond 'surface' activity to examine aims, motives, decisions and the thinking which goes into the acting out of roles. Such matters are by their nature non-observable and although it was hoped to compensate for this problem by undertaking follow-up interviews, these interviews did not successfully fill the gap in the manner envisaged. We would argue that this is a limitation which is inherent in this particular methodology rather than the way in which it was put into practice.

What then are the implications of the study for developing future models for SMT appraisal? If the approach adopted is considered to be worthwhile one has to consider whether there exist the individuals who can offer the service, not only in terms of time but also the skills, Given the highly confidential nature of the activities observed, it would be difficult to envisage members of staff at the school carrying out a similar exercise. Furthermore, it is probable that they would not have the necessary skills. Perhaps the main argument against the use of internal staff, however, is the advantage of having the perspectives of persons outside the school. Therefore one would be thinking in terms of persons from industry, social services, universities or colleges, or from the LEA. Of course much depends on whether there are people available and willing to offer the necessary service. A further consideration is whether it is best to have a perspective from personnel within the LEA or from outsiders.

Given the amount of time which might be necessary in order to undertake a thorough appraisal of a management team, we should perhaps ask whether this kind of exercise needs to be carried out every year. Rather than having a full-blown appraisal every year a better strategy might be to operate on a longer cycle. A three-year cycle, for instance, might go as follows: in the first year there could be discussion and interviews geared to an appraisal of the SMT's policies. This could be followed in the second year by the shadowing of the team in order to investigate how far policies were being put into practice. In the third year there could then be interviews with a range of staff, with Governors and with parents and LEA officials in order to consider the effectiveness of the SMT's approach. This is only a suggstion, but it points to the possibility of having a very comprehensive and thorough approach by breaking it up over time into handleable self-contained units.

In conclusion, it should be said that a useful test of any particular strategy for appraisal is whether those concerned consider it to have been worthwhile. As far as this study is concerned, the benefits can perhaps only be assessed in the long term. Will the SMT see it to have been of benefit in three years' time, we wonder?

Chapter 11

Teachers' Perceptions of Appraisal

Introduction

In preceding chapters we have offered a portrayal of appraisal in action with individuals at all levels of institutional seniority and collectively at the level of a senior management team. As we have done so, inevitably we have touched incidentally on their perceptions of it in the widely different forms in which it has developed. We now turn to a detailed examination of those perceptions.

Such perceptions are likely to be different from those of a random sample of teachers, the key difference being that they will be informed perceptions, based on a degree of first-hand experience or at least close observation of appraisal in practice. Many were not easily able to articulate these perceptions, however, even when they had had direct experience. Some admitted that they were uncertain in their view or had mixed feelings. In advance of the event, many teachers who took part in an appraisal in the case study schools had not known what to expect. After being appraised, some were still unsure as to what to make of their scheme and perhaps needed more time to reflect on it. Thus when asked about their perceptions of appraisal, or of their school's scheme, not all teachers could offer a well-worked-out view. Here are the comments by way of illustration of this:

T1 It's difficult, I mean I've got mixed feelings about the whole process of the staff review, I suppose.

T2 I have to be frank and say I haven't thought through the implications, I don't think fully, of appraising. It's something that's new to me and I've found it this year to be a very time-consuming extra.

T3 I've been here four years and so I've had three appraisals, I think. I didn't really know what to expect when I had the first one and I think in fact that the year I had my first one was the first time that the system was under way and it was a bit strange.

T4 It was a case of well I don't know what an appraisal is, I've never had an appraisal before.

T5 It's quite difficult because it's something new to me in a sense that I haven't got much to compare it with.

Positive Views

At the simplest level, it is possible to divide teachers' perceptions broadly into those which are positive towards appraisal and those which are negative. Many teachers were receptive to the introduction of an appraisal scheme from the very beginning. The perception of such teachers was that there was nothing particularly new about appraisal and that it was just a matter of systematizing a process which had always gone on and which otherwise operated in a covert and arbitrary fashion:

> T1 Appraisal's going on whether or not you have a scheme. I mean if they're purely subjective judgments that you're making, it's got an element of appraisal about it. The fact that you're doing it on a formal basis is neither here nor there. The formality of it does regularize it, if you like, but it's here all the time.

> T2 I've never felt reluctant to go and talk to the Head about the development of my career, or the subject that I've been involved in and this is just formalizing a situation which I've always taken for granted anyway.

Other teachers were supportive of the idea of an appraisal scheme because they saw appraisal as an aspect of their job and therefore as something which should be done anyway:

> T1 Evaluation and assessment is obviously important and it's right that we should look at ourselves and be critical, so I have no objections to it.

> T2 I've never been critical of it, I'm a supporter of appraisal. I'm all for improving standards of teaching at whatever level.

> T3 I think most teachers welcomed the idea of this sort of thing, because it hadn't been done in the past in the school, I don't think. I think most people welcomed the opportunity.

> T4 I am in favour of it. As it is an issue which is alive nationally, I think it is better to get it off the ground, developed by teachers themselves and demonstrate that it works, rather than wait for something to emerge. It is also useful to have a discussion about your own position.

> T5 Initially I was very pleased that something was being done about appraisal within the school because I think it's something that the profession should take on.

Communication

For some teachers appraisal is perceived as an opportunity which otherwise would not exist to have a chance to discuss one's progress, uninterrupted, with the Head or a senior member of staff:

T1 I just felt that it was an opportunity to have a chat with the Head with no interruptions, you have a hundred per cent because often you talk to him and somebody else comes to speak to him.

T2 Well, I think it's worth while. Yes, I'm glad that they've brought it in. I think it's good. It does give you an opportunity to sit down and talk with someone on your senior staff, about things which concern you, perhaps. I think this whole aspect of job satisfaction is quite important in teaching and you should have an opportunity to discuss where you're getting some satisfaction, where you're not and what you can do or what you'd like to be done.

T3 In a comprehensive school, links between Headteachers and members of staff are not always that easy because of the size of the school, so I saw it as an opportunity for him and me to come together to discuss my job.

Support

In addition to communication, appraisal can be seen to be advantageous from the point of view of support for staff. Senior staff can use the opportunity appraisal provides to ensure that subordinates' conditions are such that they can do their best:

A I think it's a very good exercise if you're interested in putting people in situations where they're giving their best. (Head of faculty)

Self-appraisal

Teachers who had positive attitudes to appraisal tended also to stress the opportunity provided by a formal scheme for facilitating teachers' self-appraisal. Comments from those interviewed included the fact that teachers rarely have a chance to take stock of what they are doing in the long term and that as a preliminary to any appraisal by another member of staff, teachers inevitably carry out some measure of self-evaluation, which is useful:

T1 I think that if it doesn't do anything else it makes you stop and think about exactly what you have done in the past year.

T2 Well I think it's a very good thing. I think it's very heart-searching. I mean you could go on and on and on but I think it does make you sit down and it makes you stop and think. It's about the only time, probably in the year, when I do stop and think about what I've been doing and how I've got on. You appraise yourself really, don't you, first?

T3 I would like to see self-appraisal. I think it's something that teachers should be doing anyway. I think you've got to ask yourself the question, 'Am I doing a good job, how can I improve it, am I capable of doing a better job, where am I going?' I think you've got to do that because it's very easy to get into a rut and just do the same sort of things over and over again. I'm sure everybody has a tendency just to do the same thing as they did last week, last term, last year, because they can get by with it. And before you know it, you find everything you're doing is on that sort of ticking-over level and certain chronic difficulties can carry on almost unnoticed like that.

Some appraisers deliberately attempted to create a situation in the appraisal where they were enabling the person concerned to appraise their own performance:

> HT The theory as I see it is that, in my role as appraiser, I wish to act as a facilitator in assisting the appraisee to a self-evaluation of their strengths and weaknesses: areas for improvement, development. That would be the approach I would seek. I would wish to withdraw from the scripted view whereby I act as the boss appraising the underling. I would wish to withdraw from that particular perception.

Benefits from appraisal

Teachers who took a positive view of appraisal also tended to stress the benefits or potential benefits of having an appraisal scheme. To be able to demonstrate some positive outcome from appraisal is to many teachers an 'acid test' as to whether it is worth having an appraisal scheme or not. The question of how far appraisal has any tangible impact will be considered in the next chapter. For the present we will simply quote one teacher who felt that all staff who had been appraised had benefited in some way:

> T I felt everybody involved wanted it to work and wanted it to be successful and the results have been positive in the sense that something has been done with each person that I am aware of, having been appraised. Each person has benefited, including myself.

'Lukewarm' enthusiasm for appraisal

By splitting this chapter into two sections, positive and negative perceptions of appraisal, we should not exclude those teachers who do not have a strong opinion one way or the other. Many teachers' views could best be summed up as 'lukewarm': not exactly opposed to the idea of having an appraisal scheme, but not greatly enthusiastic either. The quote below characterizes this particular view:

> T On the whole, yes, I am in favour of it, without being absolutely over the moon about it; a definite yes without being ecstatic about the idea.

Many teachers were enthusiastic about appraisal provided it was conducted in a particular way. They did not think appraisal was either acceptable or unacceptable but wished to add certain caveats. A common view among teachers, for example, was to claim to be enthusiastic about having a scheme providing it was in no way connected with disciplinary measures:

> T Yes, I think it's good, as long as there's no place for disciplinary matters in an appraisal. In this form it's a positive thing, which I don't think anybody could object to. If it came to a situation where you felt that he was just sitting down and criticizing you, then that would be a different story altogether.

Many teachers stressed that they were in favour of having appraisal as long as it was conducted in a positive way. That appraisal should be constructive in the sense of helping teachers to solve problems, and not just a 'knocking exercise', was a prevalent view:

> T I don't mind being appraised or whatever, so long as it's done in a thoughtful, constructive manner and not done just like a knocking exercise, like, 'Oh that is bad', or, 'Three out of ten', or whatever. If it's done like that it is not very good. But if you look at the possibilities for solving problems, then that's great, that's what I want.

Other teachers argued that they were in favour of having appraisal as long as it was a two-way process, enabling the appraisee to bring up his or her concerns as well as the appraiser:

> T I think it's a good idea. I think so long as it is a free and frank and two-way exchange of views, that's fine because a lot of the discontentment that one feels is because you don't really feel that you're able to go up and say, 'Look here I'm not really happy about this!' and in a formalized situation like this, in the ideal sense, that is free and frank, then I feel quite at liberty to say anything I like within reason.

Appraisal as a two-way exchange of views can also make for a more open system. Teachers seemed to be in favour of open records and such a system might well be perceived as part of an appraisal scheme:

> T I've supported the idea of appraisals since the first time the Head brought the idea up, which was a good eleven, twelve years ago. I've supported it because I believe when you've got an appraisal system, which is a two-way appraisal system, then there is the opportunity for both people to put forward their points of view, both the appraisee and the appraiser. In fact the appraisee is appraising the appraiser at the same time, so it isn't one-

sided. And I believe that we ought to have the right to have a say what goes in our records, because sometimes things go into records when they are secret that are inaccurate. Even given the best intentioned Headmaster on earth, he doesn't know all his staff perfectly, particularly in a school the size of ours, and his impressions are not always correct. That is no criticism of our Headmaster. I think that is true of any school above a certain size that it's impossible for the Headmaster to really be knowledgeable about every member of staff. So, I think that this sort of system is the only way you can develop an accurate record of the teacher and of the way the teacher is progressing in their teaching.

Negative Views

Despite attempts by senior management to 'sell' the idea of appraisal and to point out its merits, many teachers viewed appraisal negatively, or at least had very serious reservations about it. Just as some teachers took the view that appraisal was merely formalizing or systematizing something which already existed in some form or another, there were teachers who argued that there was no need to have an appraisal scheme because such existing procedures worked perfectly adequately. Some teachers believed that a scheme of appraisal is constraining. They preferred to have purely informal discussions when they wanted to:

> T I know him [the Head] quite well — we have chats from time to time about this and that, pretty informal but I think the more informal it is the better. You see I don't like that structure that the Head gave out because it makes you feel automatically that you've got to do your homework before you come in and you've got to adhere rigidly to it.

It was also argued that having appraisals at specific times during the year precluded, or at any rate reduced the possibility of going to see the appraiser at a time more appropriate to the person being appraised. Some teachers expressed considerable irritation at having to wait until the appraisal to be able to voice their concerns and to have feedback about their performance:

> T1 I don't think you should have to wait for meetings and official times when you can raise the worries, complaints, praise, whatever, I think it should just happen as and when.

> T2 You shouldn't have to wait twelve months to know how you are doing, you should know well before that.

Threat

Perhaps the most common negative perception was that appraisal was a threat to teachers. It would be used in order to find fault, to spot weaknesses, to catch people out and would induce fear and paranoia:

> T I can't help thinking that putting it on a formal basis as they're [the DES] suggesting is going to do more harm than good.
>
> R For what reason?
>
> T People will get worked up about it, people will get agitated and some people will have good assessments and some people might have bad ones and generally disturbing experiences.

There was no shortage of teachers who did claim to have found the prospect of appraisal to be a very threatening one:

> T1 I'm absolutely paranoic about it. I think half the members of this establishment have gone a bit paranoic about staff assessments because it's been put before lots of other things.
>
> T2 I know that, just talking to colleagues here, everybody puts on this big sort of act, 'Oh, it's my appraisal to-day' and afterwards it's all, 'let's go down the pub'. Although those sound very glib remarks they do indicate a tremendous amount about how people really do feel about it. Even when you've got a great Head, there's still that feeling of personal competence on the line and something that you're going to have to prove. I can imagine that if you did work for someone who was an authoritarian, and there are a lot of them still around today, that it could be a destructive process, and I think that's something that has to be borne in mind.
>
> T3 Just a pure personal reaction, I felt a certain amount of vulnerability because in the end you can't help but feel that you are on the line and that your motives are being questioned and that your performance is being questioned and you never quite know what's going to be said to you as you come in through the door, even though within this school, which is a very, very 'comfy' school in terms of staff relationships and in terms of communication with the Head and from the Head throughout the school.
>
> T4 There's a growing feeling amongst our members of staff of 'big brother'. In fact there's a joke going round at the moment that we should put in a resolution saying there ought to be monitors in every classroom linked to X's office so he can switch on at any time and see what's going on in the classrooms.
>
> T5 Some people were worried about it. They saw all sorts of things in it, for example it would be an opportunity for your Head of faculty to find out all the things that you're doing wrong and put it on a record.
>
> T6 Anything new off the ground is bound to be viewed with apprehension I think, especially in the light of the current national mood, so people were

bound to be threatened by it and the general feeling I think was not to be part of it because it was threatening and if you weren't part of it it might go away.

The extent to which individuals perceived appraisal as a threat differs of course. Perhaps it depends on how secure — or perhaps how ambitious — teachers are:

T1 I think it depends completely on the individual and how secure he feels in the work he is doing at the moment. I'm quite secure — I'm sitting back and I enjoy teaching and I am enjoying what I am doing and I am not worried about my future so I just sit back and let the world go by and sort of smile, but I don't know about others. I mean, there might be some others who have got things that they want to hide.

T2 I'm quite happy to bare my soul to anybody because what I say I mean and I'll repeat it to whoever, so it bothers me nought. I mean as far as I was concerned he [the Head] could have my interview in the staffroom because I've got nothing to hide.

T3 I don't mind — the Queen of Sheba could walk to the back of my classroom if she wants and whether we're discussing something or whether the kids are working or whether I'm actually involved teaching, I don't mind because I feel I can justify anything that goes on in my room. I don't have that many discipline problems, I have very, very few discipline problems, so I don't worry in that respect but there again I'm only speaking for myself.

Some teachers were reluctant to be appraised because they believed it could have negative outcomes: what was said in an appraisal might be held against them at some time in the future:

T As I'm personally committed to positive forms of staff development I was keen to get on with it. Other staff have been somewhat more reluctant to get involved: they feel they wouldn't want anything on tape or on record which could later 'be held against them'. I think they would fear that if they didn't want to do something, that the Head would turn round on a future occasion and say, 'Ah but you agree that you wanted to take this part and that part and that's what we're doing' and that sort of thing. So I think some staff have feared that the review might close down options even though the intent in my opinion is to open up options.

Other teachers believed that appraisal would be open to manipulation and that particular individuals would come out of it well, not because they were good teachers but because they could 'charm' the appraiser:

T At the start I felt quite hostile towards it, you know, what's the point of this, and the feeling that the person who comes out well from an appraisal is probably the person who's got the 'gift of the gab' and that is probably the key to the appraisal and the fact than an appraisal is only as good as the appraiser. I wasn't very keen as you can gather.

The appraisal bandwagon

Some teachers were sceptical about the introduction of an appraisal scheme because it seemed to be following a fashion:

T1 A lot of rot. A lot of balderdash. Jumping on the bandwagon. What Keith Joseph wanted.

T2 I think it's become a gimmick of the establishment. It's become the latest thing that we all ought to be interested in.

T3 I thought, 'Oh my God it's another one of these modern fads, what have we got now?'

'Just a formality'

Several teachers argued that appraisal would be a passing phenomenon and/or would quickly become just a formality:

T1 I think it's all very artificial at the moment. I think the general feeling in the school, well, within the staffroom, is one almost of sheer boredom by now. I think it's just got past a joke, nobody's bothered about it now. The people who are ambitious think this is a good thing to get on to. They're the ones who've taken part in it.

T2 I think it's purely an academic exercise in the way it takes place at the moment, I think far more of it should be actually at the grass roots level, that is within the classroom.

T3 I think that we skimmed over a whole load of things and it was very superficial.

Subjectivity in appraisal

A further concern was that, despite the attempt to make appraisal a more systematic process, it would still operate in a very subjective way and even give more weight to subjective opinion:

T1 Any form of testing, any form of appraisal, any form of assessment, evaluation, whatever you'd like to call it, is bound to get a little subjective. I mean it's got to because it's people talking about other people and being very interested in people you know that the truth with anyone is only as it stands at the time.

T2 I think inevitably there's going to be some element of subjectivity built in on the part of the person doing the review. Whether that can be overcome or the extent to which it can be overcome by skilful reviewing techniques being employed, I don't know.

T3 I'm sceptical — mainly because no one is qualified to do it. It needs firm guidelines especially if you don't get on with your Head of faculty. It is difficult to cut out the subjective, personality element.

There is also the problem of at least ensuring consistency, if not objectivity:

T Then of course we get difficulty there with not having the different standards of appraisal and knowing whether people are going into it in the same sort of depth and so on. This is one of the difficult areas isn't it, training.

The need for safeguards

Because of the danger of subjectivity and inconsistency, and to limit the consequent possibility of bias, some teachers argued that safeguards needed to be built into schemes. Some of the schemes included in our case studies do include safeguards, for example the right to go to another appraiser if relations with your designated appraiser are not good:

HT If they feel they can't go to their Head of faculty for whatever reason, and there have been a couple in one faculty who felt that, then I've made it quite obvious that I'd rather they selected somebody in whom they had confidence and still produced all the various documents and still had the benefits of appraisal than not do anything.

Alternatively a third party could be present at the appraisal to ensure fair play, as was the case in another of our case study schools:

T I'd had previous experiences in industry so I thought always the presence of a third party is very useful. I was quite happy about a third person.

Other safeguards concerned confidentiality and the writing of records:

R What kinds of safeguards did the committee want to build into the scheme?

T That anything which was taped or put on to paper would be shown first, in its final form, to the person being appraised and that they could choose not to have the office staff type the final draft: all of us can type with one finger.

LEA input

Despite perceptions of threat sometimes associated with involving the LEA in appraisal, something we noted in Chapter 8, some teachers believed that one way to avoid subjectivity and bias in appraisal is to extend it beyond the boundaries of a particular school:

> T1 I'm only expressing my own point of view. I don't mind appraisals but I don't like the idea personally of its being confined to the staff in the school, because people are human, people do have biases, whether it be a Head Teacher, Senior Mistress or a scale 1 RE teacher or whatever.

> T2 I didn't like the idea of the Head as the final judge, if you like: the person making the final appraisal, because I feel that if I was appraised by him and I didn't agree with his appraisal I should have a right of appeal. What I would expect would be that I could say, 'I don't agree with this and I'd like to see the County appraisal man.' If you're going to have an appraisal system it's got to be based on something wider than individual secondary schools. The idea of appraisal operating in primary schools to my mind is ludicrous. In this LEA some of these places have only got three or four teachers. So if you give Headmasters that power, I don't feel the people have a fair crack of the whip.

However, in the view of a minority of the teachers interviewed, whatever system of appraisal was adopted and whatever safeguards were provided, appraisal just did not seem to be appropriate for the teaching profession:

> T I think when people are in a profession rather than just a job, and I still believe that teaching is a profession, I think you attract to it people with perhaps a little bit more in the way of sensitivity. I often hear it said that teachers couldn't stand the rat race of industry and I think that's true but I don't think it's because they haven't got the guts or whatever, it's because they do feel things very keenly. I think the action now [i.e. the teachers' industrial action over pay and conditions] for example shows you how teachers feel at the grass roots level and I think having said all that about sensitivity I think it's almost impossible in the establishment in which you work to be assessed objectively. I've seen it work in a factory, same thing people work together all day, people have their ups and downs, they have their arguments with management, middle management, lower management and their bonuses and sometimes their pay structure rely on their assessment and I'm quite aware of that but I still don't think those people

have the same sensitivity: I don't think they have the same sensitivities and pressures and tensions going on as people who work with children. It's a very stressful job.

Changes in Teachers' Perceptions

We said at the beginning of the chapter that teacher perceptions of appraisal are likely to change and there is much evidence from our interviews to show that many teachers, having experienced it, have changed their view of appraisal. In most cases, teachers seem to have changed their view from a negative view initially to a more positive one.

> T1 Well, I was apprehensive about the appraisal last year because this was the first time it had been done.

> T2 I don't think appraisal when looked at in the right way is quite so threatening as we thought it was going to be. I think it will take a little while for that to get through for all of us because a lot of us here are basically classroom teachers and not high-fliers who are looking for deputy Headships and Headships.

> T3 There are very few people who seem to be fervently against it. There's one or two but not too many now, they seem to be coming round.

> T4 Last year I found it really threatening because I suppose I really didn't know what it was. This year I was more relaxed about it and it was more an exchange of views.

> T5 I think we find it less difficult this year than we did last year. It's just the unknown, isn't it? I think it's the same with a lot of things, it's fear of the unknown.

> T6 The scheme is totally internal and tries to be non-threatening. When we started, we didn't know what an evaluation process was and felt very sceptical about it. We now see that it doesn't have to be the way Sir Keith talks about it.

In these cases, teachers had been largely reacting to the fear of the unknown. Others had initially adopted a negative view of appraisal because they believed that it would take up a lot of their time and not produce any benefit. Some of these had come to see that there was value in it:

> T I think it's a good idea. Initially I suppose I thought, 'Oh God, more administration to do, just another little job to add to the thousand others, but I think there are parts of it that are of value. I think it's of value to actually sit down and think what have I done, where am I going and actually make a note of it and have it in some sort of order if only in your mind.

We noted earlier that there were teachers who were of the opinion that formalizing appraisal would be detrimental and that the system was best left ad hoc. Having experienced a systematic approach to appraisal, however, some teachers claimed that formalizing it was perhaps a good idea after all:

T1 Having a formal situation in which to discuss things struck me at first as not being particularly useful because, you know, I could talk to him [the Head] any time over a cup of coffee about anything that was bothering me but there was a certain amount of feedback which was very useful.

T2 When the appraisal business came up I was sceptical. I thought, 'Well the system that works at the moment has always worked well for me, why change it?' but I was aware that many members of staff were concerned over the subjectiveness of some of the testimonials and references that were written about them.

Those who could point to their appraisal being followed up with some form of in-service training also tended to adopt a more positive view of the process, subsequently:

T Having been through it once, I feel far more confident in dealing with it, and also this year as well, having been on courses, it does make a difference, it makes you feel that you're doing your job better, even though it doesn't have any direct bearing on the school for a while until things filter through. For me personally it has really changed my view. Appraisal is necessary and right and it's reinforced my confidence in actually going through it.

These examples demonstrate the ways in which teacher perceptions of appraisal have changed and how experience of appraisal has convinced certain teachers that the process is after all a worthwhile one in which to participate. This is not to say that all teachers who had adopted a negative attitude to appraisal came to be 'converted'. For some teachers experience merely confirmed their suspicions, whilst in other cases the appraisal turned out to be a negative experience and changed staff opinion in the opposite direction. Some teachers who had initially been open-minded about appraisal came to view it negatively. As to those teachers who were strongly opposed to appraisal, few of those seem to have changed their views. As one advocate of appraisal schemes accepted:

T As you probably know, some teachers have just got a deep-seated opposition to teacher appraisal.

Conclusions

In this chapter we have examined the varied perceptions of appraisal of the teachers in the case study schools. Such perceptions were broadly classified into positive and negative views, whilst accepting that teachers do not have just one view of appraisal or necessarily a well-worked-out attitude which they can readily articulate. However, it is evident that, from the earliest stages of experiencing an appraisal scheme in their school, some teachers are receptive to the idea whilst others are hostile.

Of those teachers who adopted a positive view of appraisal, many saw it as merely formalizing what already was happening in an informal fashion. Teachers claimed that there were many advantages in having an explicit system of appraisal, such as improvements in communication between staff at different levels in the hierarchy, especially in large schools, and a system of support. The importance of an appraisal scheme in helping teachers to appraise their own performance was also noted. Moreover, some teachers could point to some positive benefit resulting from appraisal. Of course teachers vary in how positive they are, from those who are highly enthusiastic to those who are merely lukewarm. Furthermore some teachers were in favour of having an appraisal scheme providing it met certain conditions — for example that it be geared to helping them improve rather than as a disciplinary measure, and that it operate as a two-way process with an open system of record keeping.

Many teachers on the other hand expressed a negative view of appraisal. They did not believe that the instituting of a formal scheme would bring any advantages and it might even constrain appraisal within a narrow and inflexible framework. Perhaps the most prevalent perception was one of appraisal as a threat to teachers — as an instrument of accountability which could be used to check up on them, to find fault, to criticize or whatever. Some teachers took a very cynical view, seeing appraisal as a way of manipulating staff, whilst others saw it as a 'bandwagon' — the latest fashion to be involved with. Underlying such cynicism was the belief that appraisal would become simply a formality or a very superficial exercise. Many teachers expressed concerns about how fair and objective an appraisal scheme could be, some suggesting that an appraisal scheme needs to include certain safeguards to ensure 'fair play'. One or two teachers even suggested that appraisal should operate beyond individual schools — at LEA level, something which others were anxious to avoid. However, there were some teachers who were not in favour of appraisal whatever safeguards were built in, seeing appraisal as inappropriate to teachers.

Having looked into positive and negative views of appraisal, we noted also that many teachers' perceptions of appraisal had changed as a consequence of experiencing appraisal. Many teachers seem to have come to adopt a more positive attitude, some seeing appraisal as less threatening than they had anticipated and others having been convinced that there were benefits in having a formal scheme and now perceiving it to be a valuable exercise. That is not to say that some teachers did not have negative experiences. For some teachers experience of appraisal merely confirmed their suspicions and it is noteworthy that those who had been strongly opposed to appraisal did not seem to change their views significantly. Bearing in mind that the success of any national scheme of appraisal will depend to a great extent on the perceptions teachers have of it and their willingness to collaborate open-heartedly, evidence from the case studies we have conducted suggests that whilst perhaps a majority of teachers will be favourable to a national scheme of appraisal, or may become 'converts', a significant and potentially vociferous number are likely to remain implacably opposed to the idea.

Chapter 12

The Impact of Teacher Appraisal

Introduction

We turn now to what might be seen as the most important issue of all: the impact appraisal has had on those teachers who have experienced it. Many teachers we interviewed argued that there is no point at all in having appraisals if nothing tangible results. In the literature one can also find this view expressed: Trethowan, for example, argues that, 'the appraisal meeting can become an irrelevant annual affair unless action is agreed and taken following the interview' (Trethowan 1987). In fact one of the main single objections to the introduction of appraisal systems in the case study schools was that it would all be a waste of time.

Follow-up to Appraisals

By its very nature appraisal is a retrospective activity, but of itself, reviewing past performance changes nothing. Yet it is a necessary component in forward planning for the simple reason that in order to plan ahead it is necessary to take stock of the existing situation. As we saw in Chapter 6 when looking at appraisal interviews, the balance between retrospective review and forward planning has to be decided by the parties concerned. Moreover, if changes are to be effected, there might have to be some kind of formal follow-up to the appraisal. It seems that the failure of many appraisals to produce any changes relates to the absence of systematic follow-up.

Follow-up to appraisal can take many forms, but perhaps the first essential is an agreed plan of action. This may seem obvious but in some cases where appraisals were observed no such agreed plan resulted. In one school, even though provision was made for follow-up in the form of a second meeting between the appraiser and appraisee, these meetings often did not take place. The problem here was that the necessity to complete all the appraisal interviews left senior management with no time to undertake the follow-up sessions. Where appraisals are all undertaken by senior management, lack of time for follow-up is an ever-present possibility. It may be better in such circumstances for the SMT to conduct fewer appraisals over the course of a year and to ensure that those conducted are properly followed up.

Another way to ensure that there is follow-up to the appraisal might be to place the responsibility for this with the appraisee. In an informal way appraisers in the schools visited had resorted to this strategy on the grounds that staff development was the responsibility of the individual. Here are some comments from appraisers:

A1 I certainly intend that, at the end of that period, we will go through the process again and see what progress has been made, if any, since the last time. I don't intend to let it rest but it is up to the individual teacher to ensure that it doesn't rest there.

A2 I think the first thing is for the appraisee himself to do the follow-up because I think he'll be thinking about it and I would expect him to soon come up with some ideas.

A3 I would hope that it might have given him more of an idea about saying, 'Can I do so and so, can I take over that?' that he would follow that up, which is the constructive criticism which will hopefully help him and take him where he wants to go.

In procedural terms, whether there is follow-up can depend on whether a record of the appraisal is made and to what extent that record sets out clearly what lines of development need to be pursued. If there is no written summary or record, then it is all too easy for both appraiser and appraisee simply to forget much of what was discussed and agreed. We observed appraisal interviews taking place where no written record of any kind was made:

T There wasn't a summary afterwards, I didn't give in anything, I didn't write anything down afterwards and I wasn't given anything afterwards as far as I can remember.

Yet just a few notes might suffice to ensure that action does result from the interview:

A Afterwards? No I don't make a report but what I do is to make a few notes to say, must see so and so, such and such a time in the year, if I put it in my diary, some time this month, see so and so about such and such.

A major source of dissatisfaction among teachers was the lack of systematic follow-up to appraisal throughout the year:

T1 I would like follow-up. There was follow-up to a certain extent last year but very much on the periphery: only on little things. I would like to feel there was a bit more in-depth follow-up throughout the year.

T2 I would have liked it if he'd have spelled out clearly what I can do, or what I should be doing at this stage and I don't think that was spelled out very clearly.

T3 The follow-up? I don't think the follow-up was adequate. We didn't complete the summary sheets and it was left up in the air. You feel it is quite rushed and it would be more clear what exactly you should be doing and what they're going to do or whatever but there just didn't seem to be time for that, we rushed through that bit at the end.

Even if appraisal is entirely voluntary, the view of most of the teachers involved is that follow-up should be seen as an essential part of it:

> T If you go through the appraisal process then follow-up should be a part of appraisal. So it's voluntary: fine, but if you opt for it then you should know what to expect. Like I say, it seems a sensible thing: to have five minutes, ten minutes at the least deciding what's going to be done as a result of what's been discussed.

Setting targets

In some case study schools the follow-up was in the form of a 'target setting' (Trethowan 1987). This might be thought certain to ensure that some action was agreed which could be undertaken over a specified period. However, whilst the notion of target setting as spelt out by Trethowan sounds straightforward enough, in practice some appraisers found it very difficult to get staff to set themselves specific targets. Trethowan stresses that targets should be specific, identifiable and that a set time should also be agreed by which they need to be achieved. Again, in the schools studied some appraisers had problems in getting targets down to something specific. Teachers would adopt targets which were difficult if not impossible to evaluate, such as, 'I will contribute more to discussion at meetings'. Furthermore, setting targets which are achievable in a specific time, for instance one year, was also sometimes difficult.

Perhaps as a consequence of such difficulties, some appraisals did not result in any targets being set, despite the willingness of those teachers being appraised to set them. One teacher noted that after his first appraisal interview:

> T When I was reading through the scheme it surprised me that there was no follow-up because it seemed the natural thing. The interview just stopped and I went away and thought about things that had come up in the interview. But I've not actually got a list of three or four things I've got to work on, whereas in industry for example, they'd insist upon that in their schemes. Also they'd want to see you in three months' time to see what you'd done about it, whereas this morning it was a very nice, it was a very pleasant interview but if I make no progress in any of the areas discussed or if I don't even try, I wonder if anybody would say anything.

Tangible outcomes

How far then did appraisal in the case study schools result in tangible outcomes? The problem here is that of expectations. The impact of an appraisal may not always be immediate, nor may it be as wide-ranging or as significant as teachers would like it to be. Some teachers, when viewing their appraisal interview retrospectively, were inclined to take a cynical view of the whole process. There was no shortage of evidence to suggest that little or nothing tangible seemed to have resulted. Below are comments from teachers, representing different schools, different scale posts and different phases of education:

T1 I can't really see the purpose of it. You have a piece of paper that goes towards your references and that's that.

R What have you got out of it?

T I've not got anything out of it — it's a formality. Going through the list of questions on the form, I didn't say anything the Head of faculty didn't know. I see him if I need to, anyway.

R What about setting targets for the future? Isn't that useful?

T With regard to INSET I have said I wanted sixth-form training three years on the run and pastoral guidance also for three years and nothing has been forthcoming. You view it with some cynicism since we can only go on courses which are sent to us.

R Do you think that anything tangible has come out of it, that's been of value?

T2 When you look at all the things that we planned to do last year, they all have been inhibited by NUT action, we just haven't been able to do them. That or the school organization has been such that we haven't been able to physically get round to doing anything.

R To what extent did that interview provide you with something tangible?

T3 No way.

R There wasn't a discussion of where you and the Department might go to from here or a pinpointing of areas which needed to change or anything like that?

T3 Nothing that I didn't know already before, no.

T4 I can only speak for myself, I don't think there's any great benefit to me at all. It was more of an irritation. I felt when it was over, now I can get on with teaching.

R What did you get out of this morning's session?

T5 A couple of things I knew already.

R What about previous appraisals?

T6 I think, looking back, one asks the question, 'Was it worth it, has anything been improved because of it?' and the answer is not a lot.

T7 I think it was a lot of manpower with little result. I mean the real question is has the department improved since then and the answer is, 'Not tremendously, no.'

There was a reaction on the part of some teachers that appraisal was something set up merely for effect — something that would make the school appear to be making strides in terms of monitoring performance and improving practice, but in reality a form of 'window dressing', with appraisals themselves little more than a formality which would be unlikely to produce anything significant:

T1 I'm very sceptical of it. I feel that the scheme is being run because it looks good from the school's point of view.

T2 It should have some spin-off for the individual involved, it shouldn't be a window-dressing exercise like when the Inspectors come we put the posters up and things like that. It must be that something is going to happen otherwise I can understand why teacher unions will want to stop it.

It is likely, however, that teachers' views about the impact of appraisal are influenced by their preconceptions about the nature of appraisal itself. If they see appraisal as something which is done to them by somebody else, then they are likely to see the outcome as something which is in the hands of the appraiser. If on the other hand appraisal is seen to be a two-way process then the outcome is in the hands of both parties. Some teachers took quite a proactive stance in ensuring that there was a tangible outcome from their appraisal:

T I wanted a tangible outcome and I took on extra responsibility. The timetable was changed so that I took on more of the older children.

Given that many of our interviews with teachers took place immediately after the appraisal itself, it was perhaps too early to expect much in the way of a tangible outcome. On the other hand, anything tangible proposed for the future would probably have been mentioned. We did, however, interview many teachers some time after their appraisal had taken place and with them there was the possibility of evaluating longer-term developments. The main problem in such cases is identifying what outcomes were attributable solely to the appraisal. Many teachers found it difficult if not impossible to single out the impact of the actual appraisal, given that so many other factors also related to the changes reported.

R You did in fact move on to Scale 2 last year . . . ?

T1 Yes, but I wonder whether that was to do with my appraisal interview or whether it was my application for a Year Tutor's post, which was a separate issue but happened at the same time.

R What about tangible outcomes, benefits, improvements or changes that you can actually pinpoint, have there been many of those?

T2 I'm on a course. I had been thinking about it for some time, so I talked about the possibilities of it at the appraisal interview and it was agreed that I should do it the following year. I suppose I would have applied anyway really but it was discussed at an appraisal interview so we both knew what I was going into.

T3 A lot of the things that were mentioned were things that I'd already considered but it was actually people pigeon-holing them for me and saying well this is what your option is in this direction, this is another possible option in this direction, this is how you go about it and I found that extremely useful and to a certain extent it's broadened my outlook but I think to a greater extent it's helped things to congeal into something useful.

R Are there matters over which you can point to something tangible?

T4 Yes, definitely, plenty of improvements. Although I might have picked them up eventually by other means, I've been able to pick up things earlier than I would have been able to before and able to follow them up and pursue them through the year.

Where tangible outcomes from appraisal could be indentified, those in senior positions in the school were anxious to ensure that staff did link the outcome with the appraisal since this would then give credibility to the appraisal scheme. Such sentiments are evident in this discussion between a Headteacher and a Head of faculty:

HF Some of the appraisals actually produced some very positive benefits both to the school and the staff concerned. People like — — who said he would be very interested to branch out, well we hadn't really thought: he was sort of reticent. He wanted to do General Science and he was interested in the technology. Well he got both of those and in a big way, didn't he?

HT Do you think he links that fact that he got that with what you talked about in the appraisal interview?

HF Yes he does, because we talked about it at the Science Department meeting the other day and I said, 'Well, if people are interested in doing things then they've got to say it.'

HT Sometimes people are not quite sure why they've got these things. They're pleased they've got them but they haven't equated it. If people appreciate that it is part of the process for them to get what they want, then obviously the process goes up in their estimation.

The sort of outcome being discussed here is purely personal as opposed to institutional, of course. The notion that appraisal is solely about individual teachers getting their professional heart's desire is a limited one to say the least!

Communication and Planning

One obvious outcome of the introduction of a scheme for appraisal is that a system of communication is created which may well be more effective than the previous ad hoc arrangements. It could be argued that this enhancement of communication itself constitutes a tangible benefit of appraisal. Thus sometimes the major impact is on the appraiser, in the sense that it helps inform future planning:

T1 It helped him get to know a little bit more about me and my circumstances and my aspirations and all the rest of it.

T2 It's just that I've informed him about what I'm doing next year really. I mean probably he's got more out of it than I did.

HF It has actually forced me to look at the work that members of staff within the faculty have been doing during the year. So it's forced me to take an interest in my own members of staff.

A1 If they come to see me in their appraisal with a request, I will say, 'I'll see what I can do for next year, I won't give you any promises about this but I'll try.' In the particular case I'm thinking of, somebody said they wanted to develop in a certain direction. I said, 'That's great, because that will just be handsome on our timetable, it will fit in beautifully and it will be great for your own type of development.' Now this is a prime example of how appraisal is useful. (Headteacher)

A2 I want the senior staff to be aware that there are a number of members of staff in the school that are concerned about discipline and I would hope that they will do something about it. I would hope that they would bring back the detention system but then that's a management decision and it's up to them. How they would approach sanctions, I think is for the management to decide, having been made aware of what the staff feel about it in appraisal interviews. (Headteacher)

A3 This year it has raised issues with regard to certain staff, of whom I wouldn't otherwise have been aware, to seek wider experience and what kind. This obviously will be helpful to me in 1987 and in planning for 1988. (Headteacher)

R Have you made any arrangements to facilitate specific changes as a consequence of last term's reviews?

A Yes, with — —, for example, I deliberately involved him far more than he was previously with our primary liason project that we've got going with the Heads of department. He really is our main link person there with regard to the language policy document which we're trying to produce and hopefully implement. (Head of Department)

In cases where communication is poor, appraisal can lead to better coordination of activities. It may also lead to some clarification of precisely what are a particular teacher's responsibilities so that they know what is expected of them. A member of staff can hardly be expected to make progress with something they did not think was their responsibility and in an appraisal interview certain misunderstandings can come to light which can be put right:

> T She [the appraiser] said I should have volunteered for more things but prior to this morning I was just of the opinion that I wasn't expected to do them and that she didn't want me to do them. I wasn't aware that she was waiting for me to say, 'I'll do this, I'll do that . . . ', and so yes I'll do that now.

Staff Relations

Linked with the issue of communication and planning is that of relationships between teachers. The question here is whether appraisal can act as a basis for improving relations between staff. Some teachers were able to identify problems in their relationships with other staff and there were examples where a course of action resulting from an appraisal had produced an improvement either in terms of relationships with staff generally or with the Headteacher:

> T1 People were prepared to look at me as a different type of person having done the appraisal and either their attitude towards me changed, or I changed or both. Certainly this year has been considerably more friendly as far as my relationships with staff are concerned.

> T2 You only talk to the Head occasionally when he pops into your classroom and says, 'Everything all right?' or discuss a book, or a child. If you've had in-depth discussions beforehand, I think it's easier for you. I've found that I don't feel so constrained. I feel I can just put my cards on the table more than perhaps I could two years ago.

> T3 Before we started appraisals a colleague went through a particular horrendous experience. No one had ever pointed out to his colleagues the situation that he was in and we'd gone merrily along thinking everything was fine whereas he was in a grim situation. Then the crunch came and they said, 'Look, hang on, we've got a serious problem.' I very much doubt that that situation would arise again now that we've started appraisals.

> T4 It has made me much more aware of how I communicate thoughts, and ideas.

Appraisal might also help to create the kind of relationship for a senior member of staff to be able to deal with a subordinate whose performance leaves a lot to be desired:

A When I had that chat with — —, I thought beforehand, 'Now how much do I say to this man?' In essence, all I said to him was, 'Now look, the way you present yourself is just not really good enough. You look as if you're falling apart. You look depressed, your shoulders are drooping. You know what's the matter with you, pull yourself together.' Not quite as bluntly as that, but it seemed to transform the man. I was amazed by this. I was anxious myself because I wanted to be constructive and help him to look at himself and afterwards I thought, 'Well there's another example of how talking to people in a reasonably direct way is good for them.'

The other side of the coin is where a member of staff has a grievance which they are unsure about bringing up with senior staff. The appraisal might provide such an opportunity, as was the case below:

T I felt I wanted something sorted out.

R So it was the opportunity to do that, was it?

T From my point of view, yes. I wasn't sure of the right way to do it because . . . It could have been within me to take it through the Union, but again I was only fresh into the Union. There was probably a reluctance within me to take it through Union procedure because I was unused to Union procedure. So it seemed to me an appropriate opportunity.

Morale, Motivation and Incentive

Other teachers identified outcomes in terms of improved morale, motivation or incentive:

R What have you got out of it so far that's tangible?

T I don't know, it's just the incentive, I think. I've probably needed a kick. I think the Head probably decided to talk to me because I've done quite a lot of things on my own, like doing the MA and things like that and I did feel I was starting to stagnate again but I couldn't quite think what I should be doing. I mean, I'm involved in a lot of science-based committees outside school but none of them were really necessarily going to lead anywhere. I'm involved in them for my own interest and it's essential but I think I probably needed some direction as to what I could be doing in my own self-interest rather than just a general interest, I suppose.

Such outcomes seem rather vague. However, many teachers argued that it is unrealistic to expect appraisals to result in instant outcomes. One should not expect too much from appraisals, and anything which is improved as a result — no matter how vague — merits having such a scheme:

T1 I can't really expect that because of this that kids will suddenly change but I think it will be worth looking at the points that have been raised and seeing what's happened as a result.

T2 There's no doubt at all that if you read the ten points that were drawn up at the end of my initial appraisal, all of those sound very, very vague. This is the problem, they don't come up with instant answers which will immediately make everything right and a lot of people are not satisfied, they'd like to be told, 'Start doing this or that and your practice will magically improve itself ', or something of that kind. It's very difficult to tell some people that something that isn't as specific and definitive as that can in fact be helpful and useful.

HT3 I think it has achieved much but I don't think necessarily that the scheme would have to stand by the magnitude of problems that it resolves. I think that it has given staff the opportunity, which I know they very much value, of sitting down and talking in a planned, structured way about their own career and the future. I know it has raised issues of resource implications, both human and material for the future. (Headteacher)

Motivation and morale in connection with career development is dealt towards the end of this chapter.

Improvements in Teaching Technique

What perhaps would be the best test of the impact of any appraisal scheme is how far it has produced improvements in teaching techniques, since this is where the effect would immediately be felt by its clients. Those who would like to see appraisal have a direct impact on what is actually experienced by pupils themselves would obviously feel this. From our interviews, it is clear that in many cases appraisals did not seem to have much direct relevance for teaching techniques. One reason for this is the general lack of direct classroom observation in the schemes studied and its frequent omission as a topic on the agenda for appraisal interviews. In the words of one teacher:

T As far as classroom practice is concerned, I don't think it is in my experience thorough-going enough to have such effect there except for very general things.

Where teachers did claim that their appraisal had affected their actual teaching techniques, it was often because they themselves had chosen to look into this in some depth. In the College of Further Education, teaching staff were encouraged to review their teaching methods by giving a questionnaire to students. Some staff claimed to have used it and to have made changes to their teaching as a result of what it revealed. The usual strategy for schools was to use the appraisal interview for constructive criticism from the appraiser and advice as to how changes might be made. For this to be possible the appraiser must be somebody who is sufficiently in touch with the class-room practice of the person concerned. Where claims had been made for changes in teaching methods, as might be expected it was amongst teachers who were appraised by their Head of faculty or the Headteacher in a small school.

> A Last year I drew the attention of the member of staff concerned to a weakness in her approach to teaching. This issue arose again this year because she herself drew reference to it, and how she felt she was beginning to see the early benefits as a result of our criticism of twelve months ago. I must stress that criticism was of a positive nature, identifying an area where an alternative approach could be more helpful. (primary school Head-teacher)

> R Have you made any changes in your teaching?

> T1 My classroom practice has changed enormously. I used to be very formal and I have now changed to an integrated day. I have still been able to keep my individuality and the way I work with the children. I used to shout and bellow things out, but I've discovered different ways of communication with the kids. There has been a change in the quality of knowledge and what the kids have produced. I now know they can take on much greater things.

> R How have you found it in terms of improving practice?

> T2 In terms of self-development, making me take things in smaller steps, to review and ask questions and to look to mistakes and see what I can learn from them. It has made me slow down. I have a lot of ideas and it has made me look more at the kids' ideas. Also ideas of how to teach in different ways — drama etc. I got some ideas from the Head. Before, the product was there but I tended to roar ahead — I now look at the process as well.

Some teachers noted that their appraisal had had its main impact on pastoral matters:

> T We had a few minutes of discussion in the interview over my attitudes towards discipline. At times I adopt the approach of a martinet but I will be a literalist when it comes to applying rules. I also tend to be occasionally selective on my literalism, depending on whether the offender is a known villain as it were or whether they have a clean slate. I was able to learn from the other people's views of the way in which I react on that, and while I haven't changed totally it has given me something to think about in terms of how I develop that side of me.

Career Implications

So far we have tried to identify the impact of appraisal in terms of changes in individual practice or institutional arrangements. A further, very important matter for consideration is what impact appraisal might have for the careers of teachers. The emphasis on individual performance and development, characteristic of most appraisal schemes, suggests that the implications of appraisal for career could be considerable. However, the extent to which appraisal should be concerned with career development is a matter which is open to debate. Most teachers we interviewed saw career development to be an important part of appraisal and the fact that career prospects would be discussed was one of the reasons that many teachers opted in, where appraisal was voluntary. Here are the comments of one such teacher:

> T I looked to see what it offered and it seemed to me to offer an opportunity to talk to my Head of faculty about how my career was going and how my work was developing and how it is at the moment.

Promotion

The controversy about the place of appraisal in career development seems to stem from concerns about the potential link appraisal might have with promotion. Although the notion of merit pay has come in for criticism (see, for instance Suffolk Education Department 1985) it is arguable that there always has been an implicit link between pay and appraisal insofar as promotion in teaching is geared to perceptions of the professional worthiness of teachers. There are concerns among teachers and teacher unions (see NUT, 1981) that a direct link between appraisal and promotion would be to the detriment of good teaching and could lead to an unfair system of rewards. In examining the data we have collected from schools, we need to consider the extent to which there was such a link in any of the schools' schemes.

There seem to have been few cases in our case study institutions where promotion had occurred immediately after appraisal. For this to happen, the opportunity has to exist in terms of additional money (scale points) available for use at the Headteacher's discretion. Between the time of the research and the writing up of this research, the system of scale payments for teachers changed. Our data thus refer to a defunct system. This must be borne in mind in reading what teachers had to say in this regard, although it seems likely that the spirit of what they said still holds true under the post-1986 system of payment. Below is an extract from an interview with a teacher who felt that his own appraisal had resulted in immediate promotion:

> T As a result of the interviews I did get my scale point for developing field work but that was in a way an artificial scale point, it was a temporary scale point. So it wasn't something which the hierarchy in the school recognize as being a scale point that is always going to be there for Geography. I think it was more a case of this person deserves a scale point, therefore, we'd better think of some way of giving him one.

INSET

As mentioned earlier in the chapter, another direct outcome of an appraisal interview might be to send someone on a course. Although the opportunity might ostensibly be provided to help improve their performance, most courses also improve teachers' career prospects whether or not they result in better qualifications. Being sent on a course does not guarantee promotion, but it places the individual in a much stronger position to seek it. The teacher below noted how being sent on a course was viewed both by himself and his Head as a lever for getting promotion:

> T The Head suggested that I did a further degree, an MSc in Computer Studies, because computing is coming strongly into the school. I'm the one who teaches computing, so he suggested I did something to further my own education in computers so that I could take this further and it would be another lever for getting me promotion. The degree I'm starting this October. I've been accepted on an MSc course, day release, starting from October and that is a direct result [of the appraisal].

Another teacher went on a specific course purely in order to become a Head of department:

> T One thing that I wanted was to become Head of department and I went on a course, the expenses of which were paid by the school. I found it very interesting and realized how much I needed to add to my knowledge to become a Head of department.

Sounding out senior staff about future prospects

Another way in which appraisal can be linked with promotion is senior staff signalling whether or not future promotion for a member of staff is a possibility. Many teachers find it very difficult to make a realistic estimate of what their actual chances are in terms of promotion. Thus an appraisal interview is an ideal opportunity for teachers to find out what senior staff consider their prospects to be. Teachers can also find out if senior staff consider they have the potential for the type of post they are hoping for. Again such appraisals do not lead to any guarantee of promotion, but they might make it clear whether or not a particular teacher is 'in the running', as was the case in these examples:

> R What did you feel you got out of it, first of all as regards the career aspect?

> T1 Well, I got answers to a fair number of my basic questions: 'Yes' to Head of department potential. 'Yes' to further potential at higher levels if I go in for some further training, which they strongly advised me to do.

T2 I was obviously very much interested in career development and that really was all I had in mind. There were certain ideas that I wanted to get clarified . . . What I really wanted was help in clarifying my own position within the school and where the people who ought to know me fairly well would see me going. In a sense it was asking for help, that was really what I was in there for, and to that extent my expectations were fulfilled.

And an extract from an appraisal interview in a comprehensive school:

HT You've put down here you're possibly thinking of Head of science eventually . . . ?

T Eventually, yes.

HT Well, certainly that doesn't seem to me to be a totally ridiculous ambition, by any means.

Career counselling and advice

As distinct from seeking advice about their prospects in relation to specific promoted posts, teachers often asked for, or were offered, advice of a more general nature about where their future career might lead. This career counselling took on many forms. At the simplest level it consisted of the Headteacher or a senior member of staff helping an individual to plan his or her next career move, suggesting what areas of responsibility within the school they might take on as well as what courses might prove to be beneficial:

T1 The appraisal interview went on to my career prospects and getting ahead and we talked a little bit about that. He [the Head] made a suggestion about trying to find some sort of area of responsibility which I could take over and this sort of thing.

T2 Last year I said to the Head for the first time, that I wanted now to further my career. I said I thought I'd got to the point in teaching where I either looked for something else to do or I go on and try to achieve promotion and he said, 'Well, what had you in mind?' and I said I wouldn't mind being Headmistress of a smaller school, or a deputy Head of a small school, and he said, 'Fine, I think you could do that,' and he suggested things that he could do to help me get the necessary additional experience.

T3 The appraisal interview came to the important question of whether I go on to pastoral or administrative or whatever sort of work, which made me think very hard. They all saw me as a person in contact with the children through the subject that way, i.e. as a worker through the department and not as one who is somewhat less classroom orientated, and that made me think and stop and pause quite considerably because I've been thinking about how much higher can I go, and they've said yes you can go higher if you want to, but their impression was of me with the young people in the classroom through the subject and that's where my strengths lie.

T4 One of the things that was raised by the Head was that my weakness as far as going for further jobs such as being the deputy Head would be that I've not got enough experience on the general side of the school. I mean, I'm a chemist and I do the timetable but I've no pastoral responsibility.

Below is an extract from an appraisal interview in a comprehensive school. At the end of the session the Headteacher provided quite detailed advice on possible career development strategies:

HT In immediate career terms, firstly you ought to be applying for posts and you ought to be extending your field of application. Secondly, they should probably be pastoral but you shouldn't exclude necessarily Heads of department, English department. Thirdly, you should be taking a serious look at courses and/or additional qualifications but paying particular attention to the course, a course that involves you actively and a course from which you are going to get satisfaction. Fourthly, perhaps you should consider how intense your ambitions are apart from the financial side of them and whether in fact it is sufficiently meaningful for you to take all these steps, and fifthly perhaps you should look at other things, using your job perhaps as a base but doing other things like writing, examining, perhaps some lecturing somewhere.

Another aspect of career advice might be alerting staff to potentially ill-informed decisions. An appraiser who has a good knowledge of the range of jobs available in the education system can not only suggest what might be a sensible and realistic goal, but can also warn staff away from what might turn out to be a mistake:

T I think one thing [the Head] did do was made me see that going into admin., even though I'm considered to be a reasonable organizer, is not the sort of job I would like to do. I think I'm more subject orientated and I like contact with the kids, so I think if I did stay in teaching then it would be in a school situation as opposed to sitting in an office somewhere.

School needs versus individual needs

Of course, the difficulty with such advice and counselling is that it is offered by senior staff in the context of what is available within the school and in the light of their views of the needs of the school. Headteachers in particular have to bear in mind that the needs of the school as a whole may not always correspond with the needs of individual teachers. In this sense the appraisal is not just an opportunity for staff to sound out what their prospects are within the school, it is also a chance for senior staff to persuade teachers to satisfy such institutional needs. The view of the teacher below was that this was what the Head was doing in his appraisal:

> T The interview was led really by the Head who really wanted to talk about which way I ought to go forward because my interests were pastoral really, I taught English and I also taught Technology and I think the Head was taking the opportunity to find out which of those I really wanted to progress in, which area, because he wanted to increase the school's strength in these areas.

Obviously a Headteacher has to consider to what extent the career goals of individuals can realistically be accommodated within the school. If they cannot be, then the teacher can be advised to seek promotion outside the school. In small schools this can be a particular problem, as evidenced in the following extract from an appraisal interview in a primary school. A lengthy extract from the interview is given to demonstrate how the Headteacher identifies the teacher's career goals and then the advice he offers in the context of these not being easily accommodated by the school. The teacher is left with the dilemma of how to achieve the goal given the desire to remain within that particular school:

> HT Would you have any clearer conception since last year of where promotion might take you? Last year you had a sort of two-pronged thrust: one into Advisory work and one through the school itself. Would you see any, I don't like the expression, firming up of the view about which particular route?

> T The school-based position would be attractive because I enjoy the range of school activities, but the opportunities that are available seem diminished really.

> HT They are certainly not increasing very much, though I think they are likely to in the future. To what extent would you see your future needs being met outside the school?

> T I ought to be pursuing my next grade and a more 'managerial' position within the staff. I'm not sure whether the present structure within the school allows for that kind of progression.

> HT Could you give any kind of indication of what you think would be realistic for short-term, long-term future?

> T I'll go back to when I came here three years ago, with my aim to firstly establish myself and secondly to acquire some status on the staff, which I feel I've done.

> HT Right, both of those things obviously have been manifestly achieved.

> T Right, but I'm still on a scale two and considering how long I've been teaching, that doesn't seem a very successful position to me.

HT Which of course relates actually to declining rolls, which is the situation for . . .

T Well, the answer to that lies within myself and it's something that I've got to put a little bit more effort into pursuing.

HT Can I come back then to the point that in the short term, let me put this proposition to you and see whether this relates to your perception of the situation. Would I be realistic in thinking that in the short term you see your future in this school, but in the long term with further responsibility elsewhere, or is that not a fair comment?

T Long term I would be looking towards a Senior Mistress position, possibly a deputy Headship position.

HT Right, fair enough, but with an existing position filled in this school, possibly for ten years, then obviously that isn't a realistic option for you within this school.

T Right.

Given current reduced opportunities for promotion within schools, and the education service generally, one of the functions of career counselling might be to help staff to cope with potential disappointment, both with regard to opportunities within a school and beyond. Nowhere does this seem so pronounced as in seeking a Headship or deputy Headship. The extract below is one of many where the message is clearly that things are not as easy as they used to be:

HT Let's look at career position.

T I now feel about 300 times more confident to apply for deputy Headships. I don't just want to go to another school to get it.

HT I think you will have to psyche yourself up for a lot of disappointment. A lot of us here walked into jobs — but it's not like that anymore.

Dealing with Incompetent Teachers

Much has been said in the media and elsewhere about the controversial issue of using appraisal as a means of removing incompetent teachers. In most of the case study schools, appraisal was not seen as having this function. However, if in the opinion of senior staff a teacher is incompetent, it is difficult to see how this issue can be avoided in that teacher's appraisal. Obviously it is not in the interests of the school, or of the education service generally, for an incompetent teacher to be promoted. Steps can of course be taken to remedy a position of incompetence, either through further training or advice. However where this fails, the best solution for the school is probably for that teacher to be removed. It is not just a problem for a Headteacher if a member of staff is incompetent. It is also difficult for those staff who have to work closely with the teacher concerned. Yet, although the existence of an incompetent teacher can make the work of other staff much harder, staff will sometimes seek to protect the individual interests of the person concerned.

The role of appraisal in dealing with incompetent teachers might best be seen as one of counselling. If such a teacher can be made aware of his or her weaknesses it may be that something can be done about them. However, a teacher in such circumstances may be well aware of the problem and be evasive. In our interviews with teachers, the point was often made that those who are incompetent in teaching have a very difficult time indeed from pupils and surprise is often expressed at how such teachers manage to continue. However, motivation might not be so much a matter of job satisfaction as financial imperatives! Thus it could prove impossible to pursuade a teacher judged to be manifestly incompetent to leave the profession.

Some of the teachers interviewed criticized their school's appraisal scheme for failing to grapple with the problem of staff who are either incompetent or whose performance at any rate leaves much to be desired. It was argued that where schemes are voluntary, poor performers will opt out and yet it is precisely such teachers who need most to be appraised. However, since the schemes were introduced to staff in most cases in such a way as to allay fears about appraisal being a punitive instrument, it is only to be expected that dismissal of teachers as a result of appraisal did not happen in any of the schools.

It is interesting to consider what is meant by 'incompetence'. Whilst in a literal sense an incompetent person is one who cannot do his or her job properly, in teaching it is not always a straightforward matter to decide what is proper or improper. In any profession, a degree of discretion and individual judgment needs to be exercised in performing professional duties, and there is always the possibility that fellow professionals may disagree about what is appropriate. Decisions by senior staff as to what amounts to incompetence can therefore be a matter of internal politics. The appraiser is someone who has power, by virtue of seniority, to decide what is professionally appropriate. The danger, as some teachers saw it, is that appraisal can become an instrument for enforcing conformity to the demands of the Headteacher or SMT in cases where there is genuine professional disagreement.

In one school, staff beleived that an appraisal had resulted in a Head of Department leaving the school. It was beleived that the SMT disagreed with him about how he ran the department and as a consequence had presented him with an unfavourable report following his appraisal, suggesting certain changes be made in the department. It was thought by many staff within the department that he decided to leave the school because he did not agree with the changes suggested but could not ignore the report. Here are some comments by members of the department:

T1 It was very, very unfavourable on him and I think we'd all known it was going to be, including himself. He'd developed the department in one way and that wasn't the way that seemed to be acceptable by the people doing the appraising and the changes that were asked for . . . he just for one reason or another didn't want to make.

T2 The Head of department at the time didn't agree to make the changes that were suggested, not because he wasn't able to, I think. He was a very complex man. You can't pinpoint exactly why these things happen but it was one of the reasons why he left the School, I think, in the end.

R And so it was then a question of whether the Head of department was going to effect those changes or ignore the recommendations?

T2 Yes.

R He chose to ignore them and then he left?

T2 He was hoping it would just go away, I think.

T3 I think what it did, it got rid of a man that wasn't wanted by senior management and then it all kind of died a death after that.

That not all staff agreed with the SMT is evident from the following comment:

T I felt it resulted in the Head of department eventually leaving. I think it was a great loss.

Just as it is impossible for appraisal to result in clear targets for the future if parties disagree, the outcome of a major disagreement might be that certain parties are unable to pursue their future career goals in that particular school and make their decision to leave.

Career Consciousness

There are some staff who claim not to be ambitious or even overtly conscious about the path their career is taking. For such teachers the appraisal interview might not be an occasion where they might be encouraged or even persuaded to take a more pro-active view. The issue of gender and appraisal is closely linked here since in our case studies, those who tended to opt out of promotion tended to be women. Some female teachers leave their jobs in order to have a family and come back into the profession in many cases at a less senior level than when they left. The following extract is taken from an interview with such a teacher. For her the appraisal interview was an occasion where the Headteacher tried, in vain it seems, to persuade her to seek career advancement:

R Career is a part of the emphasis and yet I remember you saying you weren't particularly ambitious and yet career seemed to be so big a part of the appraisal. Do you think it's made you think more in career terms?

T Well, the trouble is, I'm not one of these ambitious people who wants to be a deputy Head or a Head. I'm happy as a class teacher. I don't want to administer, I don't want to get on into any other area, I don't want to be a lecturer or get into college work. I am a class teacher and I want to stay a class teacher and I'm quite happy with that. Now having said that, I've come back into teaching, I've dropped back on to a Scale 1. I was on 2 before I gave up teaching to have my children and having dropped back you feel, 'Oh, I really ought to get on and get a Scale 2 again!' You feel you've gone backwards. So I mean, yes, I would like a Scale 2 post but I think in that there's an element of self-pride really: you had it once before and it's been taken from you and you want it back again, but I'm not the ambitious type, I'm basically a class teacher, I enjoy being in the classroom, I'm not one who would be happy doing anything else, particularly on a long-term basis. On the other hand the Head always manages to make me feel guilty that I say I don't particularly want to go on courses and I don't particularly want to do degree work or anything. He always makes me feel guilty when he asks me about it and he keeps asking me about it. I think he feels I ought to and I probably could do it, academically I'm quite capable of doing it, it's just I am not interested. Yes, he pokes it at me every so often and I get guilty feelings for a day or two and then I think, 'No, why should I feel guilty, I'm basically happy as a class teacher, I'm not ambitious to get on into other areas of teaching.'

Some female staff, however, claimed that appraisal had acted as a spur to their careers and had motivated them to take a more proactive position as regards seeking promotion. Several female teachers felt that if they had had appraisals earlier in their professional lives, the course of their careers might have been different:

T1 I think it's a pity that, in my case, I just feel that to a certain extent in my career I've just drifted along and I've moved wherever my husband's gone to. I think it's a good thing that people have some idea of how they're going to develop their career. I feel that (in an appraisal interview) you sit down and you think about what you're doing and where you're going and I wish now that I'd probably had been able to do that further back.

R Do you wish you had had it before, earlier on in your career?

T2 Yes, I think so, I've been going a long time now. When I look back, thirty years ago when I started, my attitude was so different.

T3 You know, I've been here all my teaching life. I've been here all the time the Head's been here. But yes, I feel I might have been pushed more. I'm sure if I'd have had this a few years ago, I'd have made more effort.

Many teachers, men and women, faced with appraisal for the first time towards the end of their professional lives could only acknowledge that it was probably too late now to try to develop their career further:

T Well, in my heart of hearts really I think I shall be retiring from here because I'm getting too long in the tooth, I think, for people to accept me in other jobs.

A I think that's maybe true. (Headteacher)

T Yes, I'm sure.

In some cases there was disagreement between the appraiser and appraisee in this regard. Appraisers did not always accept the conclusion that individual teachers had reached. This applied not only to career prospects but also to where a teacher's strengths lay:

T As regards my future career I did intimate to you the other day that I feel that having had a family comparatively late in life that it really isn't going to facilitate my career . . .

A You said you'd missed the boat and I then came back to you afterwards and said I totally rejected that perception of it. I think in the next appraisal that ought to be a matter for considerable concern and attention.

T As you know, I've never really been terribly keen, or felt any desire to gain promotion along a traditional line, deputy Head or Head . . .

A That is consistent with last year's appraisal.

T I feel that my skills are definitely more on the curriculum side than on the organizational and management.

A I would disagree with that.

For some teachers, if career development was not considered a possibility, the appraisal might be seen more in terms of motivation and morale within the existing possibilities:

HT One of the things that in the long term ought to be borne in mind is that the challenge that you alluded to earlier on is still there in different areas. One of the things that this school is big enough to be able to offer is a variety of challenges in a way that maybe another school couldn't. I'm really saying to you that within the ethos of the school and with the size and what it can offer that indeed I would see it obviously as being able to offer you opportunities if they do not appear outside the school.

Appraisers can also help staff to decide the right time for a career move. In many cases teachers claimed that they were not currently pursuing a career move but were consolidating their position within the school. In such circumstances appraisers might seek to identify how far staff had long-term career goals and, if not, to encourage them not to lose sight of their career development in the long term. Many teachers find it difficult to make long-term career decisions as is evident from this extract from an appraisal interview:

T I think I'm consolidating my position at the moment and trying to resolve the problems that we've got.

A Right, that's fair comment. Now what about the longer term?

T I'd like to develop further responsibilities.

A In what area?

T Well, I'd like to be within Lower School, I wouldn't want to go outside that. I feel I would like to go on from where I am, I wouldn't like to remain static for the rest of my teaching career, quite honestly.

Other teachers might see their career development as in some way inhibited. Many who were interviewed believed that they were stuck in a particular position and they faced the choice of whether to try to pursue promotion from a position of limited possibilities, or whether to make the most of their current post and seek job satisfaction and personal development within it:

T In terms of professional development, career development, in many ways I've reached a plateau. I'm at the top of Scale 4 and unless the right job comes along, I don't see myself moving from being Head of faculty but I wanted to emphasize and to talk with the Head about the ways in which I could improve things. One of the aspects of it which I think is the greatest benefit is talking to him about improving management skills.

Conclusions

One of the main concerns teachers have about appraisal is that it will prove costly in terms of time but will have little impact in terms of bringing about improvements. In this chapter we have drawn on data from the case studies to show the concern of many teachers that if there is to be an appraisal of a member of staff there must be some kind of follow-up and that this can be in the form of 'target setting'. Despite such concerns it is evident that in many cases appraisals were not followed up and produced little or nothing that was tangible. The lack of any decisive change produced scepticism on the part of many teachers as to the real value of having an appraisal scheme.

In our examination of the impact of appraisal, it was noted that appraisal has in some cases enabled senior staff to be made aware of the views and concerns of those for whom they are responsible and this has had implications for future planning decisions at a whole-school level. By improving communication processes, appraisal has also in some instances improved staff relations. However, in terms of an impact on actual teaching techniques, although there is some evidence of this, in the main appraisal does not seem to have had any great impact.

Although in our original project proposal, we noted that we would try to investigate the use of appraisal in connection with the dismissal of teachers, we were not able to do this in any direct way in the case study schools and college, although we were told of an instance where a Head of department had left a school following an adverse report on his departmental policies from his appraisers. We were not able to verify this. For the most part, the schemes in use in the case study schools and the spirit which surrounded them were foreign to such purposes.

The main area of impact of appraisal in the case study institutions seems to have been on the career development of individual teachers, not in the sense of directly effecting promotion but in terms of career advice, counselling and planning. Teachers had been made aware of what senior staff considered their future prospects to be; senior staff had learned about their career goals. Obviously the career goals of individual teachers do not always correspond with the needs of the school as an institution. Furthermore, what is in the career interests of one teacher may be to the detriment of another. However, some teachers have been able to plan their careers more realistically as a result of appraisal and have gone on courses or taken on responsibilities which have improved their career chances in the long term, either within the same school or by helping them seek a position in another school.

It is apparent that as a result of appraisal some teachers have been encouraged to take a more positive line in furthering their career. Women staff in particular note that they have become more career conscious. However, others have warned against the dangers of too narrow an emphasis on career in the appraisal process and stress the importance of job satisfaction and helping teachers to improve their performance. Although most teachers do see career development to be an important aspect in appraisal, the link between promotion and appraisal in the schools studied is far from a direct one and many would argue that this is how it should be.

Chapter 13

The Costs of Appraisal

Introduction

That appraisal is not a cost-free exercise is something easily overlooked by those not directly involved. In examining the schemes operating in the case study institutions, for example, the fact that none of them received any extra finance from their LEA to cover the cost of appraising staff makes it seem that no costs in financial terms were in fact incurred. Whilst in a direct sense this is true, there are costs of an indirect nature on time and resources in these schools which could and probably should be counted in financial terms.

Like many activities in school, appraisal tends to be 'lost' in the accounting system, leaving no easy way to make an accurate estimate of its real financial implications. The 'true' cost of appraisal is also debatable. Some would argue that appraisal can occur in free periods or during after-school time and need not require any other resources. If provided for in this way no additional costs of a financial nature would in fact be incurred. Others would argue that time spent on appraisal might otherwise have been spent on some other school-related activity or that teachers should be compensated financially for time spent on it outside of school hours.

Whatever view one takes on this, the fact that appraisal has a cost in terms of people's time cannot be denied. This is particularly important since much of the recent controversy over teachers' pay and conditions has been fuelled by the claim that already teachers do not have sufficient time to undertake all their professional duties during the school day.

In this chapter we shall attempt to estimate the 'costs' of appraisal in the case study schools. The definition of cost which we shall adopt does not only include accounting in a monetary sense: opportunity cost is also included and this too is relevant because we can approach the question from the point of view of what schools find they had to set aside ('sacrifice') in order to make room for appraisal.

Time Taken

Perhaps easiest to estimate is how much actual time the teachers we observed spent on their appraisals. This of course varied from teacher to teacher and from school to school. In some cases the time which could be taken on an appraisal interview was prescribed by the length of a non-teaching ('free') period. The use of free periods, a tactic generally not possible in primary schools, does at least ensure that appraisal interviews will tend to be confined to a prescribed time, if only because one or more of the parties has a class to take immediately afterwards. However, that may mean that the interview is curtailed before all the relevant matters are fully explored. A free period even of an hour may prove to be insufficient, and in many schools free periods are shorter than that. Here are comments from two teachers:

T1 The problem is, it's thirty minutes, or whatever it was, forty minutes, and there's so much you could discuss and there just didn't seem to be enough time for everything to take place that should have taken place and we very quickly went through it.

R How long did the interview take, about an hour?

T An hour, yes and we could have gone on talking longer than that but there just wasn't time.

In some cases appraisers arranged a second session to continue the interview, thereby doubling the time taken. If constraints on time are entirely removed, however, an appraisal interview can go on for several hours. This was particularly the case where interviews took place after school. Two of the interviews we observed went on for two and a half hours and another took three hours, according to the teacher appraised. The view of this teacher was that three hours is too long:

T Mine took three hours, which I thought was dreadful, and he'd [the Head] said at the beginning, as it's after school we want to keep it to an hour and I said, 'Great, fine.' Well, we'd only moved on to the second heading when the hour was up, so I said to him look, we're way behind time . . .

R It took three hours . . !?

T It took three hours. Okay there were interruptions but that to me . . . All right, I was still thinking clearly at the end of it but I thought it was too long.

The time taken up by the actual appraisal interview is not, of course, the total time spent, but what other time is involved is much harder to estimate. Time for preparation for the interview, which might entail completing a *pro forma*, varies but still needs to be taken into account. The appraiser also has to spend time on preparation. One appraiser estimated that this takes about an hour in addition to the interview itself:

A You've got to prepare yourself. For instance, for the interview I'd probably spent the best part of an hour anyway preparing for it, that is in booking it up, in ensuring that the member of staff had their record of last year, that I've got a copy of that, that I've read through it, that I've prepared the questions I want to ask and that I've actually sat down and thought about things. I should say that probably does take an hour.

As well as preparation, there is the follow-up to the interview. Even if this merely entails writing out a brief report it takes time. Many appraisers had come to the conclusion that more in the way of follow-up was necessary. In one school a further session to discuss targets was included in the programme of appraisals. However, finding time for this follow-up session was often difficult:

HT Well, the problem is time for the interviewers, I don't mean the time to get the interview done but also the time to follow it up, the time to summarize, the time to see someone for a subsequent interview and to agree on aims and goals for the following year or just to agree on what was actually discussed, that sort of time. There's too many other things to do.

Consideration of the appraiser's time raises the point that of course in an appraisal interview we are talking about at least two people's time — both the appraiser and the appraisee. In any estimation of how much time appraisal takes over the course of the school year this has to be borne in mind. In one school one of us (researchers) discussed with the Headteacher the total amount of time their appraisal scheme was likely to take over the course of the year. The conclusion reached was daunting:

HT I guess probably from the point of view of the interviewee at least three-quarters of an hour preparation, some of them must have spent at least that, say it's three-quarters of an hour on average, at least a quarter of an hour my preparation and then I think if we were following it up much better than we are, I'd guess probably another hour in total.

R For each one?

HT For each one. So what's that that's something in the region of . . .

R Three hours per person, that adds up to . . .

HT More isn't it, because the hour interview is in fact two people, isn't it?

R Ah, so it's about four and a half hours per person multiplied by the number of teachers in the school which is . . .

HT Sixty.

R Sixty, and that's over the year period, so two hundred and seventy hours, working on the basis of say a thirty five hour working week. So it's a fair number of working weeks overall of staff time. If you were to extend the scheme so that it took in an element of direct and deliberate observation this would scale it up enormously again wouldn't it?

HT Absolutely.

Observation

The point about introducing formal observation as part of appraisal suggests considerable additional time implications would be at stake. One teacher who had been observed as part of an appraisal described the total activities as follows:

> T It was observation of several lessons by the Headmaster, then a full after-
> noon's appraisal chat and then a debrief which took about an hour and a
> half, and a written report.

Whether any Headteacher could undertake such a process with all the staff in a large school is questionable. Even a limited amount of observation is time-consuming, and if we allow for proper debriefing, the total time needed can work out as double the time taken up in actual lesson observation as one appraiser discovered:

> A Every lesson I observed we then had something like an hour's debriefing
> and talking and . . . (Head of faculty)

> HT So you're really multiplying the time by two, that's a valid point, isn't it,
> that if you are observing the time it takes is twice as long as you observe
> really?

Appraisal panels

The time needed for appraisal is also increased by the number of people involved as appraisers. In several places earlier in the book we have considered the advantages of appraisal by a panel of staff. However, if as many as three appraisers are used a one-hour appraisal interview amounts to four person hours, plus whatever preparation and follow-up each of the individuals has to undertake.

Duplicate appraisals

Some schools have added even more to the time required for appraisal by instituting a two-tier system of pastoral and academic appraisal. Here, each individual is appraised by both academic and pastoral team leaders. From the point of view of time needed this does not only mean that each appraisee has to take part in two appraisals but that the number of appraisers is doubled. Appraisal of middle management and senior staff may be even more time-consuming. In one school, not only did it take three hours but it required an input from both the Headteacher and the senior mistress. He described it as follows:

> T It was a long appraisal, it took from 1.15 p.m. to 4.15 p.m. and it was done
> two-fold. The first session was dealt with by the Head and then at half-time
> a senior mistress, who was in charge of the pastoral side of the school, or

responsible for it shall we say, came in and then it went on between the three of us from about 3.30 p.m. to 3.45 p.m. and the last session, which was the Head and myself, the senior mistress went out, we stayed for a quarter of an hour.

Delegated systems

Senior management teams have been able to reduce the amount of time they have to spend appraising staff by developing a delegated system. Whilst this effectively reduces the time the Headteacher and deputies have to spend on appraisal, it does not reduce the total amount of time that the institution has to invest in the activity. It merely spreads the load.

What is Sacrificed?

Having identified the considerable amounts of time many teachers have spent on appraisals without any extra financial provision we need to consider what tends to be sacrificed in order to make way for it. This is also a difficult thing for teachers to pin-point, but it was accepted by many of the teachers we interviewed that in an occupation where all the time available is already spoken for in some way, something has to go in order to make way for appraisal. The concern of some teachers was that time spent on appraisal would inevitably be to the detriment of contact with the pupils. Here is one such view:

> T The problem is that one's main aim in life is to do as much teaching as possible and anything, however valuable in itself, that cuts across that is a frustration and a nuisance.

In some cases appraisals have been made possible by the use of staff cover, that is at the expense of another teacher's 'free period' (non-teaching time), even at a time of industrial action, as described below:

> T By and large appraisal interviews take place in free periods but we do have to arrange cover for cases where both persons are not free at the same time. It is affected by union action then, but we have been able to use 'acquired' free periods and therefore we have been able to continue with it during the action.

Having to cover for a teacher, however, almost inevitably means that the class loses the benefit of specialist tuition. What is sacrificed in this sense is the education of the children, at least in the short term. There are many other ways in which educational provision might be affected adversely by appraisal. Planning of lessons, for example, might also suffer so as to allow time to prepare for appraisal. Here is a comment from a Head of faculty in a secondary school:

R Is it the amount of time put into it worth what comes out?

A Yes it is, but that doesn't mean that it isn't being done at the expense of other things. I mean, there's loads of other things piling up at present. I don't know how many appraisals I shall be doing altogether now, I think it's about ten or a dozen I should say. So it's a whole week's worth of things, it takes over half of all my free time, in this half of the term.

R So, what gets pushed out?

T Lesson preparation, that's one thing which doesn't get done. Other things which should be done, perhaps preparation of a work sheet for something or other, you make do with last year's work sheet, which you know has faults or whatever. Things like that don't get done.

Resourcing Appraisal

If appraisal cannot take place in 'free' time in school without having a detrimental effect on the quality of educational provision, perhaps the best solution is to estimate the cost of appraisal and ensure that adequate resourcing is provided. On local authority scale such resourcing might need to be quite considerable. Sheffield LEA, for example, estimated the potential cost of appraising its entire teaching force in 1986 to amount to £1 million per annum (Wilcox 1986). Although the cost might be reduced by adopting a broader notion of the teacher's year (see Naismith, 1984), that appraisal has to be facilitated by an extra financial input has now been recognized by the DES (Rumbold, 1987).

If a national scheme of appraisal is to meet with the broad approval of the teaching force and teachers' associations, resourcing adequate to allow teachers time to undertake appraisal will probably be the least that has to be offered. As we noted in Chapter 11, the principle objection of many teachers to appraisal is the fact that it will turn out to be very costly in terms of their time. In setting up schemes of appraisal, most of the case study schools had to confront the question of the time implications at a very early stage. One teacher described staff concerns in his school when trying to 'sell' the idea of appraisal at a staff meeting:

T Well, our concern in a school like this where we have seventy plus members of staff is the amount of time that this could take. In fact I spoke briefly to some of the members of staff in an after-school meeting last year and explained what I'd been through and why I felt it was basically a good thing and the first and immediate reaction was the amount of time that had been put in by those who were involved.

It was evident from our interviews that most, if not all, teachers believed that there should be extra resourcing to allow staff adequate time to conduct appraisals. Here is a sample of the comments made by teachers:

T1 A lot of the appraisal we did was done after school. I think my feeling is that we've got to face it in the long run, I think people have got to realize that staff need time during school hours to do these things, not necessarily always in the holidays or after school.

T2 I think that time has got to be allocated for it. I don't think you can appraise staff properly unless that time is allocated. I think it's wrong to expect people to spend hours and hours after school on top of marking, which does happen. I think its's wrong.

T3 An appraiser should be given time off because it takes a very long time to appraise somebody, it isn't just the hour and a half interview, it's the writing, the reading, the discussion perhaps with other members of staff about the person being appraised. They should have time off just like somebody going on a course to learn something new.

The implication of adequate resourcing for appraisal was seen by some teachers to mean that extra staffing would need to be provided in many schools:

T It's very evident that to establish any sort of significant appraisal scheme we're going to have to have more hours. Whether that means promoted Heads or whatever is perhaps but one example. It would need to be more hours and more people, there's no doubt.

Of course, resource implications will vary according to how thorough-going the appraisal scheme is. If the observation of teachers is to be included in appraisal, that would require considerable resourcing in addition to what would be needed for appraisal interviews. One Headteacher calculated the time resourcing of including observation by team leaders below:

HT One of the things which was introduced into the role of Head of department is seeing colleagues in the department teach.

R And are you making any timetable provision?

HT We haven't made any timetable provision, no, but I do think that would have to be part of the final scheme.

R Can you speculate on how much timetable time you might write in, just speculating about the management structure as it is now. I know it's in the melting pot, but taking the present hierarchy how much time might you want to allow people for this?

HT Well if you are talking about a management structure which had something like ten senior or middle management staff, I would reckon that each of those people would require half a day [a week].

R For that purpose?

HT Half a day is where you would spend one double lesson observing someone, another double lesson either interviewing or following up in some way.

R They are each responsible for six people, that's the way you're thinking of it?

HT Yes six to eight.

Resources and the Frequency of Appraisal

The resourcing of an elaborate system of appraisal such as that envisaged by the Headteacher above might of course be reduced considerably by reducing the frequency of appraisals. This was what some proposers of appraisal schemes had in mind. The teacher quoted in the extract below suggested a very thorough-going approach with several stages of follow-up. The scope of this scheme was perceived to be more important than the frequency of appraisal interviews:

T Obviously if everyone went into a complex system then the time element would become very, very difficult. I think that a spacing of something like two or three years is reasonable when we're doing something of this nature.

Resourcing the Training for Appraisal

Another aspect of resourcing, to which attention is increasingly being paid, is the training of appraisers. Devolving appraisal to middle management certainly reduces the burden of senior staff, but once additional people are brought into the job of conducting appraisal some time has to be spent preparing them for this new role. Either some form of in-house training will need to be provided or such staff will need to be sent on a course. Whichever strategy is adopted, the training of appraisers has cost implications. Residential courses in particular can be very expensive. Even the one-day courses provided by organizations such as the Industrial Society cost around £60 and in addition to that there is the cost of travel and the need to cover for that person for a whole day if the course is run in school time. There is a cost beyond the pure financial here in that covering for a senior member of staff is very difficult. Supply teachers tend to have limited experience and cannot take over duties such as running a department. Thus for a senior member of staff to be out of school means that that person's skills are simply lost for that period.

The training of appraisers is likely to have considerable cost implications for LEAs once a national scheme of appraisal is introduced. Whether central government would adequately resource such training is something many teachers and Advisers were concerned about. Here is a comment from an LEA Adviser:

It is unfortunate isn't it that we've got this Government interested in appraisal, which in many ways I find is a wholly admirable thing, but there's no indication of what resources, what amount of in-service provision is going to be made available to help train people to undertake this properly and if it is simply going to be something that is loaded on to Advisers, this is going to be an additional burden.

Resourcing the outcomes of appraisal

We have so far considered the resource implications of setting up the processes of appraisal in schools. What is easily overlooked is what resourcing might be required to follow-up the courses of action resolved upon in an appraisal. In other words, what are the cost implications of the outcomes for the individuals involved?

One of the most frequent outcomes of appraisal in school is the identification of in-service training needs. If such in-service training is not adequately funded, much of the value of appraisal is lost. Thought needs also to be given to funding other possible developments proposed in appraisal interviews. Sometimes the steps which need to be taken to solve a particular problem or bring about a desired change have quite considerable resource implications. If there is no possibility of finding the necessary finance then appraisal can become a purely academic exercise.

There are many examples in our data where changes simply could not be made because of the sheer cost of implementing them. Within the existing resources of schools certain desirable developments are out of the question. For example, as is made clear in the extract below from a Headteacher appraisal, better provision for children with special needs was seen to be impossible within existing resourcing:

HT Children with special needs, remedial and the very able, I just cannot put any better way than the way I've put it here, inadequate resources prevents the proper development of children requiring specific support. Setting in groups and procedures within the existing structure of the school do help a bit, but we're playing at it. We spend a lot of time with our children requiring special needs, we involve them with the medical authority, with the school psychological service, with the Special Needs Officers, consulting with parents, which is extremely time consuming. I feel that we probably tackle that side better than we do the more able child . . . but I think that the existing resources of the school should be improved.

A Yes it's lack of resources again really isn't it?

HT Yes.

One Headteacher pointed out that there were likely to be occasions in appraisals where the appraisee would have no choice but to accept the situation as it was because of constraints on material or human resources within the school:

HT There are times when things are going to occur where the reality of the situation has to be accepted, simply because there is nothing that can be done about it within resource constraints, whether those resources are material resources or indeed human resources. For example, if one was to take say a relatively simple example that if one wanted to develop a higher order of musical skills within a school where you had no specialist musician, I think you would be foolish to embark upon that kind of course of action which doesn't relate to the reality of the situation and the constraints which are imposed upon you.

The problem here of course is that appraisal interviews can raise expectations and lead staff to believe that desired changes can be made. As the Headteacher quoted below was at pains to stress, appraisers must strongly resist the tendency to make promises they cannot fulfil:

> HT If somebody says, 'I wish to develop this particular area, can you support me by giving me £500?' and the short answer is that there is not £500 available, then it is dishonest to encourage that development.

Resourcing promotion

In addition to requests for extra material resources, the desire of particular members of staff to gain promotion can present appraisers with a difficult job in avoiding the raising of expectations where promotion possibilities are extremely restricted, but the appraisal might have underlined the teacher's undeniable merit. Here are comments from two appraisers on the subject of promotion:

> A1 For example, a negotiated agreement about the future, about somebody's career aspirations. I was at pains to point out that this particular person's career aspirations were impossible from an organizational point of view in that the person concerned was seeking greater responsibility and promotion on to a higher scale. I had to show, by actually going through the current staffing with them and explaining why there would be no promoted posts available and therefore for me to promise that would be totally dishonest, though it was merited!

> A2 Well you've only got a certain number of chiefs and a certain number of Indians haven't you, and if everybody is looking for promotion, they're not all going to get it. I mean, you've got to have some system whereby you sort out the ones who are going to go for promotion, if they're all looking for promotion, they're all getting suitable things put on their c.v. and so on then okay it just becomes more competitive, but you only get a certain number who are going to get promotion.

The 'cost' of institutionalized appraisal may thus be the creation of more promoted posts to be awarded at the discretion of the appraiser (with appropriate safeguards), or a considerable increase in frustration amongst those noted to be meritorious but who nevertheless cannot be offered promotion. Teachers who believe that they are passed over unfairly in this regard may well start to give far less than their best from then on, believing that they are undervalued. From this point of view appraisal can have a cost in terms of the morale and motivation of staff. As well as boosting morale and motivation, an appraisal scheme can create the reverse effect by raising expectations but then not being able to satisfy them.

The 'Acid Test'

The question that remains to be asked is whether the costs of appraisal, be they in time, resources, or sacrificing other activities to make room for it, are justified by its benefits. This question cannot be answered in any objective sense without extensive research to establish empirically the value of appraisal as a means of improving the quality of education actually 'delivered' to the clients. What it is possible to do for the present, however, is to ask teachers about the balance of time they would deem appropriate between appraisal and other important activities. It seems that many of the teachers in our case study institutions remain to be convinced of the value of time spent on appraisal or preparing for appraisal. The view of such staff is summed up by the following comment from a senior member of staff:

> T If I saw a piece of paper in my pigeon hole saying that there was going to be a staff development workshop on appraisal skills for example, I'm sure I wouldn't bother going to it. I wouldn't want to spend an hour, let alone an afternoon, in a room thinking exclusively about that, simply because there are always a hundred more important things I could think of to be doing.

On the other hand other teachers expressed the view that appraisal could have the effect of saving valuable time for staff by pointing out inefficiencies or highlighting more effective ways to use time. If there were benefits such as these, appraisal could well be cost effective in the long run. There were teachers who thought that this might be the case, but their comments were speculative:

> T Maybe the benefits that teachers get by looking at their aims more clearly and rectifying weaknesses, perceiving weaknesses and spending less time concentrating on aspects which they're doing well already, maybe the benefits will outweigh the time it takes, in the long run.

Conclusions

In this chapter we have considered the question of the cost implications of appraisal, whether in financial terms or in terms of opportunity costs.

The most obvious way in which the cost of appraisal can be estimated is in terms of teacher time. This includes not only the time taken up with appraisal interviews but also the preparation and follow-up required. Where observation of teachers is included in the system of appraisal the amount of time taken up in increased considerably.

It needs to be acknowledged that appraisal takes up the time of the appraiser as well as the appraisee, and those who are responsible for a large number of staff will have to spend a lot of their time on appraisal. If a panel of appraisers is used, or the scheme requires more than one appraisal session, then the amount of time is increased accordingly.

There are other costs related to the time taken up in appraisal. If staff already find that much is competing for their limited time then other fundamentally important activities, such as curriculum planning, lesson preparation and marking and even contact time itself, may have to be sacrificed in order to make way for appraisal. The concern that important matters would suffer as a result of appraisal activities led many of the teachers we interviewed to argue that additional time needs to be 'bought' specifically for appraisal.

An estimation of what level of additional resourcing might be needed for appraisal took up the second part of the chapter. It was noted that resourcing would be influenced by the scope of the appraisal scheme but that a thorough-going scheme might be attainable within reasonable costs if the frequency of appraisals was reduced from every year to once in every two or theee years.

Resourcing would need to take account of the outcomes of appraisal as well as the process. The cost of training for appraisal would also have to be taken into account. Appraisal might also highlight the need for changes within the school which could have quite considerable resource implications. Unless there is scope to make such changes, appraisals could merely induce or heighten frustration on the part of teachers. The same would apply where scope for promotion was severely restricted by lack of funding for staffing. Appraisal will raise personal expectations which if frustrated, might lead to hidden 'costs' in terms of the lowering of motivation and morale.

We concluded by considering whether the time taken up in appraisal was perceived to be worthwhile in relation to other valued activities by teachers in our case study institutions. Although some argued that appraisal could be cost effective, that increased efficiency could outweigh its costs, many more seemed to be of the opinion that there were far more important matters competing for their time than appraisal.

Chapter 14

Conclusions

Introduction

In the preceding chapters we have looked at school- and college-based teacher appraisal in terms of a set of issues (see Introduction) arising from the classification used in our *Review and Register*. In doing so, we have given primacy to the views of participants, wherever possible presenting these views in their own words. Our conclusions concerning these issues considered separately are included at the end of the relevant chapters and we do not therefore propose to restate them here. Instead, we shall now briefly draw overall conclusions about teacher appraisal based on the integration of these separate issues. In doing so, we shall consider the potential of teacher appraisal for bringing about improvements in the quality of the education provided in schools and colleges generally and the implications for the introduction of teacher appraisal nationally. Before doing so, however, we shall restate the nature of our approach to researching this topic because of the bearing this has on our conclusions.

The Nature of the Approach

The origins of interest

Our interest in teacher appraisal was not stimulated primarily by the political and professional attention which it was receiving three or four years ago. Rather, it arose out of the programme of research into school self-evaluation (SSE), which we had been conducting for the previous several years, now reported in Clift *et al.* (1987). In the early days of this programme, SSE did not include any direct form of teacher appraisal. Indeed, in the foreword or preamble to a number of the booklets on SSE produced and published by LEAs in the late 1970s and early 1980s, it was firmly stated that school self-evaluation was about institutions not individuals and should not be confused with the appraisal of teachers. As our programme developed, however, increasingly it seemed that schools were finding difficulty in sustaining this distinction. Judgments about schools and colleges, and more particularly the departments within them, necessarily imply judgments about the work of those employed in them. That such judgments about individuals were not explicitly called for in the various LEA schemes did not alter this.

The distinction probably had less to do with rationality than with educational politics: with the acceptability of SSE to the teaching profession. At the time of its introduction in the late 1970s, SSE was sufficiently radical to arouse suspicion and hostility in schools. At that time, openly to have associated it with the appraisal of individual teachers would have drastically curtailed its implementation. In our subsequent research, however, we found that direct experience of SSE, with its characteristically fraternal, even egalitarian ethos, had done much to allay initial perceptions of professional 'threat' amongst teachers and in places seemed to have created a climate of opinion in which the appraisal of teachers was acceptable, even desirable. Thus it was that individual schools and colleges developed and implemented schemes in which both featured. An early example of such a scheme is described in 'The Art Department' in Clift *et al.* (1987). One conclusion from that study was that the explicit inclusion of direct forms of individual appraisal seemed actually to have reduced feelings of professional threat rather than the reverse.

An alternative explanation for the development of teacher appraisal in places where SSE had been practised is that it represents a reassertion of hierarchical control over the process of institutional evaluation. This notion will be developed later.

In contrast, then, with SSE, where our early interest was in researching the impact on schools and colleges of LEA-based initiatives, the form of teacher appraisal which we decided to investigate was school- or college-based.

The nature of the sample

Having made this decision, our next task was that of sampling. With SSE, differences in LEA policy were evident from quite early on. Thus we were able to draw samples enabling us to contrast the impact of voluntary schemes with mandatory ones, and with mandatory ones followed by external 'audit'. These represented the major differences in LEA-based school self-evaluation. At the outset of our research into school- and college-based teacher appraisal, however, no such clear-cut distinctions existed to guide us. We therefore began by collecting information from as wide a range of schools and colleges as possible. The strategy we adopted for obtaining this information was to advertise in the educational press, inviting schools and colleges having a scheme for teacher appraisal and willing to share information about it to get in touch with us. We had replies from about eighty institutions all told. This information served two purposes. Firstly, it provided us with material for our *Review and Register*. Secondly, it enabled us to develop a frame from which a 'theoretical' sample could be drawn for subsequent detailed study. The nature of a theoretical sample and the characteristics of the one which we studied are discussed in Chapter 2. It is worth noting that, because of the way in which they were selected, in all likelihood these institutions are at the forefront of development in practical teacher appraisal in England and Wales, despite what might be seen by purists as somewhat simplistic policies and methods.

The way that the data were collected and analysed

We began by collecting copies of all the documentation associated with appraisal in each institution. Our main approach to the collection of data about teacher appraisal, however, was observation and interview. We were privileged to be able to 'sit in' on a number of appraisal interviews and follow them up by interviewing both parties to further elucidate issues which had arisen. Most of the interviews were tape-recorded and subsequently transcribed as word-processor files, using a microcomputer. The microcomputer was subsequently used to analyse these transcripts. This involved classifying and labelling the dialogue. This classification was then used to investigate and elaborate on the range of issues first arrived at in the preparation of the *Review and Register*. Finally, the microcomputer was used to retrieve examples of classified utterances for use in the presentation of the report, letting the participants 'speak for themselves', as it were. The process was thus empirical rather than theoretical (an important point to note) and is discussed in detail in Chapter 3.

The way that the data are reported

Since ours was a theoretical sample, the data we collected derived from the widest possible variety and range of circumstances within our knowledge, rather than representing what was typical. Because the number of institutions involved (eight) was so small, however, any attempt to claim that particular responses to appraisal were systematically associated with particular circumstances would have been improper. We have therefore not attempted to cite causal links between types of scheme, types of institutions and particular reactions and responses to teacher appraisal. Our data are thus reported in such a way as to characterize the range of responses to aspects of teacher appraisal, not to indicate how prevalent those responses were or whether they seemed to derive from a particular approach in a particular school or college. Thus this report is an early portrayal of teacher appraisal in action and an early attempt to assess its potential contribution to the improvement of the education provided generally in schools and colleges.

Integrating the Issues

Fundamental to the nature of any scheme for the appraisal of teachers are the purposes which it is intended to serve. These purposes determine the way that it is introduced, the procedures to be adopted, the evidence to be collected and the nature of the outcomes. Thus they will also determine the costs of its operation.

It was evident in our study that participants had different perceptions of the purposes of appraisal, different expectations of the outcomes, hence different views of what evidence ought to be taken into account. Thus it was that there was a wide divergence of opinion about the value of appraisal, as practised, in relation to its costs. These differences were of two main types: between appraisers and appraisees and amongst appraisees.

Differences between appraisers and appraisees

The main difference between appraisers and appraisees was over whether appraisal should serve institutional or individual needs. For the most part, appraisers were the senior members of staff. The outcomes which they desired were concerned with the maintenance and improvement of the performance of the institution as a whole. The evidence which they sought was to this end and the procedures which they favoured were those which threw light on how this might best be achieved. For these people, appraisal was thus viewed mainly, even exclusively, as a tool of management and its costs were evaluated accordingly. There is obvious potential for conflict between the management view and the aspirations of individuals and this was often the case in our studies.

Differences amongst appraisees

Amongst appraisees, the main difference was over whether appraisal was concerned with professional development or career development. Professional development is an orotund phrase with a variety of interpretations. The means by which it was sought were by in-service training and by the broadening of experience, within a particular institution or in another. Career development was seen as promotion, with more responsibility and more money. Both purposes have resource implications. The former incurs the direct and indirect costs of in-service training, the course fees, the cost of cover and the 'cost' to the pupils of their teacher's absence. Where the broadening of experience is concerned, this may still incur the cost to the pupils if no other. Career development implies the institutional cost of a higher salary for the appraisee or the loss of a valued teacher to another school or college. In the case of both perceptions of appraisal, denial of expectations may incur the hidden 'cost' of a reduction in morale and commitment.

The stringency of procedures

The procedures adopted and the evidence collected to serve the summative ends such as career development must necessarily be more stringent than those for the formative ends of professional or institutional development. Clearly they must be fair and be seen to be fair. We found little of the summative side of appraisal in our studies, though we were told of a negative instance where a Head of department had been coerced into resigning by an appraisal. In that case his colleagues were by no means convinced that justice had been done and the whole affair had left an unpleasant atmosphere. We were, however, able to observe appraisees being counselled about their career prospects and the nature and strength of the evidence taken into consideration in this regard was a cause for some misgiving.

Clearly the issue of evidence is intimately bound up in cost and it is this which we now turn to. It is probably the most serious issue to do with teacher appraisal.

The Costs of Appraisal

Throughout our study there runs an assumption that the value of appraisal, whatever its purposes, is directly proportional to its cost. An attempt was made to quantify these in the previous chapter. Costs were seen as being of two kinds: direct money costs and opportunity costs. At its most elaborate, the process of teacher appraisal certainly incurs heavy costs in all its aspects. The collection of reliable and valid evidence about the professional performance of individual teachers is inherently labour intensive. The people expected to be involved in this activity are senior professionals, the most expensive labour in the service. These are the people who are then involved in the various kinds of follow-up deemed to be necessary in order to ensure that targets set, in-service training or other agreed outcomes are achieved.

The curtailment of costs

One way of curtailing labour costs which we saw developing in secondary schools was to reduce the 'professional distance' between the appraiser and appraisee. Instead of involving the senior management team in all cases, appraisal was being devolved to 'line managers'. In secondary schools and colleges, the line managers for the assistant teachers are the 'middle management', the Heads of departments or faculties. The most senior professionals in the institution are thus only involved in the appraisal of the middle management. For most primary schools, the problem is less pressing, with Headteachers typically having similar numbers of subordinates to the Heads of faculties and departments in the secondary and tertiary sectors.

The effect of a devolvement of appraisal is to reduce the need for elaborate measures for the collection of evidence concerning the professional performance of the appraisees. It avoids the need, for instance, for the consultation with 'third parties' practised by some of the Headteachers in our study. It might well also avoid the need for systematic classroom observation.

As noted earlier in the book, the systematic observation of teachers as they went about their professional duties was conspicuously absent from most of the institutions which we studied, despite claims of its centrality to appraisal. The main reason given for its omission was that, in the frequency necessary for obtaining a reliable picture, it would have been too costly in senior staff time. It was also considered to be professionally very threatening to teachers for senior staff to intrude into their classes and distorting to the very picture of relationships between teachers and pupils which it sought to capture. The devolution of appraisal to line managers greatly increases the similarity to industrial and commercial appraisal systems, in which deliberate and systematic observation is rare. The assumption is that Heads of departments and faculties are fully aware of the way in which their subordinates conduct classes because they are constantly visiting them on a casual basis. They would not therefore need to make special provision for the collection of evidence of this kind. The universal validity of this assumption at the present time is open to question, but it would certainly be relatively inexpensive, in terms of human resources, to incorporate it into the job descriptions of middle managers in schools and colleges. It is, of course, suggested in the ACAS proposals (ACAS 1986) on teachers' pay and conditions.

As well as curtailing the costs of obtaining evidence, in secondary schools the devolvement of appraisal also spreads the load of appraisal interviews and the responsibility for the setting of targets, endorsing requests for in-service training and opportunities for broadening experience more widely across institutions. In our case study institutions this was one of the ways in which schemes in secondary schools were developing.

The credibility of devolved appraisal

Unfortunately, the evidence from our study is that this ready solution to the problem of the costs of appraisal would not be acceptable to many appraisees. Most of the teachers to whom we spoke expressed a keen desire to be appraised by their Head-teachers. In some cases they said this was because they lacked faith in the skills of their 'line manager' in this regard. In other cases, familiarity with their Head of department or faculty had led to a lack of respect for their professional abilities, generally. Other objections related to their perceived impotence over matters to do with career development, access to in-service training and institutional arrangements. Yet more serious objections related to the assertion on the part of some assistant teachers that the problems which they experienced were wholly or partly attributable to their line managers' policies and practices. In all, these objections add up to a lack of appraiser credibility.

Training for Appraisal

Doubts and anxieties over their skills and credibility raises the issue of training for appraisers. This includes training in the collection of valid and reliable evidence about teachers' professional performances, in carrying out appraisal interviews and in the dealing with the outcomes of appraisal. One of the main conclusions of our programme of research into SSE (Clift *et al.*) was that teachers are generally ignorant of the techniques of educational evaluation, which of course apply equally to teacher appraisal. What we observed in the case study institutions underlines this conclusion. The range and quality of the evidence brought to bear at interview was a cause of serious concern in many cases, many appraisal interviews were mis-handled, with possibly detrimental consequences, and counselling and target setting were often inept. The national implementation of appraisal will need to be supported by wide availability of training.

The Criteria of Teaching Quality

Training in the methods of educational evaluation raises the issue of the criteria by which teachers should be judged. Our brief review of the literature on appraisal (Chapter 1) concluded with the statement that:

> Whatever the purpose or origins, however, it seems clear from a review of the literature that the greatest problem associated with the appraisal of teachers is that there is virtually a total lack of validated criteria. The seriousness of this lack should not be underestimated.

In none of the case study institutions was this problem acknowledged. Indeed it is fair to say that the existence of such a problem was hardly even suspected! The evidence taken into account in arriving at judgments, whether it was of hearsay origin or specially collected, was concerned with matters which it was assumed related to 'good practice'. These assumptions were questioned by appraisees mainly in connection with the devolved schemes, when the 'professional distance' between the parties was relatively small. It was expressed in statements such as, 'I don't agree with (Head of department) over the way I should deal with the ''slow learners'' ', or 'I don't agree with his views about how the subject ought to be taught'. The more general and extreme views about the professional competence of appraisers included such comments as 'I wouldn't accept any criticism of my teaching from him'.

At a greater professional distance, this lack of faith in the appraiser as a judge of professional competence was expressed in appraisee's comments such as, 'I would like to have had the Art Inspector involved: none of the senior management team have any experience or training in the teaching of Art'.

Statements such as these are an implicit admission of the lack of validated indicators of quality in teaching. It is an intractable problem to which we do not offer any solution. As noted in the review of the literature, research seeking to establish empirical links between teaching processes and pupil outcomes has been universally disappointing. This inevitably undermines faith in outcomes of appraisal which purport to set targets intended to directly benefit the students or pupils.

Evaluation and Hierarchical Control

Earlier in this concluding chapter, we suggested that the inclusion of teacher appraisal in on-going school self-evaluation might represent a reassertion of hierarchical control over what was seen as a fraternal, even egalitarian approach to institutional management. In contrast with SSE, teacher appraisal as seen in action in our case study institutions is essentially a 'top down' process. Even where peer appraisal occurred, it was additional to appraisal by superiors. The comment that we have to make here is that teacher appraisal seems to us to have a better chance of becoming institutionalized than SSE ever had precisely because it coincides with rather than challenges current modes of management. It acknowledges the responsibility that senior, better-paid staff have for their junior colleagues, reinforcing existing lines of accountability and professional care.

Access to reports

The ACAS document on the appraisal of teachers, to which reference was made in Chapter 1, recommends that the officers of the LEA should have access to records of teacher appraisal. The general view amongst the teachers involved in our case studies was that, other than with the express permission of the appraisee, any written reports resulting from an appraisal should be restricted to those actually involved. This view is currently supported by the teacher unions. There is of course nothing to stop teachers making records available to their LEA, or anyone else, on a voluntary basis. We imagine that they would be quite willing to do so when the record showed them in good light, thus enhancing their claims for promotion. At this stage we can only comment that the data from our study indicate that there is likely to be considerable resistance to any attempt to enforce LEA access.

Extrinsic Versus Intrinsic Outcomes

The discussion so far has proceeded on the assumption that teacher appraisal is directed towards extrinsic outcomes and that in order for these to be appropriate they must be grounded in valid and reliable evidence about a teacher's professional performance, collected by senior staff at considerable cost. We would like now to question this assumption. In doing so, we will turn first to a parallel in our earlier study of school self-evaluation.

Much of the data collected concerning SSE suggested that it rarely produced tangible changes of any real magnitude or permanence in the schools involved. And yet it remained a persistently popular activity with teachers, despite the time and energy it undoubtedly absorbed. Allied to this, in virtually all the schools and colleges where it had occurred, those involved claimed that it had led to improvements in communication. When questioned closely about what this meant, teachers were generally vague. Factor analyses of the data from questionnaires suggested that SSE was seen as a desirable end in itself and not as a means to an end: that it was the actual process that was valued. Following four years of collecting insights and evidence about SSE from various countries, Robert Bollen, the Dutch convenor of the SSE working group of the OECD-CERI International Schools Improvement Project concluded that 'introducing SBR [school-based review: SSE] into a school, not just at the managerial level but as a normal function of the school, will bring about structural and functional change in the school which can itself be perceived as school improvement' (Bollen 1987).

Whatever their views about the outcomes of their appraisal, and some were sceptical as to whether anything of value had resulted, the teachers in our study almost invariably expressed deep satisfaction with the time of exclusive and uninterrupted discussion with their Head afforded by the appraisal interview. It is sobering to realize that for some teachers, this was the first opportunity for such a sustained discussion since they had been appointed to the school. Teaching can be a lonely business, with remarkably little daily contact with peers (in the cultural, maturational and intellectual sense) and scant feedback from superiors, except perhaps of a negative kind. In such circumstances most teachers might be expected to value the opportunity, afforded by the appraisal interview, for feedback and communication about their work from someone whose professional credibility they respect and who has the power to bring about changes. Furthermore, irrespective of the empirical validity of headteachers' criteria of judgement, they are the ones which determine the outcomes of appraisal.

The general conclusion which we draw from our studies is that even in its most elaborate (and costly) form, teacher appraisal will not necessarily lead to excellence in the education provided by schools and colleges. On the other hand, regular appraisal interviews, without over-elaborate preparation and follow-up, could well be of considerable benefit to schools and colleges and those who work in them, and at reasonable cost.

References

ACAS (1986) *Teachers' Dispute, ACAS Independent Panel.* Report of the appraisal/training group. ACAS CA1, June 1986. London, Advisory Conciliation and Arbitration Service.

Barr, A.S. (1935) 'The measurement of teaching ability', *Journal of Educational Research*, 288, pp. 561–9.

Bollen, R. (1987) 'School-Based Review in the Context of Educational Policy', in Hopkins, D. (ed.) (1987) *Improving the Quality of Schooling: Lessons from the OECD International Schools Improvement Project.* Basingstoke, Falmer Press.

Borich, G.D. (1977) *The Appraisal of Teaching: Concepts and Process.* Reading, MA., Addison-Wesley.

Borich, G.D. and Madden, S.K. (1977) *Evaluating Classroom Instruction: A Sourcebook of Instruments.* Reading, MA., Addison-Wesley.

Brophy, J.E. and Everston, C.M. (1974) *Process-Product Correlations in the Texas Teacher Effectiveness Study: Final Report.* Austin, Texas, The University of Texas.

— —(1977) 'Teacher behavior and student learning in the second and third grades', in Borich G.D., op cit.

Bunnell, S. and Stephens, E. (1984) 'Teacher appraisal: a democratic approach', *School Organisation*, 4, 4, December.

Burke, B.T. (1982) 'Merit pay for teachers — Round Valley may have the answer', *Phi Delta Kappan*, December, pp. 265–6.

Byrne, C. (1983) *Teacher Knowledge and Teacher Effectiveness: A Literature Review; Theoretical Analysis and Discussion of Research Strategy.* Paper presented to the 14th Annual Convocation of the Northeastern Educational Research Association, Ellenville, New York, October.

Clift, P.S., (1987) 'The Art Department', in Clift *et al.* (1987), op cit, pp. 110–35.

Clift, P.S., Nuttall, D.L., and McCormick, R. (eds) (1987) *Studies in School Self-Evaluation.* Basingstoke, Falmer Press.

Coker, H., Medley, D.M. and Soar, R.S. (1980) 'How valid are expert opinions about effective teaching?', *Phi Delta Kappan*, October, pp. 131–49.

Darling-Hammond, L., Wise, A.E. and Pease, S.R. (1983) 'Teacher Evaluation in the Organisational Context: a review of the literature', *Review of Educational Research*, 53, 3.

Delaney, P. (1986) 'Teacher Appraisal in the Primary School', *Junior Education Special Reports.* Leamington Spa, Scholastic Press.

DES (1972) *Education: A Framework for Expansion.* London, HMSO, Cmnd 5174.

DES (1977a) *Education in Schools: A Consultative Document.* London, HMSO, Cmnd. 6869 (the Green Paper).

DES (1977b) *Curriculum 11–16.* London, HMSO.

DES (1978) *Primary Education in England: A Survey by HM Inspectors of Schools.* London, HMSO.

DES (1979) *Primary Education in England: A Survey by HM Inspectors of Schools.* London, HMSO.

DES (1983) *Teaching Quality.* London, HMSO, Cmnd. 8836.

DES (1985a) *Better Schools.* London, HMSO, Cmnd 9469.

DES (1985b) *Quality in Schools: Evaluation and Appraisal.* London , HMSO.

DES (1987) School Teachers Pay and Conditions of Employment. Dd 8935511, EDUC JO119NJ, March 1987, HMSO p.14.

Elliott, J (1983) *Teacher Evaluation and Teaching as a Moral Science.* Cambridge Institute of Education (mimeo).

Evans, K.M. (1951) 'A critical survey of methods of assessing teaching ability', *British Journal of Educational Psychology*, 21, pp. 89–95.

Farrar, E., Neufeld, B. and Miles, M.B. (1984) 'Effective Schools Programs in High Schools: Social Promotion or Movement by Merit?', *Phi Delta Kappan*, June.

FEU (1982) *Competency in Teaching: A Review of Competency and Performance Based Staff Development.* London, FEU.

Flanders, N.A. (1977) 'Knowledge about teacher effectiveness', *British Journal of Teacher Education*, 3, 1, pp. 3–26.

Florida Department of Education (1983) *Domains of the Florida Performance Measurement System.* Office of Teacher Education, Certification, and Inservice Staff Development: Tallahassee, FL.

Galton, M, Simon, B and Croll, P (1980) *Inside the Primary Classroom.* London, Routledge and Kegan Paul.

Georgia Department of Education (1984) *Teacher Performance Assessment Instrument.* Atlanta, GA, Georgia Department of Education, Division of Staff Development.

Gill, D. (1977) 'Appraising performance: present trends and the next decade', *Journal of the Institute of Personnel Management*, 9, 2.

Glass, G.V. (1977) 'A review of three methods of determining teacher effectiveness', in Borich, G.D. (1977), op cit.

Glazier, J., Campling, G., Miles, J., Snape, P., and Swallow, J. (1986) (Committee of Heads of Educational Institutions) 'The Appraisal of Heads and Principals', *Education*, March, p. 271.

Good, T.L. and Grouws, D.A. (1977) 'Teacher effectiveness in fourth-grade mathematics classrooms', in Borich, G.D. (1977), op cit.

Gray, J. (1982) *Making More Sense of Examination Results.* Course E364, Milton Keynes, The Open University Press.

Green, H.E. (1984) *Developing a Policy and a Programme for Staff Evaluation at Henry Box School.* Witney, Oxon, The Henry Box School (mimeo).

Haefele, D.L. (1978) 'The teacher perceiver interview: How valid?', *Phi Delta Kappan*, 59, pp. 683–4.

Haefele, D.L. (1980) 'How to evaluate thee, teacher — let me count the ways', *Phi Delta Kappan*, 61, pp. 349–52.

HMI (1982) *The New Teacher in School: A Report by HM Inspectors of Schools.* London, HMSO.

James, C. and Newman, J. (1985) 'Staff appraisal schemes in comprehensive schools: a regional survey of current practice in the south Midlands and the south-west of England', *Educational Management and Administration*, 13, 3, Autumn, pp. 155–64.

Kauchak, D, (1984) 'Testing teachers in Louisiana: a closer look', *Phi Delta Kappan*, May.

Klein, S.P. and Alkin, M.C. (1977) 'Evaluating teachers for outcome accountability', in Borich, G.D. (1977), op cit.

Kyriacou, C. and Newsom, G. (1982) 'Teacher effectiveness: a consideration of research problems', *Educational Review*, 34, 1, pp. 3–12.

Lloyd, K (1981) 'Quality control in the primary school: the head's role in supervising the work of classteachers', *School Organisation*, 1, 4, pp. 317–29.

McDaniel, T.R. (1977) 'The NTE and teacher certification', *Phi Delta Kappan*, November, pp. 186–8.

McDonald, F.J. (1977) 'Research on teaching: report on phase II of the beginning teacher evaluation study', in Borich, G.D. (1977), op cit.

McMahon, A. (1982) 'The GRIDS project', *Educational Management and Administration*, 10, 3, pp. 217–21.

Medley, D.M. and Mitzel, H.E. (1959) 'Some behavioral correlates of effective teaching', *Journal of Educational Psychology*, 50, pp. 239–46.

Metcalfe, D. (1985) 'An examination of some of the issues involved in staff appraisal in secondary schools', *British Journal of In-service Education*, 2, 2, Spring.

Naismith, D. (1984) Speech to the Conference on the Professional Appraisal of Teachers. Croydon, July.

NUT (1981) *A Fair Way Forward: NUT Memorandum on Appointment, Promotion and Career Development*. London, National Union of Teachers.

Powell, M. and Beard, J.W. (1984) *Teacher Effectiveness: An Annotated Bibliography and Guide to Research*. New York, Garland.

Rosenshine, B (1970) 'The stability of teacher effects upon student achievement', *Review of Educational Research*, 40, 5, pp. 647–62.

Rosenshine, B. and Furst, N.F. (1971) 'Research on teacher performance criteria', in Smith, B.O. (1971) *Research in Teacher Education: A Symposium*. New Jersey, Englewood Cliffs.

Rumbold, A. (1987) '*What has happened to appraisal?* Speech to the Conference of the Education for Industrial Society, February 1987.

Samuels, G. (1984) *Assessment for Staff Development*. Paper given at the Conference on the Professional Appraisal of Teachers, Croydon, July.

Schools Council (1984) *School-based Staff Development Activities: A Handbook for Secondary Schools*. York, Longman for Schools Council.

Scriven, M. (1977) 'The evaluation of teachers and teaching', in Borich, G.D. (1977), op cit.

Soar, R.S. (1977) 'Teacher assessment: problems and possibilities', in Borich, G.D. (1977), op cit.

Soar, R.S., Medley, D.M. and Coker, H., (1983) 'Teacher evaluation: a critique of currently used methods', *Phi Delta Kappan*, December, pp. 239–46.

Suffolk Education Department (1985) *Those Having Torches . . . Teacher Appraisal: A Study*. Ipswich, Suffolk Education Department.

Travers, R.M.W. (1981) 'Criteria of good teaching', in Millman, J. (1981) *Handbook of Teacher Evaluation*. New York, Sage.

Trewothan, D.M. (1983) *Target Setting*. London, Education for Industrial Society.

— — (1987) *Appraisal and Target Setting*. London, Harper and Row.

Turner, G. and Clift, P.S. (1985) *A First Review and Register of School and College Based Teacher Appraisal Schemes*. Milton Keynes, The Open University (mimeo).

Turner, G. and Clift, P.S. (1987) *A Second Review and Register of School and College Based Teacher Appraisal Schemes*. Milton Keynes, The Open University (mimeo).

Turner, G., Nuttall, D.L. and Clift, P.S. (1986) 'Staff Appraisal', in Hoyle, E. and McMahon, A. (eds) *World Yearbook of Education*. London, Kogan Page.

Wilcox, B. (1986) 'Context and Issues', in Dockerell, B., Nisbet, J., Nuttall, D.L., Stones, E. and Wilcox, B. *Appraising Appraisal*. Report of a Conference organized by the British Educational Research Association, Sheffield, 11th March 1986.

Wood, C.J. and Pohland, P.A. (1983) 'Teacher education and the "Hand of History" ', *Journal of Educational Administration*, 21, 2, pp. 169–81.

Woods, P. (1979) *The Divided School*. London, Routledge and Kegan Paul.

Wragg, E.C. (1984) *Classroom Teaching Skills*. London, Croom Helm.

Index